Strategic DevOps

Strategically scaling organizations through effective and efficient DevOps culture

Benjamin Abrams

Sean Riordan

Jay B. Abrams

bpb

www.bpbonline.com

First Edition 2025

Copyright © BPB Publications, India

ISBN: 978-93-65892-338

To View Complete
BPB Publications Catalogue
Scan the QR Code:

www.bpbonline.com

Dedicated to

*To all the professionals out there who seek better
outcomes for their organizations and projects*
- Benjamin Abrams

To my wife, who meets every test by returning grace
- Sean Riordan

*To my parents, who brought me into the world, showed me the way, and
funded my education at the University of Chicago, my professors, who
taught me how to think, and my children, who taught me how to love*
- Jay B. Abrams

About the Authors

- **Benjamin Abrams** was born in San Diego, California, and later became a wandering nomad, traveling throughout the United States, Canada, and Thailand.

  Although he attended college during his career, he left to take a good job without completing his degree. He is primarily self-taught. Open-source is part of his DNA; he has contributed to open-source projects throughout his entire career and has served as a maintainer for many of them. If he could speak to what early retirement would look like, he would spend all his work time donatinged to the community. With over a decade of experience, he has gained a unique perspective that motivates him to share his experiences. He began sharing his work publicly through conferences, webinars, and blog posts as early as 2016. He loves discussing automation, operations engineering, security, observability, culture, and scaling teams. He is incredibly grateful that he has had the opportunity to use these experiences to refine his craft before deciding that he wanted to tackle something a bit meatier. These experiences led him to start writing High Performance DevOps. This book has been in the works for a decade; he just needed to decide to write it. He decided to bring along two experts to help deliver the best outcome, which he will introduce shortly.

  He looks forward to taking you on a unique journey and providing a fresh perspective on the various cultural and technical aspects of the DevOps philosophy. Before diving into the nitty-gritty or how-to aspects, we will introduce the necessary vocabulary, concepts, and theory for each topic. In each chapter, you can expect us to use real war stories from our experiences to reinforce the topic. We will focus on helping you produce the correct answers rather than providing them for you. We will bring value to various engineering-related personas by carefully weaving themes, concepts, stories, and hands-on exercises that are relevant to their specific needs.

- **Sean Riordan** was born in Anchorage, Alaska, and received a BS in computer engineering from Montana State University in Bozeman. Fond of ensuring things work as expected, Sean began his career out of college in the oil industry, where he specified safety system instrumentation and developed hardware test plans to ensure their functionality. After moving into software, Sean spent the next ten years writing tests and guiding teams across IoT and health tech on how to build a scalable and performant test suite.

- **Jay B. Abrams** was born in Los Angeles, CA, and received an MBA from the University of Chicago, where he also took graduate courses in the department of economics. He possesses numerous qualifications that make him the ideal person to address questions related to valuation. He is an **Accredited Senior Appraiser (ASA)** with the **American Society of Appraisers (ASA)** and a **Certified Public Accountant (CPA)** (inactive status). Has been valuing businesses for more than 40 years. Valuation is the science and art of determining the amount an investor should be willing to pay for business ownership or a set of assets. His very first assignment was valuing Columbia Pictures, which was acquired by Coca-Cola in 1982 and later sold to Sony. Thus, he has experience valuing very large and small firms. As a published author in valuation, he has a lot to bring to the table. He has written four books on valuation and more than 20 quantitative journal articles. He invented more than 160 mathematical formulas, valuation models, and algorithms. He can help us provide some missing and much-needed language to bridge the gap between engineering, management, and sales.

About the Reviewers

❖ **Babafemi Bulugbe** is a dedicated DevOps and cloud engineer with over five years of hands-on experience in optimizing and managing cloud environments across Microsoft Azure and **Amazon Web Services** (**AWS**) platforms. He is highly proficient in designing, deploying, and maintaining scalable, highly available, and secure cloud infrastructures tailored to business and operational needs.

Babafemi is skilled in automating CI/CD pipelines, provisioning **infrastructure as code** (**IaC**), and applying industry best practices to ensure infrastructure reliability, performance, and security. His work consistently drives efficiency and resilience in modern cloud-based systems.

He brings strong expertise in scripting with PowerShell, Bash, and Python, enabling him to automate workflows, streamline deployment processes, and manage complex environments with precision. Known for his attention to detail and a proactive approach, Babafemi collaborates effectively with cross-functional teams to deliver high-impact cloud solutions.

His passion for continuous improvement, combined with a solid understanding of DevOps principles and cloud architecture, makes him a valuable asset in any technology-driven organization.

❖ **Ron Veen** is a seasoned software engineer with extensive experience ranging from Microservices to mainframes. His passion for software engineering and architecture has been his guiding force throughout his career. With over 20 years of expertise in the JVM and the Java ecosystem, Ron is an **Oracle Certified Java Programmer** (**OCP**) and a certified **Sun Business Component Developer** (**SCBCD/OCPBCD**).

A dedicated Java enthusiast, Ron also has a keen interest in alternative JVM languages, particularly Kotlin. At Team Rockstars IT, he serves as a special agent and lead developer, frequently speaking at international conferences. Ron is the author of books on Java cloud-native migrations with Jakarta EE and on virtual threads, structured concurrency, and scoped values. He has also co-written a book on Kotlin.

Acknowledgements

The author would like to express his sincere gratitude to all those who contributed to the completion of this book.

To the co-authors: It was a pleasure and an honor to have you join forces and give you space to speak to areas the author thought you would excel in. This is the first of many collaborations ahead of us.

To the publisher: Thank you for giving the author this opportunity and supporting him through every step of this process.

To the authors' friends who provided feedback during the writing process: Thank you to everyone who took the time to read portions or the complete work and provide feedback. You made it possible for the author to create the best outcome. Specifically, Michael Atencio and Aaron Granovitz for their outsized contributions.

To the readers: The author knows time is valuable, and he appreciates your interest in the book. He knows that you will now be better armed to head out into trenches and improve organizational culture and outcomes.

Preface

Have you ever tried to wrap your head around what DevOps is and been confused? It is understandable! DevOps is not a team, technology, role, or tooling. Its culture and philosophy bring developers and operators together to achieve better business outcomes.

In short, it is a cultural philosophy that utilizes communication, collaboration, and feedback loops to enhance processes in software development and maintenance, ultimately aiming for improved business outcomes. Join us as we explore several key areas of technology driven by DevOps culture. We will emphasize automation, testing, security, continuous integration, and continuous delivery. Once we have deployed, we will examine the questions we must ask ourselves to ensure our systems are still operating as desired.

Most importantly, this guide seeks to help you understand the why more than the how. There are many great resources on how to perform a specific engineering task, but they rarely take the time to explain why you should or should not do something. You should expect a 70/30 split of why vs. how. This will enable us to be agile when applying the DevOps philosophy and avoid limiting ourselves to what we can fit on a page.

Chapter 0: Navigation- Welcome to your journey of exploring DevOps. Thank you for entrusting me as your guide. This will be a brief guide to some of the book's structure, including unique navigation techniques that will help you get the most out of it.

Chapter 1: Introduction to DevOps- You may have heard or read about the term DevOps before, or perhaps this is your first introduction. Either way, you are looking to understand what it really means. It can be confusing. The definition changes depending on whom you ask.

Before we dive into the implementation details of how to, we need to take a step back and understand a bit of the why that drives the mindset, we will start by defining DevOps and exploring how the movement emphasizes building and sustaining a culture of empathy, continuous communication, collaboration, and delivering value. It recognizes that while it is essential to scale technology, it is really hard to do so without a culture that enables it. Having worked at both smaller and larger organizations, we will examine how things are structured differently and how to avoid the pitfalls of applying solutions that work well at companies like Google and Netflix to a 10-person organization.

Chapter 2: Planning and Reacting to a Changing Organization's Needs- Planning is challenging, especially when meeting rapidly changing requirements from different parts of the organization with competing priorities. We will explore what Agile is and how it can help us frame our approach to planning and managing work streams. We will compare Scrum vs Kanban and why one or the other may better fit a team or organization. Most importantly, it lets you know that these are guides to help you and are not a religion. You should create your own agile framework to meet the needs of your team and customers, rather than adopting one because a certified agile person said so.

Chapter 3: Automation- While culture and philosophy might be the heart of DevOps, you can think of automation as the arteries that allow the heart to pump the blood to where it needs to go. One could certainly say that this is the meat and potatoes of the day in the life of an infra, SRE, security, etc. Engineers who are operating with a DevOps mindset. Before we dive directly into the code, we will take a quick look at why it is so important not to rely on manual processes. We will explore the processes of gathering requirements and selecting tools and frameworks, delving into the common patterns used to minimize negative user impact during the development and deployment phases.

Chapter 4: Importance of Automated Testing- In theory, we could deploy code, but is it safe to do so? As we established in the last chapter, automation is a crucial scale component. It does come with its dangers. When we make mistakes, the stakes are higher. Instead of slowly impacting a handful of systems, we may be taking down the entire system all at once, and it may be in a way that is not easy to recover. Let us define different types of testing so that we can help build the confidence that the changes we are making are safe, whether it is Friday at 3 PM or Monday at 9 AM.

Chapter 5: Security- What is cybersecurity, and why is it important? We will quickly explore cybersecurity and its crucial historical context. Then, we will examine its core principles and discuss how to manage risk effectively. Most importantly, we will cover the CIA triad and why it is so foundational.

Chapter 6: Understanding Pipelines- We will explore pipelines and their potential value. This chapter will serve as a primer for the following chapters, focusing on CI and CD pipelines.

Chapter 7: Continuous Integration- Testing is critical at scale. Developer time is expensive, and we want to optimize the time it takes for them to get feedback from the system, whether their code behaves as intended or not. Often, setting up useful testing is challenging. Let us explore how to introduce the concept of continuous integration and code testing. We need to apply it to workstations and remote systems to reduce the time and complexity for developers to test their changes before pushing to production.

Chapter 8: Continuous Delivery- This chapter explores the realm of **continuous deployment and continuous delivery (CD)**, highlighting its crucial role in consistently delivering value to production. We begin by exploring the fundamental concepts of

CD and why its successful implementation depends on a solid foundation in CI. With this understanding, we discuss selecting the deployment tooling and frameworks that align with our specific needs and requirements to achieve continuous deployments with minimal impact on customers and stakeholders.

Chapter 9: Pipeline Mastery- Now that we know how to create automated testing and deployments, we must consider how to integrate them efficiently and effectively. We will examine what makes good pipelines and what they can help us accomplish. Much of this work involves translating the necessary business and technical requirements, such as quality assurance and change management, and codifying them.

Chapter 10: Trusting Our Metrics- It is essential to be data-driven; however, the analysis is only as good as the initial data and its accurate representation. You may be familiar with the phrase lies, damned lies, and statistics popularized by Mark Twain, which I find hits home with a lot of of this chapter. We will examine what makes a good metric, why it is created, and how we can create meaningful metrics, identify useless ones, and game the system when necessary.

Chapter 11: Valuation, Bridging Management and Engineering- Have you ever heard someone say this does not bring value, and been taken aback? You would be amazed how few people understand what value is. If our leaders, peers, and subordinates do not understand value, we must expect that they will make bad choices for the organization. In this chapter, I welcome Jay B. Abrams, who has a background in economics and over 40 years of experience focused on determining organizations' value, to have a discussion to help bridge our understanding of what value is so that it can be used as the common language across business, finance, and engineering.

Chapter 12: Observability- We will begin by exploring the differences between monitoring and alerting, as well as some high-level concepts to help you improve the quality of what you monitor and ensure that you are alerting on the right kinds of signals. I will share my unique perspectives as a practitioner and open-source maintainer in the observability space. Once we have established effective monitoring and alerts, we will shift our focus to processes related to on-call responsibilities.

Chapter 13: This Was Just the Beginning- The world around us changes, especially as we introduce new technological improvements. Let us take a few minutes to discuss how a transformative technology, **artificial intelligence** (**AI**), is starting to impact people and affect the DevOps philosophy and culture. We will briefly examine history, risks, rewards, and various impacts to make informed decisions when navigating change.

Code Bundle and Coloured Images

Please follow the link to download the
Code Bundle and the *Coloured Images* of the book:

https://rebrand.ly/uh2sbyk

The code bundle for the book is also hosted on GitHub at
https://github.com/bpbpublications/Strategic-DevOps.
In case there's an update to the code, it will be updated on the existing GitHub repository.

We have code bundles from our rich catalogue of books and videos available at
https://github.com/bpbpublications. Check them out!

Errata

We take immense pride in our work at BPB Publications and follow best practices to ensure the accuracy of our content to provide with an indulging reading experience to our subscribers. Our readers are our mirrors, and we use their inputs to reflect and improve upon human errors, if any, that may have occurred during the publishing processes involved. To let us maintain the quality and help us reach out to any readers who might be having difficulties due to any unforeseen errors, please write to us at :

errata@bpbonline.com

Your support, suggestions and feedbacks are highly appreciated by the BPB Publications' Family.

Did you know that BPB offers eBook versions of every book published, with PDF and ePub files available? You can upgrade to the eBook version at www.bpbonline.com and as a print book customer, you are entitled to a discount on the eBook copy. Get in touch with us at :

business@bpbonline.com for more details.

At www.bpbonline.com, you can also read a collection of free technical articles, sign up for a range of free newsletters, and receive exclusive discounts and offers on BPB books and eBooks.

Piracy

If you come across any illegal copies of our works in any form on the internet, we would be grateful if you would provide us with the location address or website name. Please contact us at business@bpbonline.com with a link to the material.

If you are interested in becoming an author

If there is a topic that you have expertise in, and you are interested in either writing or contributing to a book, please visit www.bpbonline.com. We have worked with thousands of developers and tech professionals, just like you, to help them share their insights with the global tech community. You can make a general application, apply for a specific hot topic that we are recruiting an author for, or submit your own idea.

Reviews

Please leave a review. Once you have read and used this book, why not leave a review on the site that you purchased it from? Potential readers can then see and use your unbiased opinion to make purchase decisions. We at BPB can understand what you think about our products, and our authors can see your feedback on their book. Thank you!

For more information about BPB, please visit www.bpbonline.com.

Join our Discord space

Join our Discord workspace for latest updates, offers, tech happenings around the world, new releases, and sessions with the authors:

https://discord.bpbonline.com

Table of Contents

CHAPTER 0
Navigation

Why chapter 0?

In computer science, we always start counting at 0, which sets the tone for this book's technical nature, even as we explore the messier nature of organizational cultures.

Cheat codes for various personas

The author is a gamer and a software developer; *cheat codes* (when used fairly) are an effective and efficient use of time. This book is about engineering culture, not technology. You can extract value without looking at a single line of code. Why?

This chapter is written for you if you are not a software engineer. Software engineers may also utilize it on subsequent reads, or if they have heard enough opinions on a particular topic and want to enjoy the first read without (re)exploring paths they are familiar with. Even if you are not a software engineer (or have not been in many years), there is value in better understanding how to build an effective, efficient, and productive (engineering) culture.

This book is not just for engineers. It is for a diverse range of professionals, including engineering executives, executives at engineering companies, project managers, product managers, QA testers, IT operations, system administrators, network administrators, and anyone else curious about building an effective and efficient culture. The author has shared excerpts with friends, family, and peers who are not engineers, and they found it insightful and understandable, even if they could not extract the complete value.

When we see a [NOTE: **GOTO SECTION HEADER**], you can **optionally** fast-forward to that section. These *cheat codes* are precious for folks who want to avoid getting bogged down in the nitty gritty. They typically contain code snippets or information that they may already know and do not need an introduction. We usually indicate a specific persona or context-specific criteria for using these mechanisms.

Different ways to consume

The author designed this book to be helpful through different lenses, allowing you to tackle one problem or another, and it does not require reading the entire book in one specific order. For example, you can consume it differently after the first run. Together, we will walk through a logical progression around topics; however, experienced practitioners may wish to skip around, and the author will try to give cues when this makes more sense. I heavily use deeply nested headers to help organize the content; the **table of contents** (**TOC**) is an index, and we can use it like any data structure to reference the contents quickly, regardless of the predefined order. The one exception is that you must read *Chapter 1, Introduction to DevOps*. If you must, you can skip the history since you know it.

Join our Discord space

Join our Discord workspace for latest updates, offers, tech happenings around the world, new releases, and sessions with the authors:

https://discord.bpbonline.com

CHAPTER 1
Introduction to DevOps

Introduction

This is a primer to DevOps for the uninitiated and technology veterans alike. We will focus on the challenges that organizations face and how we can use the philosophy and culture of DevOps to achieve better business outcomes. We will approach this through four primary questions in the *Objectives* section.

Objectives

1. What is DevOps?
2. What is the history and evolution of DevOps, and why does it matter?
3. Why does culture overrule technology?
4. How can we create a better culture?

DevOps: Philosophy and culture

You may have heard or read the term DevOps before, or this could also be the first time. Either way, we are looking to understand what it means. It can be confusing as the definition changes depending on whom we ask. Rather than going into a ton of detail already so well covered, I will try to speak to the condensed version and add my flavor based on real-world experiences in story and example formats. I am trying my best to try to distill the most essential (previously covered) aspects, focus on my unique takes, and emphasize topics that are covered but not in as much detail due to their focus and scope. At the end of this book, I highly encourage anyone interested to check out the recommended reading on the various categories of subjects.

Before we dive into the implementation details of *how to*, we need to take a step back and understand the why that drives the mindset, we will start with defining DevOps and exploring how the movement's emphasis is on building and sustaining a culture of empathy, continuous communication, collaboration, and delivering value. It recognizes that while it is vital to scale technology, it is hard without a culture that enables it. Having been at both small and large organizations, we will look at how things are structured differently and how to avoid the pitfalls of applying something that makes sense at Google, Netflix, etc., to a ten-person organization.

What is DevOps?

DevOps is a philosophy and culture that seeks to create better organization or business outcomes by tearing down silos between traditional software developers and operations engineering teams. While we focus on the context of developers and operators, many of the tactics, techniques, and procedures that we describe can be applied to other groups such as quality assurance, cybersecurity, support, product, business, finance, etc.

We can achieve these goals by creating a culture of shared expectations, empathy, communication, and processes. If done correctly, these result in reduced friction between teams (or groups), better products, better services, shorter development cycles, and even long-term cost reduction.

By embracing DevOps, we realize that developers and operators are not as different as we (may) have believed. In my experience, priorities, desire, and knowledge often govern the difference more than anything else.

What it is not!

It is not a technology, a set of tools, person(s), a team, or a title! It also does not distinguish between types of developers and operators. A realization of DevOps culture and philosophy would be an operations engineer recognizing that they are not too different from a software engineer, rather than focusing on a title or set of responsibilities. When most people hear *developer*, they often think that this means an *application* or *product engineer*; this is a bias. In the context of computers, *developers* should refer to anyone involved directly in creating the business requirements and the dependencies required to meet those objectives.

Many engineers' eyes rolled when they saw the title of *DevOps Engineer*. This is because those that created that title did not understand the DevOps movement. We will shortly look at this, but for the moment, we can say that there is no such thing as a *DevOps Engineer* any more than there is a *DevSecPlatformDataQAOps Engineer*. There are Engineers in multiple disciplines who adopt the DevOps philosophy and culture. We should stop trying to shove so much into a title and take the time to become familiar with the movement. I use *Supreme Unicorn Hunter of Planet Earth and the Entire Galaxy Besides* as my unofficial title.

History of DevOps

If you are familiar with the history and want to skip ahead, please move on to the section **[GOTO Why is culture everything?]**.

Before the computer era

This book is about optimizing relationships between developers and operators. What do you mean by a time before computers? How is this relevant?

Some developers are mistakenly under the impression that we are unique. Both application and operations engineers have much in common with other types of engineering, manufacturing, etc. We will call out some early developments used as building blocks by computer engineers later:

- *Fredrick Taylor*, a mechanical engineer, introduced the principles of scientific management in the early 20th century. His foundational work, *The Principles of Scientific Management*, was published in 1911. He primarily focused on optimizing work processes and improving efficiency in industrial settings, particularly manufacturing.

- While certainly, the car may come to mind for many, in some ways, *Henry Ford* had much more profound gifts than simply building cars. In *My Life and Work*, published in 1922, he discusses his experiences and ideas, including the revolutionary introduction of the assembly line.

Computer era

While *Fredrick Taylor* and *Henry Ford* did not directly contribute to DevOps, we built on top of many things that they showed us.

Separation of responsibilities

As software systems became more intricate and required specialized knowledge and skills, organizations assigned distinct roles to different computer engineers. Application Developers now typically focus on writing business logic, designing customer features, and providing a complete product to customers. Systems administrators specialize in managing infrastructure, configuring servers, maintaining networks, and ensuring overall system stability.

While there is no date or event to point to, this happened over some time, in the 20th and early 21st centuries. The role continues to evolve, and we invented (and defined) new terms to achieve the same goals we initially set out to solve, improving the efficiency of our ability to scale as a business.

The separation of duties can matter significantly depending on the organization's size. In many startups and smaller organizations, some application developers are also responsible for some or all of the operational functions.

Here is a story that illustrates why we may want to have a separation of duties even within the same role:

I worked for a company in the real money gambling industry. Let us call it *Take My Money Inc!* for the sake of a name. Some people think that **Payment Card Industry (PCI)**, **Systems and Organizational Controls [NUMBER]** (such as **SOC2–Type II**), or **Health Insurance Portability and Accountability Act (HIPAA)** are a compliance nightmare. The gambling industry is 100 times more complex; we had to deal with international, national, state/ province, county, and city-level regulations. There are a lot of unique aspects that I may reference in the book about this job. In this case, we will focus on one of the things we did to deter potential collusion by engineers.

To avoid speaking about any specifics of the systems, we will simply refer to two core concepts. The platform servers handled all sorts of stuff, and the game servers were responsible for running each game. We designed the system so that both the game server and platform servers could detect certain types of tampering. From an access control perspective, our infrastructure team was split and given access to the game or the platform servers, but never both. We did this to protect engineers from themselves; when we see lots of real money, it is better to remove temptation. Most of our threat model simulations required an engineer on both teams to agree to work together, to cheat the system in a way that was not easily detectable. Given the high risks associated, this acted as a strong deterrent.

Lean software development

After the *Second World War*, Japan needed to rebuild its industrial base, which was in shambles. This led Toyota to need to improve its efficiency with its production methods. To this end, they studied the Ford Motors production processes and techniques; while many aspects could be copied as is, others required modification and flexibility due to the scales of economy. This ended up bringing substantial improvements to Toyota's processes, it was now possible to change aspects of the assembly line in days, rather than months. This eventually led to the creation of the **Toyota Production System** *(TPS)*, which focuses on making life easier for workers by reducing waste and shortening lead time. *Lean Manufacturing* was heavily influenced by TPS, it focuses on improvement, waste reduction, and value creation. *Lean software development* is based on *Lean Manufacturing*. We will discuss this in further depth in *Chapter 2, Planning and Reacting to a Changing Organization's Needs, Lean Software Development*, what is important to know right now is that it had a profound impact on DevOps.

Rise of virtualization

When I started in this industry, in the late 1990s and early 2000s, provisioning was no small feat, and we considered only a fraction of the overall process. To help someone new to the field, let us see how this used to work.

We called up our representative(s) at our server, storage, and network vendors and requested **X** devices with **Y** capabilities. When can you get that for me?

It was common to plan at least 4-8 weeks to ensure that our vendor could get the required gear to us on the requested date. Then we, in some cases, travel to a data center, rack and stack, pulling all the equipment out, putting it in a rack, connecting it to the network, and then providing an operating system. One or more teams then configured it to meet the needs.

IBM's Cambridge Scientific Research Center was responsible for creating CP-40[1], which introduced the concept of virtual machines into a mainframe. This development led to the first commercial release of IBM System 370[2], which allowed a single machine to run multiple operating systems concurrently on the same hardware.

Mainframes? Yes, mainframes were the first virtualization use case.

Why did mainframes fall out of favor? Computers got cheaper and smaller, making it more feasible to decentralize. We shifted to the client-server model. While many tend to discount mainframes, they remain critical in some largest-scale organizations.

As we moved back from managing a mainframe with many systems to a more 1:1 relationship, we had to look at how to make these systems efficient to scale. In the late 1990s, we saw reason to adopt the concepts we previously learned from mainframes and looked to apply the same ideas and concepts to modern commodity hardware. By the early to mid-2000s, multiple open-source projects and commercial players were now virtualizing servers and workstations.

The saga continues in cloud computing.

Cloud computing

In the early 2000s, a lot of people viewed anyone selling *cloud* as latching onto marketing buzz phrases without doing anything new. At the time, it meant someone ran our server; hosting was an established concept.

What changed my mind? The rise of **Amazon Web Services** (**AWS**). In 2006, when AWS launched its first services, it differed from every other service I had worked with previously. I did not know why it felt different, but I do now. It was the first time someone had taken the meaning of cloud to heart and designed a system around APIs rather than human consoles. The fact that we could write a script to spin up **N** number of systems was compelling. After seeing AWS, I knew we had just stumbled upon the beginning.

1 (IBM CP-40, n.d.)
2 (IBM System 370, n.d.)

While many people refer to 2006 as the start of AWS, it started in 2004 with **Simple Queue Service (SQS)**. It followed up with **Elastic Compute Cloud (EC2)** and **Simple Storage Service (S3)** in 2006.

These combined features started a true cloud; however, there were gaps. While some workloads made sense in the cloud, others would never make sense to migrate. By 2010-2011, the industry launched multiple projects to provide a cloud platform management overlay, deployed on our infrastructure and treated like a cloud, externally hosted or internally. Fast forward to the present day of the book's writing, AWS has more than 200 fully functional services hosted in global data centers.

The other characteristic of cloud computing that people like to talk about is on-demand. From a financial perspective, it is essential to understand capital expenses and operational expenses. When we buy the hardware, we must pay for it whether we use it or not. In other words, it would take a long time to bring value due to long procurement and deployments. At the same time, this can be cheaper in the long term but requires better forecasting not to be wasteful. When we **rent** or pay for using someone else's cloud, this is considered an operational expense instead of a capital expense. In other words, we only pay for it when it is on. In private cloud setups, the hardware needs to be purchased, whether it is used or not, which is a capital expense. We can save on power by turning down services that are not required. The savings of private clouds come from other management efficiency aspects rather than pure hosting costs. One of the very compelling aspects of many public cloud providers: while most services are consumption-based based there are some that are free. This helps offset other aspects of operational complexity, such as building out the **control plane** or management functions at no cost to the customer.

10+ deploys a day, Dev and Ops cooperation

Now that we are here, can we talk about the creation of DevOps?

This historic presentation from (*Hammond & Allspaw*, 2009) at the Velocity conference highlighted how the Flickr Engineering team achieved a high frequency of deployments while maintaining stability and reliability. It is important to remember that it was common to consider annual, bi-annual, quarterly, and monthly releases at the time. Very few organizations were even doing single deployments a day to production. As you can imagine, this was a game changer; some in the audience were not initially sold, as this seemed far-fetched, however, many from both camps were captivated by the lure of what they were selling, even if they were skeptical.

This talk had many ideas that seemed outlandish then, and we now accept them as common knowledge and best practices. Here is a quick overview of some of the most essential concepts:

- They challenged the traditional notion that frequent deployments and stability were mutually exclusive. It emphasized the need for a cultural shift where development and operations teams work together towards shared goals rather than operating in silos.

- They highlighted the importance of effective communication and collaboration between Dev and Ops teams. It highlighted how close cooperation, proactive monitoring, and rapid feedback loops enabled faster and smoother deployments.

- The Flickr team demonstrates the significance of automation and tooling in streamlining the development process. They highlighted their usage of configuration management, continuous integration, and testing frameworks, which were crucial in achieving their deployment frequency.

- They also discussed the importance of feedback loops, continuous learning, and improvement. The team optimized its process over time by closely monitoring the deployments' impacts and promptly addressing issues.

Coinage of DevOps

The term **DevOps** itself seems to have been coined by *Patrick Debois* during a presentation at Agile 2008. This unifying label for the emerging movement clarified that the focus was bridging the gap between Dev and Ops teams. Having the term helped us establish a common language and shared expectations as to what this meant.

DevOps Days started in 2009 and was crucial in fostering a community among professionals interested in DevOps culture, philosophy, and practices. After that, there were dedicated conferences to discuss DevOps, and many started featuring discussions on the topic, even if that was not the focus.

Rise of containers

Containers are a lightweight form of virtualization; they are a logical next step to isolate processes while driving down cost. Containers seek to have a smaller footprint than heavier virtual machines. By reducing the overhead, we encourage process isolation while being able to deploy many services with minimal overhead for the management.

If you think containers are a recent technology, you will be shocked. Containers' popularity started gaining traction in the early 2000s when we began exploring operating system-level virtualization, which we use in systems such as **Linux Containers** (**LXC**) or Docker. In the BSD community, this comes in two forms, *chroot* and *jails*.

Chroot stands for **change root** and was introduced in the 1990s. *Chroot* allows processes to be executed within a restricted directory environment, isolating them from the rest of the system. *Chroot* laid the groundwork that *jails* would be built on top of.

Jails provided a lightweight virtualization mechanism that allowed for the isolation and separation of processes within FreeBSD. *Jails* enabled the creation of these self-contained environments, or jails, with their file systems, network interfaces, and process spaces. This isolation allowed multiple applications or services to be run independently within their respective jails, enhancing security and stability.

When most people talk about containers today, they typically mean LXC or Docker. Both of them were heavily influenced by BSD chroot and jails.

Why are containers relevant to DevOps? Containers have a lot of benefits similar to the previous forms of virtualization. Automation has allowed us to cut down on the time that it takes for us to create value and has the distinct advantage of being less resource intensive. This was made possible by sharing resources from the host rather than relying on a more *complete* virtualization option. Another thing to keep in mind is that this had a profound impact on the development process.

Docker introduced a simple way to manage the definition of a containerized application. With Dockerfiles, developers were able to run locally an isolated version of their application in a way that could resemble production. This allowed developers to better communicate their dependencies and processes needed to bootstrap and run their applications to the Operations teams.

Container orchestration and the age of Kubernetes

Like how cloud platforms formed around virtual machines, we needed to create a system to help manage the running of this complex set of containerized services.

Docker Swarm

As a company, Docker may be the most responsible for the rise of containers. They focused on trying to make the development part easy. Prior to this, our application developers were in pain. It was hard for us to get started contributing to a project. It was a lot of work to pull down the code, install all the required dependencies, update configuration files, and set environmental variables. Developer's machines were *snowflakes,* often leading a developer to declare *works on my machine, must be an ops problem.* A lot of time was wasted by operations and application developers. This meant scaling our development was difficult, especially as we spanned multiple teams with different services. There was no standard, and it was non-trivial to *handcraft* all the necessary components required to run an application locally for development and testing. Only later did Docker invest in creating Swarm, released in 2015. Swarm was Docker's answer to *how do we run this in production.* Before this, the community had to rely on production solutions elsewhere. CoreOS, Apache Mesos, and Kubernetes initially dominated the container orchestration market.

While Docker still develops Swarm, they have invested heavily in supporting Kubernetes tooling from their ecosystem.

Apache Mesos

Benjamin Hindman, Andy Konwinski, and others started working in 2009 at the University of Berkley, CA. The project was *Mesos: A Platform for Fine-Grained Resource Sharing in the*

Data Center.[3] What makes this unique, as opposed to many other container orchestrators out there, is that it is a generalized approach to what needs to run in our data center. The reality is that most organizations will often need standalone Virtual Machines even if they run much of their systems in the container ecosystem.

Nomad

It is an open-source project developed by *HashiCorp* and released in 2015. In similar principles to other HashiCorp tools, the goal was to create a lightweight and easy-to-use solution for managing clusters of computing resources. It supports container and non-containerized applications, which makes it a unique option compared to most.

Nomad was designed from the ground up with simplicity, scalability, and flexibility. Anything that can offer much functionality while keeping complexity down is not something to be underestimated or overstated.

Kubernetes

Kubernetes (**K8s**) started as an internal project for *Google* in the early 2010s to manage their large-scale containerized applications. It was built based on their experiences with managing containers using their in-house system, Borg. At DockerCon 2014, *Google* made the public announcement of the project. In 2015 Kubernetes hit the 1.0 milestone and donated the project to the **Cloud Native Computing Foundation** (**CNCF**) for long-term stewardship. *Google* has remained an active contributor.

We could now argue that at the time of writing, Kubernetes has become a larger organizations' de facto container orchestration platform. If we are looking for evidence, all the major cloud providers offer a hosted Kubernetes service.

Just because all the cool kids are doing it does not mean it is the right fit for us. It is an incredibly complex system that is flexible. With this comes complexity; many may find a more straightforward orchestration platform and scheduler, or other simpler solutions better suit us.

Where are we heading?

Now that we have covered the historical context, let us go on to understand where this industry is heading.

Self-service

The goal of complete self-service is noble. There is a lot of complexity hidden within this; in many cases, it still requires the operator to understand the underlying concepts. We should start having more nuanced conversations, especially with usability, cost, security, and compliance concerns. While we might want to achieve complete self-service in some cases, other times we want to enable it with the appropriate number of reviews, checks, etc., while keeping the outcome of the work completed entirely self-service, even if it requires collaboration to accomplish.

3 (Hindman, et al., 2009)

Sometimes the meaning of self-service changes depending on the context. There are multiple layers through which we can view this. For example, we could be building self-service automation that is only used on our own team and has one set of needs. This is different than when we are building out self-service for another group. When we are working with external groups, our goal is to often take a process that they would have manually requested we do before, and instead look to allow them to define what they want and rely on a review or approval before it can be applied. Once it is applied, the user can perform the task without further hand-holding from the team managing the process. When we look to create a self-service process, we should outline who the beneficiaries are, what self-service means to us in this context, etc.

We will look at this a bit deeper in *Chapter 3, Automation*, as well as other chapters in the book, such as security, testing, and pipelines.

Artificial intelligence

We need to slow down! An incredible amount of hype is causing people to make risky bets despite their better judgment. Rather than tossing anround *unhelpful* and *untrue* labels such as *anti-progress, anti-technology, anti-AI*, or similar anytime someone says something that does not speed up development, we should seek to realize that the people advocating for safe AI are inherrently for progress and AI. We steel ourselves against attempts to distract us from our mission, of ensuring that technology has a positive impact on the world. We will need to figure out how to slowly integrate it before we unleash it on society in an unsafe manner. We are in the initial stages of this, and there are a lot of rewards in store for us and potential dangers that need addressing.

Now that I have gotten that out, let us discuss positive things. We will focus on AI from a developer and operator standpoint:

- Write my code for me!
- Ask it to help us understand how a system is supposed to work!
- Information retrieval
- Automated code reviews
- Automated security testing

AI is not safe enough to trust entirely, but experts in their craft can best use it to augment human decision-making processes. As we progress in this field, we will see shifts in the role of software engineers. In the future, we will rely heavily on AI to generate specific portions of the desired systems and subsystems. We will be more focused on using our knowledge to instruct the AI on the construction and ensuring quality through reviewing the output, primarily focused on flaws in logic that affect the usability, performance, availability, and security of the system.

While I have personally used *ChatGPT* to create some great content, I have seen it make egregious mistakes I would never expect an expert to make. I have used it in some cases extensively, such as using it to write 80% of my documentation on the wiki when rolling out a new network brokering solution (think VPN if that term does not make sense). Whenever I use it, I review the contents carefully, see if I can spot any errors, and optimize the result even if there are no mistakes. After that, I will put the content in with a comment stating that the *content was entirely generated by AI and reviewed by a human for accuracy* or *that an AI-generated it; updated by a human to ensure accuracy and clarity*. To be clear, I have used AI tools to augment my writing, to explore potential topic ideas, spell and grammar checking, etc. All content in this book is original, except where explicitly cited to the contrary.

Wrapping up history

While the *Principles of Scientific Management*, the production assembly line, and Lean Manufacturing all predate DevOps, we would only be where we are without their efforts. They all look at taking a general production problem and breaking it down to improve the overall system.

In the beginning, all developers were responsible for administering their programs. When these systems became too complex to manage, we started separating the concerns of development and operations.

Virtualization is instrumental in automating repeatable deployments, which we will discuss heavily in *Chapter 3, Automation*. It has many variations, each leading to another level of potential optimization.

While some might expect some major event to be the birth of the movement, it was a few engineers getting together to discuss the problems they were seeing and giving a talk at the Agile conference.

All of this is in the pursuit of happiness between developers and operators, because we both prefer our sleep and holidays to dealing with outages after hours. Each of the events we went over has some connection.

Why is culture everything?

It sets the foundation for successfully implementing DevOps practices, processes, and tools. If you skip past this, you learn to write some code, but that is it. Do not get me wrong, that is an accomplishment, but a small fraction of what this offers. Things will go wrong, and when you have a great culture, you can weather the storms as they pass through you.

Communication

People often assume we are talking about language when discussing communication. At the same time, while language is important, what is critical is conveying an idea from one party to another and the process required to facilitate that. Although I do not work in this field, I understand the value communication holds and work to improve my capacity for this daily.

Many of our challenges in life stem from a lack of communication, miscommunication, or not interpreting the intended idea through the intended lens.

As someone who has worked with people worldwide, I can attest that there is more to mastering communication than language and stitching words together. Some of my favorite conversations at work are with our international employees. For now, we will focus on communication between people and teams rather than with systems, which we will cover in depth in *Chapter 6, Understanding Pipelines, Chapter 7, Continuous Integration, Chapter 8, Continuous Delivery, and Chapter 9, Pipeline Mastery.* Effective communication empowers us to share complex thoughts and ideas with each other; this manifests healthy culture through coming to better-shared expectations, improved empathy, collaboration, break down silos, and work through our more challenging issues.

Now that we understand the importance of communication, we can look at how we can improve these areas. You will notice that the topic of communication is woven throughout the book and is certainly not constrained in this section or even the chapter.

Considerations when adopting communication tools

There should be several communication tooling rules that we should ensure:

- It must support all the platforms used by the organization, not a simple majority of members, employees, and contractors.
- It allows people to have open and closed communications.
- It must protect the user from message fatigue, which we will cover in additional depth in *Chapter 12, Observability, Taming your Monitoring, Alerting, and On-call Demons, Identifying* and combatting alert fatigue.
- It must allow us to integrate messages from systems (such as webhooks).
- We must not host it, or it needs to be in a distinct set of fault domains from the rest of our infrastructure. Communication channels need to work even if everything else is down.

Shared expectations

Everyone has expectations; most *miscommunication* events can be broken down into technical failures, different expectations, dropped balls, or a *black swan*. Which we will discuss in the following paragraph. However, if we can address these, we will vastly improve the outcomes, as when people are on the same page. Unfortunately, we will not spend much time addressing the technical aspects of communication itself. Valuable resources focus on the subject, and we must focus on what we can tackle here.

In a sense, most cross-team or functional communication is about understanding others' needs and perspectives, then seeking common ground and creating shared expectations. We should always give people the benefit of the doubt that they are reasonable. The term *black swan* can have multiple meanings and definitions. Throughout the book, we will refer to a *black swan* as an event when there is asymmetric information, that is, information available to one party and not another. How does this play out? Suppose we are talking with someone, we say something that we believe is innocuous, and we are surprised that they react negatively to our comment or statement. In that case, this is an opportunity to take a step back and evaluate what is the missing link.

Story time, my DevOps moment

Why did I leave behind IT administration and embrace engineering?

I worked at a **Managed Service Provider** (**MSP**); and spent much of my time dealing with customer issues. I began noticing patterns and sought to reduce the amount of grunt work required while improving the customer experience. I categorized the common problems into several buckets and showed that we could have significantly reduced the number of customer support requests if we could solve several core issues. I proposed working one day a week (Friday) on automation to make myself and everyone else better. The solution to an identified problem looked like a win-win scenario.

After preparing this material, I presented it to my boss, who said that, unfortunately, as we billed based on how many issues we solved, this was not good for the business.

While I understood what he was saying on the surface, I struggled with this logic; it seemed so short-sighted.

At the time, I considered myself a Sysadmin who did some scripting. I did not understand it then, but it was the most profound moment in my career. It made me want to identify as a programmer who did IT things. Always do right by the customer and the business; never did I want to choose between the two in this way again. The solution was to lean into something I was initially intimidated by. This experience happened before DevOps was a thing. I was searching for DevOps even if I did not know what that was or if it existed.

When I joined the MSP, I expected that I was always supposed to do right by the customer, akin to the Hippocratic Oath, *first, not harm our patients/customers while enriching their experiences for the better*. I could not reconcile this business mindset, knowing there was a more effective and efficient way to do things. I set out to reshape myself based on this new experience.

Fast forward several years, and I identify as a software engineer focusing on operational challenges.

Story time, black swans

I will share a story from my career to help us better understand and identify *black swans*, identify misconceptions, and then get to a positive resolution. We will refer to the company in question as Cloud Widgets Inc., and we will replace all the names as they are not necessary; we will further discuss the importance of anonymity in *blameless postmortems* when we dive into *Chapter 5, Security, What is cybersecurity in a nutshell?, Shifting right and left, Right, Security Incident Response* and *Chapter 12, Observability, Building sustainable on-call processes, Blameless postmortems* and *Root Cause Analysis.*

I interviewed at Cloud Widgets Inc. and received a job offer, but I had not yet realized the chaos I was walking into. After joining, I got to work quickly, evaluating where we were. It took me less than a day to realize that we were not on track and were not where the company believed itself to be. I was informed that the company had been using an external contractor to build its infrastructure. The contractor took a year at on average of 50 hours a week, to deliver a *Jenkins-powered* (continuous integration) build server that could spin up AWS instances tagged with a desired name. After some investigation, we found an *AWS Security Group* giving access to a random IP address in Germany, which only made sense if they subcontracted the work. After reporting my findings and the necessary meetings, we ended the relationship and decided we did not have time to find additional contractors. We had to work with our existing resources with the scope of what I considered a production-ready system for the initial launch. One of the problems was that people at the company had marketed around a launch roughly 45 days from when I joined. As we had never seen our entire app work, it was challenging to devise a timeline for when that would happen. There were some severe architectural constraints, and the stack was unnecessarily complex, brittle, and needed to be simplified. For example, they needlessly built their own rather than using existing (open source or commercial) service discovery mechanisms. Applications ran on the same hardcoded ports, so we initially had to run one per machine. The applications would crash if we passed an environmental variable that it was not aware of! We broke down the existing requirements and said we wanted to launch this ASAP. Does constraint **X** affect our ability to launch sooner? If so, it was on the table to change; otherwise, we left it alone and said it needed further optimization post-launch. After introducing better solutions, which took several weeks, we devised a 60-day target to bring a production solution online.

We were effectively still launching from zero. We did not even have a network or account designated for development, let alone production. Again, we had effectively implemented a minimal feature built into the AWS console, SDK, and APIs. I was their first remote engineer, which added to the importance of effective communication and clear expectations. I needed 50% of my time to be *heads down*, writing automation. We needed to bring things online in a reliable and repeatable process that we could easily roll out to Production once we had a working development environment.

I spent 25% of my time teaching several of our application developers about the infrastructure side to help add bandwidth. I worked with leadership to quickly remove hiring roadblocks to staff up the needs. I reserved the remaining 25% for travel (required), weekly status meetings with our executives, ad hoc meetings, and anything else needed.

We brought the last core component into our development environment eight days before our target of having a working production setup. I immediately let our engineering executive know we were good. We finally had it working in our production environment two days after bringing up development for the first time, six days before our target deadline. Now, taking a step back, let us examine this and ask a few questions:

- What black swans existed that contributed to a false set of expectations?
- What things did I do to help establish or reset shared expectations?
- What were some of the direct and indirect impacts of creating shared expectations?
- What questions would you want to ask to understand the context better?

Psychological safety

Psychological safety refers to an environment or team culture where individuals feel safe and comfortable expressing their thoughts, ideas, questions, concerns, and even making mistakes without fearing negative consequences, humiliation, or punishment. It creates a supportive atmosphere where open communication, collaboration, and innovation can thrive. Psychological safety encourages individuals to take reasonable risks, share diverse perspectives, and contribute their best to the team's goals, fostering a sense of trust, respect, and psychological well-being.

Accountability

Just because we have psychological safety does not mean there is no accountability for actions, and it is certainly not OK to be a jerk, for which there are consequences. The golden rule of *treating others how one wishes to be treated* especially applies when giving critical feedback. We will explore how to do this in the unpopular opinion *with empathy*.

Experimentation

Everyone needs to sit down and determine their risk profile and how they want to balance innovation and stability. Holding people personally accountable makes them less willing to try new things. When leadership signs off on trying something out, they acknowledge our outlined risks. The buck stops with them.

Empathy

Empathy is a super-power, it is obtained through our efforts to share our feelings, perspectives, and experiences with others. By putting ourselves in another's shoes, we can better recognize their motivations. When we understand someone's motivations, it is easier to respond in a caring manner. In the context of DevOps, empathy is a core principle that we use to foster effective and efficient collaboration, communication, and teamwork across teams and disciplines.

Unpopular opinions

Organizations are a collection of people. Most open-minded people resist change at some level. Sometimes that is all it takes to make it unpopular; other times, issues are real. We must be conscious that ego and politics often play a part in this.

What would be an example where we need to voice an unpopular opinion?

Setting the stage

We are responsible for provisioning infrastructure and applications and responding to their availability problems.

We have recently joined our organization, and after participating in several on-call rotations, we observe that most of the problems come within the application rather than the infrastructure.

There are several issues in this hypothetical situation, which I have seen play out dozens of times in various shapes at different companies. We will discuss this type of scenario in depth in *Chapter 12, Observability, Taming monitoring, alerting, and on-call demons, Building sustainable on-call processes, Identifying and combating alert fatigue*.

We need to (re)route alerts so that the issues are brought to the people who can most quickly address the notification and who are able to impact future decisions based on the event. A common example is moving alerts to application developers when we previously might have had all alerts route through a central infrastructure, site reliability, system administration, support, etc. teams.

We still need teams to monitor the infrastructure, allowing respective teams to focus on their domain of expertise. Equally important is that they feel the consequences of their actions. Most often, they are unaware of the impact they are causing and need help understanding it. By voicing shared expectations around quality and support needs, we can create empathy for both sides. We can see from the other side why this idea might be unpopular. The application developers have benefited from the support already being provided, and we are now challenging that shared expectation that it is always an operations problem until we prove it is application related. They have been shielded, not facing the impact of their choices. It always should have been part of their job.

After convincing the various groups within engineering to redistribute the workload, we will need to make sure that we are there to help them with the transition. When services or responsibilities are handed over the team(s) will need time to wrap their head around what they have inherrited. During these times, the most important thing is keeping active lines of communication between these groups to ensure as smooth as possible handover.

Setting another stage

Let us say, we work for a medical software company. Some of our products fall under compliance territory, and others do not. One day we are approached by another team that informs us that we need to deploy this new service. After going back and forth a bit to understand what they are doing, we highlight the fact that this involves patients and, as such, falls under compliance requirements. During the discussion, they revealed that we would be relying heavily on a third-party API that would have access to the sensitive data we must assume is **Protected Health Information** (**PHI**). The company and product in question do not have any compliance or certifications attesting to their trustworthiness to handle our most sensitive data. According to the person who came to you, we need this running in two weeks.

There are at least two red flags in this hypothetical scenario.

- We should never trust our sensitive (especially regulated) data to a third party without vetting them.

- If this integration was actually important, there would be appropriate time given to perform a proper evaluation. We understand organizations want to react to the market, but we should not stake our integrity or reputation without proper risk management.

  [Thinking on your own]

- What other red flags do you see?

- What are some appropriate next steps to take?

Rules for feedback

Personality-wise, I cut to the heart of the matter rather than beat around the bush. We should speak our minds if we do it respectfully and have built psychological safety.

How do we go about providing critical feedback with empathy? Let us start with some rules to keep in mind:

- Never attack the person that has an opposing position.

- Always give the benefit of doubt, in other words assume positive intent.

- Always allow both sides to speak their piece without interruption.

- Always discuss the idea/specifics, not the people behind them.

- Always be prepared to be objective: back up our assertions with facts, anecdotal evidence, metrics, etc.

- While it depends on the person, I prefer to give it live rather than text-based messaging. Tonal inflexions can easily be lost and more easily misinterpreted.

- If things look to be going poorly, look to get out. Using something like *It sounds like this needs further discussion; I will set something up* has taken heated conversations away from the group.

- If we feel it necessary to escalate and need to state the unpopular opinion in public, be prepared for the fallout.

Psychological safety

Psychological safety is critical to enabling DevOps. When we create a culture where we hear each other out and do not *shoot the messenger*, we end up having teams that are more willing to innovate and can work through our challenges.

Collaboration

Now that we have teams communicating with each other and being able to set clear expectations, we can figure out how we can best work together. There are many models, each with its pros and cons. For example, it is valid to keep all a particular responsibility centralized or attempt to use embedded team members on various teams. They are correct if we figure out how to work together as part of a larger team to ensure we are delivering value. The reality is that I have yet to know anyone who has worked without resource constraints; we can choose what we want to optimize for based on that.

Enabling business and technology

Now that we better understand the relationship between developers and operators, we can examine DevOps's relationship with the business. In today's rapidly evolving digital landscape, technology is not just a means to an end but a critical enabler of an organization's success in achieving its mission statement. As organizations strive to stay competitive and deliver value to their customers, they must harness technology's power effectively. Enter DevOps, a transformative culture and philosophy focused on improving communication, collaboration, and empathy in the pursuit of efficiency at scale. DevOps is not merely about tools or processes but about aligning technology initiatives with business goals to achieve enhanced agility, customer satisfaction, and competitive advantages.

Organization and business agility

Organizations and businesses (which we will often use interchangeably) that effectively implement DevOps can expect to be able to respond quickly to market changes, customer demands, and emerging opportunities. The primary method of this is shortening development lifecycles. Often, we start with an idea and look to improve it; DevOps philosophy pushes our development and operational practices to mirror this. We ensure that we can react quickly to changing organizations' needs through automation, continuous integration, and continuous delivery.

Customer satisfaction

We put our customers near the center stage in an organization practicing DevOps. We ensure open lines of communication and feedback loops between our producers and consumers. We look to design our systems to be highly available, proactively monitor and improve them, and implement well-thought-out incident management to result in shorter and fewer customer disruptions.

Customer advisory boards (**CABs**), a group of selected customers who provide feedback, insights, and guidance to an organization or team regarding their products, services, and overall organization's strategy. CABs are often composed of representatives from key customers, and they serve as a forum for open and collaborative discussions between the company and its customers. In larger companies, we could create a CAB for internal products.

Design partners are like CABs, although they are typically expected to collaborate more regularly throughout the design process and may be limited to a specific feature. My experience with product owners via CABs and design partnerships is that they appreciate direct feedback and working with them on solutions. Some people think that product managers want to hear **yes**, they do, but only if that is how we feel about it. The purpose of connecting with these customers is to increase the product's effectiveness, efficiency, experience, etc. Put ourselves in their shoes; they went out of their way to connect with customers to ensure that their products met their needs; they certainly do not want to wait until other customers get their hands on it and say it does not meet their needs. Now, they must decide if they can modify it to meet those additional needs with constraints from previous implementations.

Competitive advantages

When leveraging DevOps, we can cut down the time to market, reducing cost and fostering innovation, giving the organization an edge over ones that have yet to bring their developers and operators together. In addition to many of the time-to-market-type advantages, we must look at how we can drive improved **return on investment** (**ROI**) through efficient design, especially when utilizing consumption-based models such as public clouds. By leveraging automation and consumption models, we can reduce waste and ensure that we can meet the scale needs of the organization.

We have discussed some ways DevOps can help an organization or business meet its needs. How about a real example?

I was working for *Doximity*, a medical software company, before the start of the COVID-19 pandemic. We had a product called *Doximity Dialer*, which was a tool used by medical professionals to call up patients, masking their number as their office or hospital to ensure that we could cut down on the time it took for a doctor to update a patient when getting results, while also ensuring that the patient would pick up. Fewer patients would pick up the call if the medical professional relied on blocking their number.

Enter the start of the pandemic: The world was in a state of panic; many places had varying levels of shutdown/lockdown. Due to the restrictions, people needed to connect more online than previously. Companies scrambled to enable remote workers, ramp up demand, and do anything else necessary to keep the lights on in their business.

As you can imagine, being a medical software company that connects medical professionals, there was an incredible influx and demand for our platform. We had to assemble multidisciplinary strike teams to focus on keeping up with a scale we had yet to see previously.

In addition to the high demand for our existing services, our customers screamed, *We need Telehealth products now!* We decided to rise to the occasion and build an initial telehealth product at *warp speed* to meet the emerging needs of our users in near real time.

After we launched this new product, it compounded our problems. We received an unprecedented amount of traffic on our platforms and had to scale many times beyond what is considered reasonable to plan for, think double-digit multiples. Thankfully, we had invested heavily in automation and were on the largest public cloud provider at the time (AWS), which could help us meet those scale needs. If we were running our own data centers, we would have fallen over and needed more time to procure the necessary equipment to meet the demand. The pandemic was a make-or-break moment for the company; due to our heavy investments into the right areas, we walked away OK, other than being a bit sleep deprived.

There is some overlap between this section and business agility, and I initially struggled with where I should put this story, as it speaks to both. Business agility is a general grouping of competitive advantages.

[OPTIONAL] Produce two answers to each of the questions below.

- How did your organization handle suddenly needing to support remote workers?
- Could your organization have risen to the challenge and met these needs?

Many times, operations are often overlooked until something goes wrong. Did you have an opportunity to change the perception that we can drive business value with these boring operational investments?

Framing DevOps as an organization or business strategy

By framing DevOps as a strategic approach that bridges the gap between technology and business or organization, we set the stage for exploring DevOps principles, practices, and methodologies to facilitate the alignment of information technology initiatives within the broader organizational objectives. While the name implies that we are focusing on development and operations, the reality is that while the specifics change, it is an approach to bringing together two or more groups with (seemingly?) competing priorities and incentives.

Incentive alignment

Operation developers support application developers and not the other way around.

We will come back to this quote shortly because it lives at the heart of our discussion. Please note, we use the terms *Customer* and *User* interchangeably, as well as *Implementors* and *Developers*.

- **What is incentive alignment?** In short, it is about ensuring that business leadership and implementers are rewarded for acting in the best interest of shareholders or *customers*, rather than their own interests exclusively.

  Throughout this section, we will make a few assumptions to simplify and isolate how operations personnel are affected by this notion of incentive alignment and how leadership might respond to optimize product development.

- **Business leadership and customer alignment:** The most sustainable, long-term relationships derive from leadership that prioritizes customers' needs, founded upon an excellent product or service. For simplicity, let us assume this is the context and culture of our team as we proceed to inspect developer dynamics.

- **Application vs. operations developers:** For a developer of any kind to sustainably contribute to a project, the value of their contributions must support the interests of leadership in both reality and perception. Although both developer personas seek to satisfy leadership interests, the perception of a persona's value is often held unequally. Let us define a few terms before we unpack this.

- **Incentives:** We define incentives as any bonus, promotion, recognition, benefit, or general addition desirable to a developer. This could include access to budgets for tooling or personnel. These incentives are dispensed according to the achievement of *performance indicators*.

- **Performance indicators vs. activities:** Developers are incentivized by achieving *performance indicators* (think new features, or server uptime), which are outcomes of *activities* recognized by leadership to add value. By contrast, an activity that adds value but is not recognized by leadership as such would not be considered a performance indicator. The effort to achieve a performance indicator is a type of activity. One is a subset of the other. Each activity carries with it the perceived degree to which it impacts our product. We will call this a *degree of separation*. The more indirectly an activity impacts our product, the greater its degree of separation.

  - **Typical (mistaken) lens of leadership**: The following figure depicts an artificial hierarchy representing a misguided leadership's perception of the relationship between operations and product development. This is a flawed perception, born in ignorance of what operations do and their contribution to the final product.

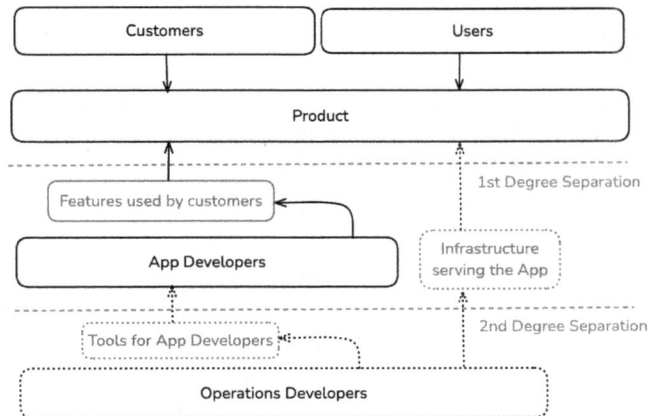

Figure 1.1: Perceived degrees of separation

Among more than one of my former employers, I would estimate the typical engineering executive understands perhaps one-half of the various contributions that operations engineering makes to the final product, and from there it falls off rapidly. A typical CEO likely understands an even smaller fraction of the contribution. Is there any wonder that they perceive operations as a mere cost center, a necessary evil to be minimized, bleeding the bottom line?

What is the solution to this perception deficit and communications gap? The first part of the solution is to make the operations' contribution to an organization's product and value clear to leadership. Providing a list of the various tools and other capabilities by category that operations provide to the application developers is a good starting point. The entire book is a lightweight response to *what value does operations bring?*

The second part of the solution is for both operations engineering and leadership to understand valuation. How does one measure the value of a business and its various components? This is a pathway for operations to command respect and restore it to a place of proper dignity in organizations that typically perceive it as an annoying necessity, even below the level of having to pay an accountant to file one's tax returns. At least the accountant can claim to be saving money with their work. We will discuss how to measure the value of the business and its various components in *Chapter 10, Trusting Our Metrics* and *Chapter 11, Valuation, Bridging Management and Engineering*.

Some executives, including our engineering ones, are lacking context to understand how value is affected by each group's contributions to the business. The degree of separation is a perception and is not proportionate to value. *Figure 1.1* paints the picture of app developers performing solo on stage, where Ops plays background music in the orchestra pit.

For example, I have assisted an operations team once plagued by poor logic concerning a project's database adapters. In this case, if there was a node replacement performed due to failures in the cluster, the application would also fail to refresh its connection pool, leaving it erroring and non-functional until someone kicked it. The product teams did not care about the impact on our customers or how it affected the operations team. After enough nights of lost sleep, we, the operations team, decided to peer deep into the bowels of the adapter. We identified the undesirable behavior and submitted a patch to the upstream provider. The developers told us that this was a feature and that they would not accept our proposed changes. After some discussion, we created our own adapter to address the specific operational concerns that modified the upstream behavior, and never looked back.

With the importance of operations activities in hand, let us shift our previous diagram to reflect a direct impact on our product.

o **Cleaning our glasses**: *Figure 1.2* paints the picture of a duo that complements each other and whose efforts are directly impactful to the product:

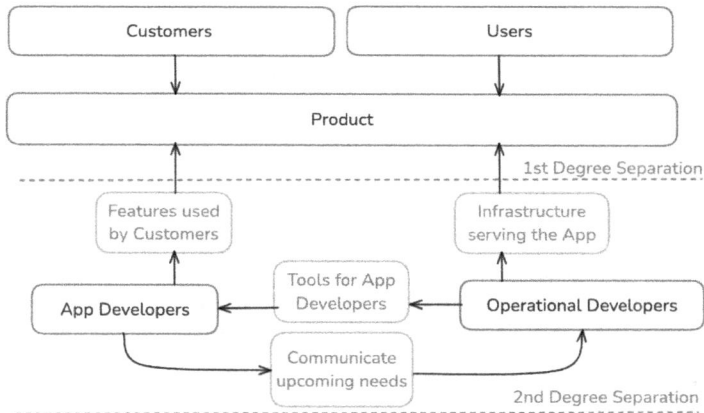

Figure 1.2: Degrees of separation

How would we modify our quote from earlier to reflect operations having a direct impact?

Leadership supports operations and application developers, whose combined efforts support customers.

- o **Epilogue**: To change the perception and get better results, we need to ensure that each persona considers the following:

  - **All developers**: Balance performance indicators with activities that ultimately improve the product. If an activity is considered necessary but is not captured within a performance indicator, then communication with leadership is needed to ensure credit is received for the effort.

  - **Operations developers**: Gather feedback from application developers to keep a pulse on any workflow issues or slowdowns they are facing. These touchpoints serve to inform the next iteration of tooling, but also give an opportunity to scout for changes on the horizon that might not have been communicated yet.

  - **Application developers**: Collaborate with operations on upcoming features and related technology. Make sure to broadcast any upcoming needs with as much lead time as possible. Approach with goals rather than solutions.

  - **Leadership**: Gather feedback from operations along with application developers to support activity orchestration. Seeking to understand the impact of an activity leads to appreciation, which in turn, will inform the appropriate incentives. For example, I have seen leaders give direction that no major upgrades should happen for the first half of the year! This obviously is not realistic, as it disrupts operations and infrastructure teams from completing their goals. Risk also increases during future upgrades since they were deferred longer, meaning we have less time to understand the impact of changes and apply them before we are forced. An upstream provider's surprise imposition or meeting a regulatory compliance requirement are examples of infrastructure goals typically at risk.

- **Reporting structure:** Reporting structure can contribute to or detract from incentive alignment. A common example of misaligned incentives is to have a security team report to the same executive who is primarily responsible for innovation and growth rather than risk management. When there are no security executive(s) sitting at the table, it is better to have security leaders report to the chief legal or finance officers, as they are more responsible for risk management than a typical engineering executive. Please note that this is affected by the industry. For example, a security engineering company's engineering executive is not comparable to most industries.

- **Job insecurity:** There are some in our industry that seek to create job security through obfuscation, intentionally making their code hard to work with, not conforming to team or industry standards, etc. When we encounter a system that is poorly designed, we must evaluate the cost of maintaining the existing solution against a refactor or even a complete rewrite. The more difficult it is to maintain, the more willing an organization is to invest resources for a rewrite, especially after the purchase of a company; the company will work to make the bottleneck go away or make it no longer critical to the organization's success. This can be true when discussing systems, processes, employees, contractors, and third-party managed services.

Differences in larger vs. smaller organizations

Not all organizations are the same, we should be careful to take our typical *this is industry standard* with a grain of salt. We will briefly take time to carefully explore myths, lenses, and teams within the organization.

Myths

When sketching this out, I called these myths. Upon re-reading the *DevOps Handbook*[4], I knew why; it was how I had heard it years ago, and it resonated with me. I spent some time searching for a better word, and it fits it too perfectly to change.

- **It only works if:** This is already well covered, so I will summarize a couple of these and speak to them all at once rather than breaking them down.

    Here are some examples:

    o DevOps only works in startups.

    o DevOps only works at small companies.

---

4 (Kim, Humble, Debois, Willis, & Forsgren, 2021)

o DevOps only works in enterprises.

o DevOps only works at Unicorns.

o DevOps only works at X, Y, Z.

- **Realities:** My experiences match the results of the various case studies out there. Organizations implementing DevOps culture have improved their effectiveness and efficiency while reducing friction between groups of people who have historically (and still have some) had competing priorities. No one suffers from improved communication, collaboration, and empathy. I was discussing this with an engineer, and we had a long conversation about not getting bogged down in manifestos. True DevOps is an *otsefinam* or the opposite (reverse) of a *manifesto* mindset.

Lenses

I have worked at organizations ranging in size from under ten to hundreds of thousands of employees. I realize that my default lens is one of a larger organization. As such, it is essential to dedicate a section to this. In addition, I will describe some differences in a smaller organization. Most importantly, if you find me saying something that does not make sense for an organization or team your size, please disregard it. Hopefully, you will have an opportunity to return here and review with a new lens. For example, please do not run an overly complex Kubernetes stack to run a handful of WordPress sites. If your business is hosting WordPress sites, that is another matter.

Teams

In many smaller organizations, operations may fall on the application development team and eventually will get a dedicated role to help this. One team becomes larger with too much scope. There are two main ways to scale it: to embed members on other teams or carve out a section to focus on. If we choose the latter, we must be conscious that we are not creating silos.

Organizational silos

In the upcoming sections we will demystify what silos are, understand why they come to be, the harm they bring our organizations, and some techniques that we can use to combat the negative effects.

What are they, and why are they harmful?

An organizational silo is a situation where different teams or departments operate in isolation, with limited communication, collaboration, and knowledge sharing. The hallmark signs of a silo are barriers and boundaries that hinder the flow of information, ideas, and resources across various parts of the organization.

As we previously established, DevOps is a culture of communication and collaboration. In a sense, the entire DevOps movement is the answer to what we do when we encounter organizational silos.

How busting silos makes life easier

When we leave teams to themselves, they lose sight of the forest for the trees. Let us look at the benefits of breaking up silos while allowing teams to remain autonomous.

- **Communication and collaboration:** The single most telling sign that we have a silo is when there is a lack of effective communication between teams or other units. When groups are isolated, the inevitable outcome is the lack of shared understanding, coordination, and alignment. When we fail at these, it leads to miscommunication, duplicated efforts, building suboptimal or undesirable features and products, and overall loss of effectiveness, efficiency, and productivity.

  To restate in a positive light, breaking down silos helps us with improving cross-unit communication and collaboration, reducing miscommunication, reducing duplicated efforts, and improving efficiency when working on common goals.

- **Effectiveness, efficiency, and productivity:** Rather than give the definitions in isolation, let us attempt to understand them in context with each other.

  o **Effectiveness**: How often are we doing the right thing?

  o **Efficiency**: How well are the resources utilized?

  o **Productivity**: How much progress can we produce within each time constraint?

  When looking at this in the context of a team, I always use the rate. No one is perfect, we sometimes make bad investments, and it is part of the innovative process.

  So, the real question then is, what is most important? While some people will tell you that there is no correct answer. According to me, the most critical aspect is effectiveness. We can optimize our efficiency and productivity if we succeed in getting the right things done.

  Teams working in isolation often have their tools, practices, and methodologies, leading to duplication of efforts and suboptimal use of resources. Breaking down silos and promoting cross-functional collaboration allows for more streamlined and efficient workflows, eliminating unnecessary handoffs and delays.

- **Innovation and creativity:** While creative exploration has a certain freedom with few constraints (a silo being one), it cannot be brute forced alone. I form many of my best ideas when discussing problems with others, especially if they have a unique perspective.

  When teams are left to solve common problems while simultaneously siloed, we end up with suboptimal solutions. We must take advantage of opportunities to leverage other teams' collective intelligence and domain expertise. We get a lot more quality innovation when we can tap into this.

- **Customer focus:** Let us revisit our story about the MSP. Our customers were companies looking to offload IT management to focus on their business, not technology. I was prevented from serving the customer first by management. I decided to put the customer first, which was an absolute requirement before jumping into engineering.

Customers do not always mean external; it is encouraged that you identify your internal and external customers.

External customers: This can vary depending on our business model. In general, this would be either the consumers of the services, goods, and platform, OR the people who might be paying for someone else's consumption.

Internal customers: This can also be up to some interpretation. In short, we refer to any internal user, team, etc., that needs to consume a service or product that another team offers.

From this point on, we will use *customer* and *consumer* interchangeably.

When there is no focus on the *consumer*, the inevitable outcome is an unhappy *customer*. The internal groups' needs and concerns often drown out those of the consumers.

It is essential to place the customer first, even though they are sometimes wrong. When we put the customer at the center of what we do, we are effective, even if we are not efficient or productive. Otherwise, we always miss something crucial.

- **Agility and adaptability:** Isolation can hinder an organization's ability to respond quickly to changes and market demands. When teams operate in isolation, adaptation and rapid improvement become challenging. Organizations can embrace agility by fostering collaboration and breaking down silos, enabling them to respond swiftly to market dynamics, customer feedback, and emerging opportunities.

Avoiding organizational silos is crucial for promoting effective communication, collaboration, efficiency, innovation, customer focus, and agility. It fosters a culture of shared responsibility, accountability, and continuous improvement, which are core aspects of DevOps culture.

How do we break down silos?

We must break down silos. To ensure that we do not worsen things, we must step back and see why they exist. We previously explored the negative consequences of silos; however, they do not form to make things less efficient intentionally. It is often from a desire to internally optimize a process without going through the red tape and external processes that these inefficiencies manifest.

The most important thing is something we have already discussed, open communication and empathy. Before judging a team or a process, ask questions to understand why it exists. Often, something may not make sense from an *outside perspective* until we have a missing piece of information. Once we understand their perspective, we can suggest collaboration in a mutually beneficial way. In *Chapter 3, Automation, Communication,* we will discuss one of the most common ways in a technology organization that helps facilitate communication and collaboration. We will communicate needs, processes, and more through code. Communication naturally has the effect of eroding silos. It is not enough by itself, but it is one of the better places to start.

Put a pin in this thought and return to this section after reading the book. I wove these themes into the rest of the book outside of what I have explicitly called out here. Try to identify what other techniques I did not expressly call out. If you cannot identify any, I suggest you re-read the book.

Is there anything to be careful of here?

There are more landmines out there than we can clear here. We will focus on allowing teams to remain autonomous, even as they specialize, as it is core to DevOps culture. As we previously discussed, at some point, organizations tend to centralize some resources even if they also have embedded team members. Centralized resources are simply a fact of scaling to achieve efficiency; if so, we need to ensure that the newly formed teams can operate in a way that can make many decisions with minimal external dependency. We will discuss how best to handle this throughout the book, specifically in *Chapter 2, Planning and Reacting to a Changing Organization's Needs, Chapter 3, Automation, Chapter 4, Importance of Automated Testing, Chapter 6, Understanding Pipelines, Chapter 7, Continuous Integration, Chapter 8, Continuous Delivery, and Chapter 9, Pipeline Mastery.*

Community and knowledge sharing

As you might imagine, being a culture focused on communication, collaboration, and empathy, there are a lot of great community resources out there to help you grow.

Many DevOps practitioners prefer open-source software to closed-source. The main reason is staring us right in the face; open-source software is the ultimate technological expression of communication and collaboration. It breaks down traditional silos between developers and operators as well as between producers and consumers.

Conclusion

Now that we have a baseline understanding of what DevOps is, the various historical events leading up to the present day, and the importance of culture in achieving our business goals and objectives. This is primarily powered by communication, collaboration, and empathy. While we discussed silo busting, you can expect to see more techniques throughout the book.

In the next chapter, we will look at how we efficiently and effectively structure large software projects and teams within our organizations. We will start with the necessary historical context before diving into the models that are more commonly used today. With this improved flexibility and predictability, we make it easier to react to our reacting organizations and markets.

CHAPTER 2

Planning and Reacting to a Changing Organization's Needs

Introduction

Planning is complicated, especially when meeting rapidly changing requirements from various parts of the organization with competing priorities. We will explore Agile and how it can help us frame how we plan and manage work streams. We will compare *Scrum* vs. *Kanban* and why one or the other may better suit a team or organization. Most importantly, it lets you know that these are guides to help you and are not a *religion*. You should create your own Agile to meet your team and customer needs, rather than because some certified Agile person said so.

Objectives

- How did we plan large software projects?
- What is Agile, and how do I pick the flavor that best suits my team and organization?
- What techniques, tactics, and procedures can we use to improve collaboration and communication?

What agile fits you best?

Before we explore how to pick the Agile best suited for you, let us take a step back and understand where it comes from and why certain practices make sense.

Agile was a response to the plan-heavy methodology of Waterfall.

Before Agile, there was Waterfall

Prior to *Waterfall*, there was no great guide for structuring large software development projects. It aimed primarily to provide predictability and control over the timeline of the project. Initially, it was adopted by hardware companies, whose development software processes were considered more linear and had fewer unknowns.

Dr Winston Royce first described what is known today as the Waterfall methodology in a paper titled *Managing the Development of Large Software Systems*, published in 1970.

Phases

Waterfall methodology is recognizable by its approach to software development through distinct phases, which we must complete before proceeding:

1. **Requirements gathering:** Working with all the required internal and external customer representatives to understand the needs and document the scope, objectives, and functional specifications.

2. **System design:** Create detailed design plans outlining the system architecture, modules, and their relationships.

3. **Implementation:** Developers write code within modules and must integrate it into the larger project.

4. **Testing:** Once it is ready, we ensure the software meets the specified requirements. This includes several types of testing, such as unit, integration, and system, which we will discuss in more depth in *Chapter 4, Importance of Automated Testing, Types of Testing, X-Driven Development*.

5. **Deployment:** Once ready, it is deployed or released to the end-users or customers, including the installation, configuration, and user training.

6. **Maintenance:** Ongoing support and maintenance of the software. This includes bug fixes, updates, and addressing any issues that arise post-deployment.

Characteristics

Let us explore the characteristics of the Waterfall methodology:

*   **Sequential approach:** The sequential progression in the Waterfall model is analogous to *Henry Ford's* assembly line. Both approaches revolve around a step-by-step progression from one phase to another.

*   **Documentation:** The Waterfall methodology heavily emphasizes extensive documentation covering detailed requirements, design specifications, and test plans.

- **Limited flexibility:** During the Waterfall's rise, the lack of flexibility and rigid nature was considered a feature rather than a bug. The motivation is that changes mid-flight are costly, and we should do the necessary upfront work to limit the changes midstream.

- **Long development cycles:** The linear nature of the Waterfall methodology often results in longer development cycles.

- **Minimal customer involvement:** Customer involvement and feedback are reserved until the latest stages, making it challenging to incorporate changes promptly or address customer needs.

Waterfall and DevOps compatibility

Due to many of the Waterfall model's flaws, it has fallen from favor in the industry and is no longer widely practiced. Agile was a movement that responded to the Waterfall model's very limitations. Specifically, it addresses needs around collaboration, deployments, feedback, flexibility, and adaptability. We will cover this in greater detail in a minute, and for now, we can summarize Agile as solving these problems in the software development cycle. DevOps extends these and more to encompass the entire delivery cycle, leading to a complete picture of producing and operating software, which is outside of the scope of Agile.

So why did we have to read all that? We must analyze what came before to understand why we do what we do.

Introduction to Agile

We can trace Agile back to the 1990s when several software engineers came together to challenge the traditional plan-heavy development workflows, such as Waterfall.

In 2001, a small group of software development practitioners gathered and produced the *Agile Manifesto*. They outlined the core values and principles of Agile software development.

There are several variants of Agile, each seeking to solve problems differently while maintaining the manifesto's core values. Over the years, Agile has continued to evolve and eventually found its way into other industries, such as manufacturing.

Worldwide organizations of all shapes and sizes practice one of the many flavors of Agile or related movements such as lean software engineering and DevOps.

Tour of the big bands: While Agile has several siblings and cousins, we will focus on the most common variants practiced at the time this book was written.

Lean software engineering

Lean software engineering is an adaptation of lean manufacturing principles, which originated in the automotive industry and became popularized by the successes of companies such as Toyota. Lean manufacturing focuses on eliminating waste, optimizing processes, and continuously improving efficiency.

Both lean models share several core principles, listed as follows:

- **Value:** There is a heavy focus on delivering value to the customer. We aim to better understand the customers' needs and develop products and services that meet those needs.

- **Eliminating waste:** Using Lean, we seek to identify and eliminate waste within our processes. Some common manifestations of waste in software engineering are unnecessary features, overproduction, inefficient processes, excessive documentation, and time spent waiting.

- **Continuous improvement:** Teams are encouraged to reflect on their work, identify areas for improvement, and implement changes incrementally. We accomplish this by performing retrospectives, feedback loops, and iterative development.

- **Empowering teams:** It is vital to promote empowering teams. We accomplish this by allowing teams to make decisions, collaborate effectively, and take ownership of their work. Teams practicing lean are to be more engaged, innovative, and capable of delivering high-quality products.

Lean software engineering sounds like DevOps?

Lean software development and DevOps appear to be the same. They share many core principles. Lean focuses on optimizing the software development process and maximizing value; DevOps extends collaboration and integration beyond software development to encompass the entire software delivery lifecycle. DevOps incorporates lean principles alongside other practices, cultures, philosophies, and tools to achieve that goal.

Jumping into Agile

Now, we are going to discuss specific flavors of Agile. There are three main ones; we will spend most of the time discussing Kanban and Scrum, the two most widely practiced flavors. The third is Extreme Programming, which emphasizes technical practices and engineering excellence.

Kanban

Kanban relies heavily on a visual workflow management system to help teams manage and optimize their work processes. It provides transparency, flexibility, and a focus on continuous workflow.

Board

A Kanban board, typically using columns and cards, helps teams visualize their workflow and tasks. It provides a clear and quick view of the work in progress, backlog items, and completed work.

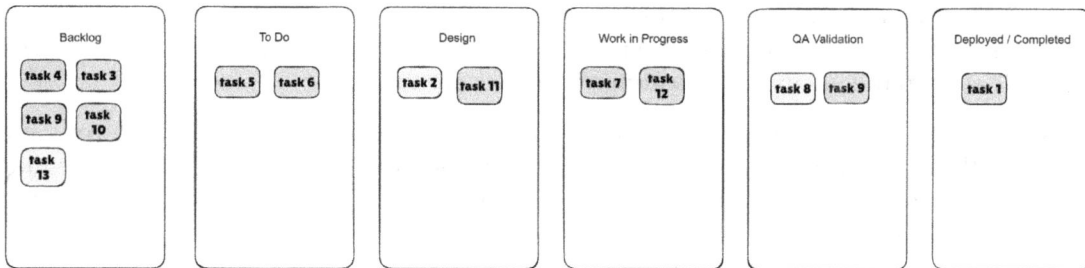

Figure 2.1: *A Kanban board represents work status as it moves through the various phases to completion.*

Work-in-progress limits

Kanban emphasizes that we can only work on a finite number of tasks simultaneously and limits the picking up of new work until we have completed other objectives.

Continuous flow

Kanban emphasizes a continuous, steady work stream to avoid unnecessary delays and wait times. Members pull tasks or stories into *In Progress* when they have the bandwidth, rather than pushing them to take on too many priorities.

Cycle and lead times

We typically measure and analyze cycle time (time taken to complete individual tasks) and lead time (time taken for a task to move from start to finish). We will discuss this more deeply in *Chapter 10, Trusting Our Metrics*. Using these metrics, we can identify bottlenecks and optimize our workflows.

Scrum

Scrum is an agile framework for managing and delivering complex projects. It provides a structured approach to software development, focusing on collaboration, adaptability, and continuous improvement.

Scrum roles: We have defined specific roles such as Product Owner, Scrum Master, and Development Team. Each has distinct responsibilities and contributes to the project's success:

- **Stakeholders:** While *stakeholders* are not an official Scrum role, they play a vital role in the process. Anyone who is an affected party of the product being developed is a stakeholder. Stakeholders have a vested interest in the project's success and can influence its direction and priorities. Stakeholders can be customers, but more often, other interested parties such as employees, investors, regulatory bodies, and other internal or external groups who are not customers.

- **Product owners:** They are responsible for representing stakeholders' interests and ensuring the development team builds the right products. They typically liaise between the business or customers and the Scrum team.

- **Scrum masters:** They ensure that the scrum team understands, adopts, and follows the agreed-upon scrum process. The Scrum master acts as a servant leader, facilitating collaboration, removing impediments, and fostering a productive and self-organizing team environment.

- **Development or scrum team(s):** They are responsible for completing the agreed-upon objectives. Typically, this cross-functional group develops, delivers, and potentially maintains the new functionality.

Sprints and iterations

Sprints are a predefined time period, typically one to four weeks. The team commits to delivering incremental value, while giving structure to review and adapt their approach regularly based on the organization's changing needs.

Product backlog

Product owners are responsible for managing the product backlog and ensuring that it meets the customer's needs. The product backlog is a prioritized list of user stories and tasks that work to define and refine the priorities as things shift.

Sprint review and retrospective

At the end of each sprint, the team demos the newly released functionality and performs a retrospective. We will look at what went well and what needs improvement.

Extreme Programming

Extreme Programming (XP) is the least well-known of the three primary siblings in the Agile family. I have used elements of XP even if I have never used them to this extreme. It focuses on delivering high-quality software through iterative and incremental development.

Iterative development

It brings value by breaking development into smaller, more manageable iterations, each delivering a working piece of software.

Continuous feedback

Regular feedback loops with the customer early in the process ensure that the software meets the customer's requirements.

Test-driven development

We will discuss this in more depth in *Chapter 4, Importance of Automated Testing,* under the *Test-driven development* section. What is important to understand now is that there is a heavy emphasis on writing our tests before our functional code. Thorough testing ensures that we meet the quality and maintainability requirements.

Pair programming

Encourages developers to work in pairs, often with one actively writing the code while the other provides suggestions, feedback, and real-time code review. Pair programming ensures quality and helps avoid knowledge silos.

Continuous integration

We will discuss this in more depth in *Chapter 7, Continuous Integration*; what is essential to understand here is we must regularly test and integrate our code to detect issues early on.

Team collaboration and communication

While many tactics, techniques, and procedures exist to improve team collaboration and communication, these are the most critical. Some are commonly covered in other works, while some are not represented in other works:

- **Stand-up:** Stand-up meetings are short and focused. They are typically held at the beginning (subjective) of the day to provide status updates, identify blockers and dependencies, and foster team communication.

  In larger organizations, we may see other standups than the typical internal team standup. Common examples include a leads standup where the leads from each team will perform a standup comparable to the daily one done by each team. Doing so aims to ensure that Leads are coordinated with each other and can highlight cross-team concerns. It is more common to see these weekly or monthly than daily.

- **Chat and collaboration tools:** It is essential to utilize chat platforms and collaboration tools such as Slack, Microsoft Teams, Zoom, etc., to facilitate real-time communication, file sharing, screen sharing, and other forms of collaboration.

- **Happy Hours:** Team Happy Hours are social gatherings where members meet informally, in person or remotely, to relax, socialize, and build relationships outside of work-related tasks. Examples include grabbing drinks, sharing a meal, playing games, or engaging in other enjoyable activities.

  It may seem odd to some to count this as a collaboration technique, but we are humans, not machines. I cannot stress enough the value of having a regular *Happy Hour* with the team in person or virtually. Team Happy Hours became even more critical during the COVID-19 pandemic as we were unable to meet in person regularly.

- **Offsites:** Many organizations these days have all or a portion of their workforce working remotely, be it in an office, home, or anywhere with internet connectivity. To bring folks together, especially in the context of hybrid and remote workers, we should bring together the team to work on team building, product development, etc. While some organizations are tempted to suggest everyone fly into headquarters, we recommend against that. Doing so negatively reinforces that remote workers are second-class citizens, and both parties miss out on the opportunity to meet elsewhere. This will significantly benefit team satisfaction, belonging, cohesion, etc., besides the more tactical conversations. The author has seen some of the largest problems an organization has been plagued with for years, which have been solved by bringing together the right group of people and letting them hash it out. While the goals and activities at an offsite differ, the common goals are improving connections with our peers, sharing our successes, creating and sharing plans, and giving ourselves a break from the routine.

- **High-impact changes:** When thinking about making high-impact changes to our systems, we should take a step back to consider who should be brought into the discussions to help come to a decision and who to communicate the changes to when decisions are made. In most cases in the technical world, we will use several forms of documentation to help us frame the shift, which we discuss in *Chapter 3, Automation, Automate all the things!, Communication*. Right now, what is important to emphasize is that we need to ensure that we give all the necessary people plenty of time to review the proposed changes, discuss any concerns, and sign off or voice disagreement with our proposal. Once we have decided to move forward, we need to ensure that anyone else who may not necessarily have been involved with the review but is impacted can be notified, and they can update their plans to match. The more lead time we can give our teams within our organization, the better, and they will very much appreciate it. No one loves changing the plan at the last minute because a dependency was not communicated to another group.

How to select and customize your flavor

This is a framework or set of guidelines to help you efficiently run your engineering team(s). No two organizations or even groups within them are the same. As such, it is essential to recognize that no one size fits all.

When we look at the various practices within our organizations, teams, etc., it is essential to ask ourselves some questions:

- What does X or Y mean?

- What does X or Y imply?—In other words:

   o   Why does that make sense?

   o   Why does that not make sense?

The most critical element is right in the name, that is, Agile! This means avoiding arguing about what color to paint the bike shed (AKA *bikeshedding*) when there are more important things to focus on. We could more easily adjust in the middle of the application sprint to meet previously uncommunicated or emerging needs.

Remember, the goal is to create an Agile approach that fits our needs while staying true to the core principles and values. Stay flexible, be willing to adapt, and continuously refine our process to achieve the desired outcomes.

Handling disruptions

Plans are to help guide us. In a changing landscape, we should refrain from holding ourselves to a plan that no longer makes sense. When it comes to changes in the plan at work, I ask myself two questions: *Does this align with my mission statement?* And *does our business benefit from this?* If both are a *yes*, then I want to support it.

At the same time, there is a cost to context switching; in fact, this was the argument for Waterfall's rigidity and its desire to reduce some of the waste caused by changing priorities, specifications, and more. While we should look where possible to optimize for reducing context switching, it is essential to optimize efficiency after effectiveness. If the business needs have changed, we need to meet them.

I have dealt with finite resources at every organization I have ever worked at. Most of the time, people were the scarcest resource. That means we must ensure that we always choose to do worthwhile projects. In the last several places where I have led teams, I have adopted a model where the product owner will set the general priorities for the planned work Monday through Thursday, leaving Friday to the engineer to pay off technical debt and explore new projects. If there is something urgent, we can reclaim the time.

Friday tasks refer to work items or items prioritized only on Fridays. These stories have a number of characteristics. The most important are that they are not urgent, bring value, and some meaningful progress can be made working on it in less than a day. If it becomes urgent, it is no longer considered a Friday task and must be scheduled in a sprint. Large Friday task projects should be discussed and approved on how we can break it down into smaller bite sized projects.

Friday tasks bring a lot of value to the organization in many ways. It allows the product owners to focus on the more significant problems, leaving the teams to self-prioritize the smaller technical debt. When engineers are passionate about spiking a new project idea or fixing a bug that has annoyed them for a long time, we empower them to make the best decisions regularly. Giving engineers Friday means they can manage their time more efficiently. Using this technique will enable us to save up small tasks that are not urgent during the week and keep our context switches down. I only ask that any project work and tech debt cleanup be written up in our project management software and tagged as *Friday* so I can review it. My rule and lens are that if it brings value to the organization and nothing is more urgent, we can do what we need on Friday.

[OPTIONAL] Please pull out something to write on, whether paper and pencil or your favorite text editor on a computer. Produce two answers to each of the following questions:

- What other benefits can you see from implementing *Friday tasks*?
- How do *Friday tasks* relate to Agile?
- What *Friday tasks* would you like to pick up at work if allowed to?

Retrospect and continuous improvement

There are lots of valuable resources out there that discuss the in-depth rituals of Agile retrospectives. Here is a TL; DR (Too Long Did Not Read) to help understand why we do it more than what we do.

- **Purpose:** When embracing Agile, we seek to understand what is happening and improve daily. When we do not take the time to take a step back and reflect, we are limited in how to improve the situation.

- **Structured format:** We introduce a minimal format to ensure that the *retrospectives* facilitate *meaningful discussions* and *actionable outcomes*. I have mostly seen this in the *What went well, what can we improve? And Action Items* format.

The role of the facilitator is to help guide the retrospective. They are ensuring that we have psychological safety and leverage additional techniques such as round-robin sharing, polling, and using *sticky notes* to ensure everyone feels safe speaking up.

Retrospectives are most effective when we do them regularly; this allows us to use this feedback loop in our next planning phase.

Conclusion

To understand DevOps, we must step back to understand what came before. Before the time of computers, we started asking questions on how to better optimize our development and production problems. Many years later, these were used as building blocks and applied to computer engineering problems. By exploring the flaws of the Waterfall method, we see why Agile came about. After exploring what it was trying to solve, we explored several different flavors. We ensure that we know there is no *one-size-fits-all* and that we must choose our own Agile flavor to be effective and efficient.

In the next chapter, we will discuss how automation brings value to organizations. This will result in more resilient systems, reduced maintenance costs, customer satisfaction, improved communication and collaboration, etc.

CHAPTER 3
Automation

Introduction

While culture and philosophy might be the heart of DevOps, we can think of automation as the arteries that allow the heart to pump the blood to where it needs to go. One could certainly argue that this is the *meat and potatoes* of the day of the life of infrastructure, site reliability, security, etc., engineers operating with a DevOps mindset. Before diving directly into code, we will quickly examine why it is important not to rely on manual processes. We will explore requirements gathering, automation as a form of communication, some personal programming rules, tool/framework selection processes, and common patterns used to minimize negative user impact during the development and deployment phases.

Objectives

- What is the value of automation?
- Do we automate everything or leave some things to humans?
- What is the relationship between automation and the need for automated testing?
- How is automation a powerful form of communication?
- How does automation play a key role in building, maintaining, and recovering complex systems?

- Why should we code for 3 AM? What does that mean, and how do we get there?

- Should we start deploying manually or fully automated processes?

- What are some key considerations for picking an automation framework?

Automate all the things!

To automate as much as possible, it is essential to understand our organization's processes deeply. As wonderful as automation is, we must be careful as it is a bit of a double-edged sword, which we will discuss extensively in *Chapter 4, Importance of Automated Testing, Why do we test?*

There are many benefits to an organization that takes processes from various domains, such as application development, operations, and other business needs, and automates them. Few opportunities pay such high dividends to those willing to make these investments.

The primary benefits include improved communication, documentation, disaster recovery, efficiency gains, consistency, scalability, reliability, quality, accuracy, time savings, risk reduction, agility, speed, compliance, auditability, employee satisfaction, and other cultural benefits.

I love automation, as there is just something immensely satisfying about only needing to solve a problem once.

Removing humans from the process

Okay, not entirely! To be clear, even though I spend a sizable portion of my life automating stuff, I still want humans driving the decision-making process in the near future. Through automation, we address inefficiencies, risks, scalability, reliability, and auditability, and focus on enabling the business to bring value to whomever the customer is. Removing the grunt work allows us to focus on more critical aspects. It enables us to protect our support teams by performing actions they would have to troubleshoot and perform manually. This is something we will discuss more in *Chapter 12, Observability.*

Human vs. computer failures

While computers certainly fail, most customer disruption happens due to operator or developer mistakes. Automating processes can help make it safer for humans to interact with dangerous processes.

We all make mistakes; anyone unable to acknowledge previous mistakes denies their humanity.

Storytime, copy, paste, delete, restore

I worked at a company on a project to migrate from Elasticsearch **2.x** to **5.x**. The project itself went smoothly. It required running two computer clusters side-by-side. The migration ran successfully, and I cut the applications over to the new cluster once we validated the integrity. We left the cluster running for a while in case there was a good reason we needed to cut back after finding a severe bug (which had happened before). At some point, the data was stale and no longer helpful from a recovery standpoint and became a minor waste of resources.

After the migration, I had several time-sensitive projects, and the cleanup got deprioritized. Less than a month after the migration, an executive said it was urgent that I take down the old cluster for cost reasons. Normally, these changes would go through two sets of eyes for safety reasons.

The executive did not care, so despite my better judgment, I decided to let them have what they wanted.

What happened next can be summarized as a typical copy/paste mistake. As I had no one to review my change, I bypassed protections that typically would have prevented me from pushing this through. The computer did exactly what I told it to do. It resulted in the complete destruction of data in both clusters. We had to restore our backups. The restore process alone took 24 hours, and the incident lasted almost 40 hours.

If I could go back, I would do things differently. This was perceived vs. actual urgency. This task could have waited until Monday morning, when I would have had a proper review and would not be under pressure, especially as I was actively working on something that was truly time sensitive. Thankfully, we had working backups since I had forced us to test our backup and restore strategy many times before.

Resilient and self-healing infrastructure

Failures happen, whether it is software or hardware. We should build systems that include proactive monitoring. In the face of failure, our automated systems should safely apply some remediation and, only if necessary, alert an engineer. We will discuss the monitoring concepts in *Chapter 12, Observability* right now, let us focus on how automation can help us build self-healing systems.

One of the primary benefits of automation is that we have taken all the necessary steps to bring the system online; why not apply this to our failing systems? For now, let us assume it is safe to proceed. In the case of failure, instead of paging an engineer, we can build systems that replace faulty ones with working ones. Automation and well-thought-out monitoring allow us to minimize customer disruption, protect our on-call engineers, and more. If this makes you think about my experience with the MSP from *Chapter 1, Introduction to DevOps,* I had advocated for this in multiple forms. After years of being responsible for automating systems, I cannot return to the manual system administration world. I treat my systems like the cattle of an enterprise rather than pets for companionship. In other words, we reserve the right to go in and modify or terminate any instance without hesitation, and the system should be capable of detecting failure, sustaining the failure, taking actions to minimize customer impact, replacing the failing deployments with a new one(s), and ensure functionality all without ever needing to wake someone up if this happens at 3 AM.

Communication

How is automation a form of communication? In computer science, we sometimes like to use big fancy words, such as *algorithms*, to describe the computational operations required to take business processes and have a machine perform them. To help us focus less on computers for a second, we will lean on the many concepts that will be easier for our less engineering-heavy audience to relate to. Most of us either must cook or know someone who does. An automation framework called *Chef* uses this model to help illustrate this. Although perhaps they took the theming a bit too far, it is beneficial in understanding the basic building blocks. We will not be using the terms specifically from that community, but rather, we will use them broadly to help understand it in a more approachable manner.

An *algorithm* is like a recipe; it is a step-by-step process that takes you from a desired dish to a shopping list and eventually to the finished product.

In the cooking world, a chef performs experiments to determine the equipment, ingredients, and instructions necessary to achieve and reproduce our desired tasty outcome.

In the technical world, we start the process by asking questions to help gather requirements. In many processes, this might be in the form of a **needs assessment (NAs)**, **request for comment (RFCs)**, or **technical proposals (TPs)**. Once we have communicated with all the relevant stakeholders or affected parties, we need to take those requirements and create the recipe to make our product work as desired.

Machine <-> Machine

Application programming interface (API) is a set of rules and protocols that allow applications or processes to communicate with each other and perform requested tasks. In contrast to human communication, which can be more flexible, APIs support a limited set of functionalities as needed. When developing systems, we can have internal APIs that are only accessible from within that system component, or we can choose to expose this API externally; this has some risks, and we will discuss this in *Chapter 5, Security, Advanced topics, Shrinking our attack surface*. Often, we call many of these programs bots, which comes from robots. We can design Bots to interact exclusively with systems, humans, or potentially both.

Human <-> Machine

We want our machines to work for us *(NOT sorry, robot overlord if you are listening)*, not the other way around. As such, we need to define ways that most greatly benefit us.

While a computer is happy to sit there continuously scanning some data and processing it, we are more limited in this sense. We simply cannot take in the sheer amount of data that a computer is capable of. Therefore, we need to protect the user from the machine. We do this by not displaying everything our programs are performing and instead, relying on various techniques to condense the information into a more human digestible form.

Developer <-> Machine

Yes, developers are humans! Yet we have a unique relationship with computers compared to *end users*. Typically, end users communicate through the paved path, such as a **graphical user interface** (**GUI**) that developers create.

We developers are expected to communicate *directly* with the machines and not through some abstraction or translation layer. That is not to say that in many cases, we have not created our own layers for our own convenience; they are still governed by logic and not purely by interface.

When our systems fail, we as developers and operators need ways to *ask* the system what its current state is, what happened prior, and what would happen if we changed **X** or **Y?** This can be accomplished using techniques and tooling such as logging, exception handling, console/shell debugging, metrics, tracing, and much more.

Human <-> Human

We need to write automated tests to ensure we meet the required specifications. We will cover this in the next chapter.

To create products, we need to know what to build. This typically starts as a conversation between two or more people. Product owners work with the customer, often with diagrams, mockups, **pseudo-code**, flow charts, test plans, etc., to be delivered to the development team to ensure we are effective and efficient.

We briefly touched on the need to have lots of lead time and communication when proposing high-impact changes in the context of planning. Let us take a closer look at some additional considerations and tips. Once the decision has been made to go forward, we should make sure that everyone who will be affected by the change has been notified; while previously, we may have had a representative from each group, we need to make sure that all members of the group are aware. Make sure we communicate the change, indicating when we expect to roll out the change. Prior to performing the change, stop and make sure that we have communicated again. This acts as a reminder to folks as the changes are rolling out; that way, the context is relevant if we see something unexpected.

Challenge yourself: The next time you need to communicate with someone, be it an e-mail, chat message, memo, requirements, proposal, etc., read it and ask yourself if you can understand what it says at 3 AM. We will shortly discuss this concept through the lens of code; the reality is that this applies quite broadly.

Familiar internet APIs

Most have heard of the terms **Internet Protocol (IP)** address and **Domain Name Service (DNS)**, even if they do not know how they work. Stay calm; we are not expecting you to understand how they work, nor will we dive into them. However, we will use these to quickly understand what an API is and how we often use multiple APIs to accomplish an overall objective.

When a user wants to access a website, we open our favorite browser and type a name, such as `starwars.com,` and hit enter. Suddenly, the site appears before our eyes. How would we get here? We will not go into much detail, as it is a fantastic interview question I like asking engineers, and it would be an unnecessary distraction.

Essentially, the user requested the address for *starwars.com*, which our networks do not understand. They understand network addresses, and in order to reduce the user's burden, our programs automate the lookup from the requested address through the API to get a network address. Once we have the address, we can route to the appropriate destination.

Documentation

Documentation is an excellent way to communicate something, but why do we need it, and how do we create quality documentation?

The importance of good documentation

Good documentation is worth its weight in gold, perhaps more! It helps us understand not only what decision was made but why it was made. Often, we are faced with something odd; we look at something and ask ourselves *why it was set up that way*. When we have the documentation for these decisions, we can look back at them historically and understand the context of the time, which may be very different from now.

We will discuss this further in *Chapter 7, Continuous Integration, Quick overview of SCM;* these decisions are often encapsulated in a pull request, a process in which a developer requests that their changes be reviewed prior to integrating them with the rest of the team.

- **Comment-generated documentation:** One common way to bring the documentation and reality closer together is to have our code contain structured comments that can be automatically turned into documentation. By keeping the documentation close to the code that affects it, we are more likely to update the documentation when we are modifying the behavior. This is very common with products that need external APIs for their customers. One of the more well-known frameworks out there is called *Swagger*. Not only can it automatically generate API documentation, but it can also create **Software Development Kit (SDK)** clients based on the API documentation. This is extremely useful as we can write our documentation once and use a tool to generate client libraries in multiple languages, allowing the customer to write in their preferred language and keeping our documentation and functionality more closely in sync.

Docs lie, in code we trust

We just said that documentation is worth its weight in gold; however, the quality matters more than the quantity. Docs can lie; code does not! I know I just heard at least one engineer groan when seeing *code is documentation*. I will not lie; I generally do not trust a lot of documentation, even if I rely on it. To be clear, I do typically start with the official documentation of a project, but I am quick to question the documentation. I cannot tell you how many times I have been working with an engineer to troubleshoot something and see this happen. They keep explaining how they think it is supposed to work based on the documentation, which does not seem to match reality. I will most commonly respond with, *OK, and What does the code say?* If they are still getting familiar with the exercise, they might try restating what the documentation says; I clarify that I am no longer interested in what the documentation says until I can confirm that the code matches the documentation.

I recall one time in my career when I had to do some extensive API reverse engineering. A major cloud provider that I will not name regularly gave incorrect information in their documentation, and their provider swallowed the error, making it hard to debug. Using a web proxy tool, I was able to inspect the generated requests, intercept them, and see the error messages being swallowed in Terraform[1]. After working with that cloud provider and the Terraform Team at HashiCorp, we got their provider into a somewhat reasonable place.

If our documentation is lying and we have good comments next to our code, these two effectively are the complete specifications. By allowing us to review them side by side, we can more easily spot the edge cases, which are where the typical places bugs typically sneak in.

Contracts

Often, the requirements gathering processes aim to introduce a *contract* or set of agreements to define the needs. This includes the scope of the automation, the objectives or desired outcomes, support responsibilities, **service level agreements (SLAs)**, data privacy or compliance requirements, security needs, **intellectual property (IP)** rights, **End User License Agreements (EULAs)**, channels for disputes and resolution, and so much more.

While we need to have contracts to understand what the desired state should be, the code tells us what we have attempted to do. Sometimes, those two do not match and are often the source of downstream problems. Wrong documentation can be worse than no documentation. Engineers (or people) lie; thankfully, computers have not yet been able to lie on their own without some direct or implicit instruction. When troubleshooting something unexpected, I always ask, *What does the code say?* Rather than *what does the documentation say?* Generally, we only document the intended functionality, and bugs are hopefully unintentional.

---

1 Terraform is an automation framework that users declare what their "infrastructure" looks like and terraform sees to make it so.

Disaster recovery

Companies often claim they *do not need a plan for disaster recovery or business continuity.* When they have a major issue, it is too late. We should instead subscribe to the mindset that *failure to plan is planning for failure.*

Planning for failure

While we should strive to build highly available, redundant, scalable, and self-healing automated solutions, we must acknowledge that some things are simply out of our control. At the time of writing this book, perhaps the most vulnerable piece of the internet runs in the AWS *us-east-1* region; when something happens there, it has a ripple effect due to the many dependencies on this single region.

We need to document all the manual and automated processes, including the necessary order of operations required to bring our systems back online.

Extensive testing is necessary to understand how all the interconnected systems work and how to restore operations. This encompasses complete environment destruction; only (data) backups remain. Most organizations require an array of technology to solve their needs; this is often referred to as their tech stack. As these systems usually leverage shared functionality, they do have a certain dependency hierarchy. While we design our systems to be resilient, bringing things up from scratch can be an entirely different recovery process than what we would normally do when we have a working system and need to perform specific maintenance to address a more acute problem. As such, I recommend that the teams responsible for **disaster recovery (DR)** and **business continuity planning (BCP)** go through regular *fire drills*, where they run through the process on a regular basis. We take an environment that replicates production as closely as possible. Hit the *Delete* button.

This may seem extreme, especially considering how much effort this was before all our investments in automation. My experience tells me *Murphy's Law* is perhaps the best mindset to adopt when planning. Many engineers have difficulty picturing complete destruction when asked to explain what recovery looks like; they tend to miss essential dependencies. For example, many processes do not handle a lack of network very well.

Storytime, simple mistakes lead to major disruption

During the mid-2010s, I worked for a company that provided a generalized platform to customers, customized applications, and managed operations of those systems within customer environments. One day, I got an alert from our *dead man switch*, a mechanism telling us that our internal monitoring system on the customer side was unable to check in with our external monitoring system.

After acknowledging the incident, I started investigating. Initially, it was unclear what had happened.

I spun up a *war room*, a dedicated set of communication channels to facilitate real-time communication and decision-making during incident response. I was unable to reach any of our systems in that customer environment. I reached out to the customer, who said they were seeing the same thing, and it was affecting their entire infrastructure.

After about 45 minutes, I got an update from the customer. They have gotten word from their cloud provider that they have sustained a massive regional failure. Many of their systems, such as the status page, support portal, and more, were hosted in that region. The only thing that still worked was their call center, which was overwhelmed with customers seeking clarity.

Obviously, that is not supposed to happen for a cloud provider, ever.

After about another 15 minutes, we got another update, this time from the cloud provider claiming that their systems were back online. Despite this, our dashboards had not yet turned green. We did not have direct access to the cloud provider (only specific instances through a VPN) and required our customer to kick the boxes to get everything running again.

The **root cause analysis (RCA)** revealed that this was initially caused by a single operator making a mistake but highlighted systematic failures that could have prevented this. Thankfully, they clearly cared about *psychological safety* and *blameless postmortems,* as they did not punish the operator and used the opportunity to improve its resilience.

While there are many lessons from this, the most important ones are that while we must strive to avoid single points of failure, even internal tooling needs data validation. We must assume that even with all these efforts, something will go wrong, and we need to rebuild everything from scratch at any moment.

Whenever I write code that accepts user input (even shell scripts), I take special care not to allow situations like the above when performing sensitive operations that would impact confidentiality, integrity, or availability, which we will discuss later in *Chapter 5, Security,* in more detail. Here is an example of some VERY old, UNMAINTAINED, AND NOT GREAT code that I wrote years ago that looks to validate against the very problems that resulted in all servers being restarted by the cloud provider in our disaster recovery story:

**https://github.com/majormoses/es_utils/
blob/273b86b4c15906c5bdf8d05a6006d382578b74f2/bin/es_utils.rb#L1218-L1238**

The following snippet was intentionally modified to be shorter for better visibility in the book. If you want to see more about this, please see the online copy for additional context. The following snippet should be enough to illustrate the point:

```
1.  if index_prefix.include? "\*"
2.    raise "not safe to use '*' in an index delete, Generate a list"
3.      elsif indices.include? "\*"
4.        raise "not safe to use '*' in an index delete, Generate a list."
5.      else
6.        #logic
```

```
7.    end
8.  end
```

Elasticsearch is a datastore implementation similar to a database, where data is stored within structures called indices, while not requiring the data to have a relationship and schema. The code in this utility is designed to prevent the risky deletion of indices by rejecting the use of the "*" wildcard character. This wildcard functions like a Joker in card games, matching any number of characters, and could lead to the unintentional deletion of all data matching the pattern.

In this utility, we wrote methods to generate a list safely and use that list as input to delete specific indices in bulk. This reduced the risk of accidental mass destruction of indices through a single command.

Now, obviously, this did not help me in my own story, where I took down Elasticsearch. That was destruction at the instance level, cluster-wide, not data loss with a fully functional cluster.

Everything as code

Manual processes are the opposite of scalable and repeatable processes; thus, we should look to automate (complete or partial) processes for our organizations.

Various terms

You may have heard of terms such as **infrastructure as code (IaC)**, GitOps, **policy as code (PaC)**, etc. In my opinion, they do not mean much on their own. What they do mean together is that there is an overall push in various tech sectors to put everything into code. As we keep automating more aspects of our systems and application management of our business processes, someone will create a new term, if nothing else, but for the marketing opportunities.

Exceptions

Blanket statements are usually false; they lack nuance. We will carve out two exceptions: *data* and *secrets*. You should look at why these two make sense and ask yourself if there are others. Even if that were true today, there is no telling what the landscape will look like in another decade.

We should use configuration management, a framework used to install and configure software and perform other system-related maintenance tasks. We need to clearly distinguish between the code used to automate a resource and the inputs required to be passed in for a particular deployment.

Similarly, we need to use *secret* vaults or specifically designed solutions for securely storing and retrieving secrets.

So, why is it wrong to store our data or secrets within source control?

Let us start with secrets. Secrets are typically used for authentication (or proving one's identity) or other sensitive functions. If we embed these secrets within our application, anyone with access to our application can take those secrets and use them outside of the context of the application. For example, it is not uncommon for quality assurance or product managers to need access to the application's source code. However, they have no business seeing some of the operational concerns of running the application. It also makes it harder to update should it need to change. Secrets that our systems (not humans) use should be rotated regularly; if we do not have such mechanisms and discipline, we will find ourselves in the future with a very large-scale security incident, and something as *simple* as changing a value becomes a nightmare. The more people that have access to the secrets, the higher the risk that they will be abused, be it an inside threat actor or a hacker compromising a workstation. We will explore this further in our chapter on security.

Okay, so what about data? Data is a very broad term. Let us try to be a bit more specific. We will discuss topics related to this in *Chapter 4, Importance of Automated Testing, Test Data Management*.

It is perfectly valid to have scripts that set up the schema (or layout) of an application's database and data that can populate the local development or testing environment with non-real data.

What is not okay is to take a dump of the production data and shove it into source control for any reason. Sadly, many companies struggle with this; they reach for the *easy* answer early on and end up shooting themselves in the foot. Refrain from taking shortcuts with test data or data scientist use cases!

Disaster recovery and business continuity planning

Anyone who tells me they have a **disaster recovery plan** (**DRP**) or a **business continuity plan** (**BCP**) that does not have a significant portion of the process automated is likely underestimating the complexity of their organization. During disasters, we need to understand aspects not typically required on a day-to-day basis. We likely have at least one *chicken or egg* order dependency challenge to solve that we are only aware of if we are testing this on a regular basis. Even then, there is a risk that something new is added between these tests.

One of the nice things about creating self-service automation is that it can make the auditing process a lot easier and can reduce the number of people who need admin permissions to perform a task. We will discuss this further in our security and pipeline chapters.

Patch management

It takes effort to keep our software up to date, which is especially important when the updates are patching known vulnerabilities. Thankfully, automation is the answer to keeping our fleets safe from hackers on this topic. This applies to direct application dependencies as well as operating system-level dependencies. While I understand that we, as developers, want to evaluate each report and decide whether we are ultimately vulnerable in our usage, one has to realize that it is not worth the time and effort to do so. It makes more sense to patch everything and have suitable testing environments to validate the changes. Only when we run into significant challenges with upgrades, meaning it will take some time to apply safely, should we concern ourselves with if it is vulnerable.

Code for 3 AM

Too often, outages have been extended by code's (unnecessary) complexity, leading me to my *Code for 3 AM* mantra.

What does that mean?

After years of providing on-call support, I realized, like many others, that stuff likes to go bump in the night rather than during business hours. My mantra is that the code should be easily understandable, especially when paging engineers at 3 AM. We must improve the code and add commentary whenever the code is unclear.

How about an example?

To keep all our audiences engaged, we will explore this without requiring any computer science background or specific language knowledge. We will explore this with **pseudo-code** or non-functional code, which is meant to convey the idea behind the flow of logic rather than focusing on syntax. Another way of saying this is that **pseudo-code** is the distillation of the objectives we would like to accomplish, while functional code is the implementation required to get us there.

Requirements

We need a simple program to help motivate employees while channeling Yoda. Keep it simple.

Indeed, the requirements are unclear. This often reflects the requirements we are given when developing systems. Good product developers, systems engineers, and product managers must take less-than-ideal requirements and translate them into something better. I am attempting to walk through this logical progression and how it relates to high- or low-quality code.

Code intent is unclear

Consider the following terse line of code. There is obviously a lot we can do to improve this. We will do this over a couple of steps, resulting in much more straightforward code.

```
1. do or not do; say "there is no try" if tried?
```

Who tried? What was tried? Why are they getting that result? This raises more questions than answers.

Unclear code with helpful comments

Without changing the code, we can make the intent clearer with a comment, though it is still unclear when this applies. Who/What tried?

NOTE: **The # indicates that the rest of the line is a comment and not processed as part of the program's execution. It is purely for the developers to understand better the technical aspects of the code or the intent. Keep in mind that you or someone will need to come back three years later and understand what was done. More important than what was done is understanding the why that drove the decisions at the time. Our memory of the relevant context erodes over time, even as the author of the changeset, while others, seeing it for the first time, have even less context. I cannot tell you how many times I have looked at some code and been very confused as to why someone would write that. Only to inspect the history and discover that I was the original author.**

```
1.  # We should not try. Yoda is saying a
2.  # commitment to accomplishing your objective is required,
3.  # not effort alone.
4.  do or do not; say "there is no try" if tried?
```

While this is a significant improvement over our initial code, there is a lot we can still do to improve it. Next, we will look to create a more understandable program, and we will seek answers to many of the questions raised.

Code intent is clear without commentary needed

With the following example, we make it clear that only when the user lacks the necessary commitment to their goal does Yoda reply to the user with his famous quote in order to motivate them to action rather than simply trying.

```
1.  when user.lacks_commitment(goal)
2.     yoda_motivational_quote("do or do not, there is no try.")
```

While this example may seem trivial, it is important to understand how this affects those responding to incidents that are inherently time sensitive. Now, put that in the context of your much more complex systems, and it makes a big difference.

Ben's ten commandments of clean coding

This next section is written for software engineers. It will be accessible to all but may not stop to explain certain terms and concepts. You can find them in the glossary. If you wish to skip [NOTE: **GOTO Understanding common deployment patterns**]

Thou shall always

These are a set of *positive* commandments or rules to follow that will help us ensure that our code is written for 3 AM:

- **Ensure the intention and function of the code is clear:** We explored this a bit above; however, there are some additional improvements to consider when speaking more broadly on this matter.

- I advocate for longer and more descriptive names of projects, classes, methods, etc. I have worked at places where we had *fun* naming conventions. For example, in one place, we used Transformers for server names, Autobots for production, and Decepticons for nonproduction environments. As someone not intimately familiar with the universe, this left me regularly googling: *is [BOT NAME] a Decepticon or Autobot?* In the context of computing, we name things when we already know something about them. This is different from when we name humans. We give names before we know much about the person. The parents can convey what they want, which is great, but different. Naming in computing is a form of communication. A good name should always seek to answer these two questions at a minimum: *Who/ What am I?* and *Where am I?* I also encourage folks to tag compute resources with the name of the team and/or person(s) responsible for supporting the system. So, what is an excellent example of a naming convention? This is complex, will not cover all use cases, and aims to illustrate what is important to consider.

```
$ENVIRONMENT-$OPTIONAL_CLUSTERING-$APP_OR_SERVICE_NAME-$SOME_UNIQUE_
IDENTIFIER
```

An example of a good name would be something along the lines of:

- ```
  production-us-east-1-k8s-cluster1-default-nodegroup-$IP_ADDRESS_
  WITH_DASHES
  ```
- ```
  production-us-west-2-auth-$IP_ADDRESS_WITH_DASHES
  ```

What is an example of a bad name?

- ```
  prod-staging-k8s-default-nodegroup-$IP_ADDRESS_WITH_DASHES
  ```
- ```
  prod-dev-app-$IP_ADDRESS_WITH_DASHES
  ```

Do not try to get clever, production is production. I have no idea what **production-staging** or **prod-dev** means. It is either production or not.

- **Ensure there is appropriate commentary if necessary:** We talked about this at the beginning of the chapter. While the code should be clear on both matters, sometimes only the *what* and *how* are clear; in this case, we may need to comment on the *why* within the code itself.

```
1.  # This wise Jedi Master is
2.  # reminding us that while
3.  # effort is appreciated; it alone
4.  # is insufficient. We must put
5.  # in the hard work and never
6.  # give up. Only then will we
```

```
7.  # achieve greatness.
8.  when user.not_acts_but_tries
9.    yoda_motivational_quote("do or do not, there is no try.")
10. end
11. # ideally, the proceeding
12. # comments could be an input
13. # in the future, if the user
14. # wanted a further explanation
15. # as they may not have access to see
16. # [LINK TO STORY]
17. # source code and can
18. # only see the output
```

We are giving future gifts to our developers. This helps explain the necessary bits in a condensed form and provides a link for more information. Anyone who wants to know more can click without overloading the developer with information every time they look at the code. We could also move more of those comments into the ticket. The danger of external dependency does exist. You decide where the balance is.

- **Handle your own exceptions:** Do not rely on the **standardError** handling in your preferred language. We should always outline what failure scenarios we have thought through and how we want to handle them. Do we want to retry, log a message, inform other services, etc.?

A common example I see people missing is handling APIs that have rate limiting, or limits on how much we can consume in each period. Most of these services will respond back with a specific status code (the standard is **429**).

We can check if we have a **429** and then make an intelligent decision, rather than keep running through the same loop and making the problem worse. Oftentimes, headers are passed back, letting the user know what their current budget is, if they are rate-limited, and when the system will reset their budget.

Using these, we can stitch together more performant processes when designing them. A good example of an excellent implementation is the AWS **Software Development Kit (SDK)**, which has a built-in rate limit awareness with an exponential backoff strategy. This means that if the system keeps telling us to slow down, we wait increasingly longer between intervals to request again. This is important in the context of not making things worse when systems are struggling to keep up with the requested load.

This also means making sure that when things go horribly wrong, we fail fast! We do not want users to sit in a foreign country, trying to get a rideshare app to work. I once had the experience of an application wasting more than 30 minutes of my time, wherein the app was telling me no drivers were available. After watching drivers come and go, there was another explanation, and after eventually getting someone to order it for us on their app, we got to our destination. After digging around online, a random Reddit thread revealed it had something to do with my credit card[2]. While we do want to fail some things gracefully, that is only if we can handle it; otherwise, we should let the user move on and stop wasting their time.

- **Read The Monitor or Manual (RTM) before asking for help:** Sorry, I am about to get a little ranty. Technically, this is not about the code we write. It is more about a regular problem I see with many software developers. To be clear, this is not true of all software developers, and I will admit that I have been guilty of this occasionally.

  Suppose we are presented with an error message, whether on-screen or in a log message, especially if it is a custom error message; please read it before reaching out for help or assuming it is someone else's problem. I cannot tell you how many times I have dropped something I was working on and come running to help an engineer, only to find the answer is staring at them right in the face. If only they would be brave enough to read the message and understand what it is saying. For example, if *the disk is full*, the error says it right there!

  Why do we have this problem in our industry? There are more reasons, but what comes to mind is specialization, increased complexity, laziness, time pressures, and lack of empathy.

  So, what can we do about it? My favorite technique for this is to ask the reporter of the problem to read me the error message. If it is too large, ask them to send it in a screenshot and text, along with a summary of their understanding of what it means. Prompting users to think about this will get them to self-help often. When they cannot, that is when they really need our help.

  At the same time, let us put a positive spin for the developer audience; this relates to handling our own exceptions. But it is more than that. It is our job to provide whoever needs to troubleshoot a problem with information about what is happening. Sadly, many products fail in this regard, leaving additional expertise from humans to make the leaps between different pieces of information. We will discuss this a bit in *Chapter 12, Observability, Taming monitoring, alerting, and on-call demons*.

- **Use internal or external modules:** While I am a huge fan of copy/paste, it is not always the best thing for our codebases. There are more scalable ways to provide common functionality through the codebase(s). We will have different options depending on the language or framework we are using. Regardless of the options, the goal is simple: **Do Not Repeat Yourself** (**DRY**), which is a common engineering principle. We will talk about this further in *Chapter 5, Security, Where Does Security fit into DevOps, Building Blocks for Reusability and Encapsulation*.

---

2 (Ridesharing App: Failure to Find Drivers, Use Cash Not Card!, n.d.)

Thou shall never

Similar to the previous rules, except that they are written in a *negative* viewpoint to help you ensure that your code is designed for 3 AM.

- **Hardcode what should be an input:** Some variables are meant to be *internal* to the application, and we offer an interface to set a limited number of external variables, typically at the launch of the process. However, there is a disturbing trend I have seen over the years. I have seen developers embed secrets or other types of external configuration from within their application or script, motivated mainly by cutting corners. To be clear, this problem also exists in the infrastructure space. We should follow the same principles and separate the configuration logic from the configuration itself.

  The next time you create an internal variable, stop and ask yourself the question, *Would someone ever want to control this externally?* If the answer is yes, move it to external. Outside of secrets, what types of other configuration parameters are best to be considered external? Most applications and services have external dependencies. If they need to communicate with those dependencies, all the required bits should be externally provided. This includes base URLs, credentials, regions, owners, support teams, etc.

- **Implement functionality best left to the experts:** While I usually do not subscribe to the *trust me, I am the expert* mindset, we need to be careful in a couple of places. Some specific subjects, such as encryption, hashing, etc., require highly specialized knowledge. In these areas, let us absolutely challenge these experts through transparent dialogue and figure out how we can best help each other accomplish our shared goals.

- **Rely on end-users for QA:** When we, as developers, choose not to write an automated test or deploy it somewhere manually, we implicitly ask our customers to test it for us. Last I checked, that was something that we share a responsibility with the QA teams to ensure that we at least attempt to catch problems before our users do.

  We will discuss the specifics of testing in *Chapter 4, Importance of Automated Testing,* and *Chapter 7, Continuous Integration, Environments.*

- **Break an interface without a clear CHANGELOG entry:** Often, in pursuit of making software better or fixing a deficiency, we need to make changes. Different projects, teams, etc., have their own ways of deciding when it is acceptable to introduce breaking changes into a project. We can all agree that when we intentionally introduce a breaking change, we need to communicate that clearly to all the affected parties.

- **Suggest breaking your versioning contract for trivial reasons:** We will discuss this in *Chapter 8, Continuous Delivery, Does Versioning Have to be Hard or Complicated?*

I am convinced that developers do not like big numbers in versions. I do not understand why, but I have seen developers suggest bumping the major version of a project many times because *it feels weird to have a* **1.200.0**, though they cannot quantify it when probed.

What is a good reason to suggest breaking our versioning contract? There is NOT! We should determine what makes sense ahead of time. The most important thing is a shared expectation that stable software projects adhere to the versioning schema and communication we committed to. We cannot change that lightly. We must first introduce the change to the rule set, and then we can attempt to push our change itself forward.

In seriousness

These are just a *random* number of specific characteristics of good coding practices and some pet peeves of mine regarding *code smell* that I picked for a good section header. Code smell typically indicates that the code might need improvement. It does not necessarily mean it is a bug; however, breaking these outlined rules is a bug, in my opinion.

Deployments

When we begin deploying our applications, starting with a manual process is okay. Once we have documented the deployment, we should determine how to improve the process. Often, our deployment is first created by the product engineer rather than an operations engineer. From there, it is common for an operations engineer to take on the responsibility of creating an automated release process. For now, we will be starting small and simple, and we will be focused on performing the tasks required to get online and go from one version to another. We will not yet be considering high availability, zero downtime deployments, and handling failures, which we cover in *Chapter 8, Continuous Delivery, Understanding common deployment patterns*.

Considerations for picking frameworks

Selecting Deployment tooling largely depends on the technology stack we are working with. Start with mapping out the requirements and include some *nice-to-have* features. Next, we ask ourselves what kind of deployment strategy we want to employ.

Let us look at some common requirements and see what matters and when they apply.

Criteria for selecting frameworks

Personally, I am a fan of using a *best-of-breed* approach. Once we outline the requirements and have our list of nice-to-haves, we select **N** number of frameworks. Research each option and perform a limited deployment that is easy to revert. After doing an initial deployment with each solution, we can do an initial evaluation, looking to eliminate the ones that do not meet our needs and those we do not like. Depending on how many solutions remain, how much we like the remaining options, and the need to go deeper, we will invest until we deem one option better suits our needs. At the end, we review the options. While the process depends on the number of stakeholders and internal processes, the end goal is to decide on a path forward.

- **Key features and capabilities:** Sometimes, there is a *killer* feature that no one else has, and it can sometimes make the decision easier, especially when two good options remain.

- **Scalability:** While my default lens is that of a larger organization, this is an opportunity to sit down and remind us that scalability is relative. Define our needs and make sure they are met. Sometimes, it is a critical consideration, and other times, it is not. Do we need to support ten users, 1 million, 10+ million, etc.?

[NOTE: **GOTO Community and commercial support**]

The rest of this chapter, until the *Community and Commercial Support* is geared towards the engineering audience. It is accessible to all but may not be of as much interest to other personas.

Some considerations when scalability is important:

o Do we scale horizontally, meaning we bring up more instances of the same size?

o Do we scale vertically, bringing up instances with more resources than currently?

o Which computing model are we?

- **Distributed**: Multiple interconnected systems working together through some internal networking or clustering.

- **Peer-to-peer (P2P)**: Clients work together through *peer* networks, sharing resources without the use of centralized servers.

- **Grid, Geo, or Edge**: Each of these distinct models is typically distributed. In the case of Geo and Edge, there is a heavy emphasis on moving the computation closer to the consumer, reducing latency and cost.

o What does our app look like?

- **Service oriented architecture (SOA)**: We treat a loose grouping of services with a larger goal in mind of providing an overall cohesive service through the communication of the interfaces between these loosely coupled services.

- **Monoliths**: They are applications where most or all the functionality is built into a singular service rather than in a more modular fashion.

- **Microservices**: They are like SOA but are even more specific in their scope and tend to emphasize decentralization. Each component can be more easily scaled independently.

- **Macroservices**: These are *wannabe* microservices but have very heavy frameworks rather than opting for lighter approaches.

- **Serverless/functions**: The developer focuses on writing code and does not have to consider the underlying infrastructure. Serverless most favors use cases where event-based architecture or logic that triggers when something else happens is desirable. While this sounds perfect, we do need to be aware of various infrastructure aspects, even if the footprint is smaller. Some models may also be unsuited for this type of development, and they are extremely inefficient compared to other solutions.

- **Extensibility:** I typically see what plugin or integration system frameworks or tooling we have available. When evaluating the current gaps, it is essential to understand whether we will be able to fill them ourselves or if we have to wait for the community or vendor to add functionality.

  These extensibility conversations often manifest when discussing APIs, SDKs, vendor integrations, and other types of plugins or module extension architecture.

- **Community and commercial support:** I am an open-source developer at heart. Although I often prefer to run open-source software, I also run commercial software and, in some cases, pay for commercial support on open-source software. *Forking* or making a copy of an external codebase to maintain ourselves has a cost. I always favor contributing upstream rather than maintaining our own fork.

  We must have a vibrant community of people who really care about our subject, whether it be an automation framework, deployment pattern, observability tooling, etc.

Conclusion

We use automation, a technical manifestation of communication, for everything we can to improve safety and stability while ensuring a consistent user experience, even during deployments. This solves part of the problem that was discussed during the presentation by the *Flickr* Engineering team. This includes using automation to augment human capability and reduce risk, leaving us in the most crucial roles; using this automation to capture all the requirements to run our business, why we need to *code for 3 AM*, and some rules to help achieve that. Through understanding various deployment patterns and essential aspects of helping you pick your direction; we can seek to increase the value our customers receive while keeping the disruption to a minimum.

In the next chapter, we will address the testing aspect. This will increase our confidence in those deployments' ability to deliver on the promise of being able to deploy frequently without compromising stability.

CHAPTER 4

Importance of Automated Testing

Introduction

In theory, we could deploy code, but is it safe? As we established in the previous chapter, automation is a crucial scale component of successful businesses, but it also comes with its dangers. When we developers make mistakes, the risks are usually much higher. Instead of slowly impacting a handful of systems, we may be taking down the entire system all at once, and it may be in a way that is challenging to recover from. Automated testing is a critical tool in our belt to balance the need to move faster, using feedback loops, and all while ensuring that we deliver quality to our customers. There is a lot to unpack, so we will be touching on a wide variety of topics within this chapter, highlighting the importance of automated testing and defining several different types of tests that support safe deployments. We will point out pitfalls along the way and eliminate worries of being called after hours, whether we are deploying on Monday at 9 AM or Friday at 3 PM in time for a relaxing weekend.

Objectives

- Why do we need manual and automated testing?
- Understanding the types of testing and when to use each of them?
- What makes a good vs. a useless test?

- How does testing influence good development patterns?
- How do we manage data in testing?

Why do we test?

Let us rephrase the above question as follows: *What is the worst that can happen to our application or system,* and *how can testing help us catch failures before they impact our customers?*

Computers do what we tell them

Most problems are caused by *developers* and *operators* rather than *end users*, despite many industry stereotypes that users are the problem. While it is certainly true that I have seen end users do things I would never expect, nor should we trust user input; however, this is akin to comparing apples and oranges. If a user can do that much damage with, or to our systems, it is because we let them, whether explicitly or through omission of controls; that is on us as developers. No end-user has root-level access to any resources on our web servers or applications unless we give them it. We will shortly focus on testing all our interfaces.

Amplification

There are two main aspects of how the impact, both positive and negative, is amplified through automation.

Typically, our automation systems run with high levels of system permissions, otherwise, they are inherently limited in what they can perform on our behalf. As our deployments are automated, they bring change, both positive and negative, more quickly. Obviously, we seek to mitigate that through the usage of testing and deployment strategies that minimize customer disruption and optimize recovery time.

Internal morale and customer dissatisfaction

What happens when we try shipping frequently and do not have a commitment to quality? The two biggest impacts are hits to internal morale and unhappy customers.

Most people do not want to spend their time fighting fires and would prefer to be building cool new features. This is especially true if we are *on-call* and being woken up at 3 AM to fix problems. This tends to snowball and have a lot of negative impact, typically affecting the velocity that we deliver in. If we are going to be forced to slow down, we might as well take the time to be proactive rather than reactive.

When customers are unhappy, it affects all aspects of the business. The impact is clearest when customers decide to part ways for our competitors, however, we often see warning signs long before it comes to this. Customers can be forgiving depending on how we handle problems. If we blame the customer, external factors, etc., rather than taking responsibility, then the customer tends to lose patience and starts looking to put together an exit strategy. Even if they do not leave today, they may be looking to reduce their reliance on the product or service.

Stories

Real-world examples of test deficiencies are not hard to find, and neither are the people affected by them. Consider the global outage that affected operations reliant on *Microsoft Windows* and using *Crowdstrike's Falcon Sensor* in July 2024. This global outage was due to a faulty update from *Crowdstrike*. The event affected an estimated 8.5 million machines and resulted in billions of (US) dollars in value lost, spanning critical industries like banks, airlines, hospitals, and beyond. Could not comprehensive testing have revealed the issue in a safe environment prior to the disaster? Let us step inside a first-hand example of how these scenarios can occur.

Battle scars

It is time to explore a scenario when I saw an engineer decline to perform testing that was requested, resulting in a lot of internal disruption. In this case, this was not a public customer-facing disruption, however, it destroyed the productivity of the development team for a day. The engineer was tasked with creating a backup solution for our internal development virtual machines, including critical systems such as our code repository. The initial backup strategy rolled out smoothly. We then wanted to create a retention strategy, meaning that we only wanted to keep a certain number of backups. Here is where the *fun* starts. There was an obvious logic flaw in the script, which was copied/pasted from the internet without testing it first. This resulted in all VMs being deleted, even the ones that were running at the time!

The developer's plight: *Wondering if the imported library or copied code from the internet will work as advertised, what was not advertised, and what could possibly go wrong.*

Testing catches a problem before production

Now that we have seen what can happen when we lack testing, let us explore a scenario in which testing really saved us.

I worked at a company on a project to upgrade our automation framework to the next minor version, which was supposed to be safe. After testing the changes across much of our codebase, I ran across a single automation suite whose tests started failing. The reason for the failure was not immediately clear. I made a note of it and made my way through the rest of my list. I circled back to the one set of failing systems, kicking the tests again, hoping that the issue was transient, but it was not. The impact was clear, even if we were scratching our heads as to why it happened. The expected configuration was not present. If this had been pushed out, it most certainly would have resulted in an outage, likely including data loss. We read through the release notes, changelog, etc., but could not find anything announced that would explain what was happening. I opened an issue to report the bug. As I attempted to upgrade multiple minor versions at once, it was unclear when it was introduced. I had reproducible code that could trigger the bug, a test demonstrating the bug, and showing which version started failing. This made it a lot easier to work with the vendor. At the end of the day, they said I was using an *undocumented* public API, and they decided to change it. They said it was not a breaking change because it was not a publicly documented API, even if it was publicly accessible. This was an example of an end-to-end test, which revealed issues existing between applications. Thankfully, with proper testing, we can catch problems before they cause disruption, even if our vendors break their version contract.

Types of tests and the value they bring

Each type of testing can be thought of as a layer of protection, adding its own specific value to our test suite. We will not explore all types; this is a quick primer on the topic.

Tip from Sean: **Every type of test has four phases in common: setup, run, verify, and teardown. Another way I like to describe this is the four A's: Arrange, Act, Assert, and Annihilate. Every type of test must have each of these phases represented to ensure that your tests verify real application behavior and do not break other tests by leaving the test environment in an inconsistent state.**

Unit

Unit tests are perhaps the first form of (non-manual) testing that developers are introduced to. Typically, a unit test takes the smallest unit of critical functionality that requires testing and ensures that it does what is expected.

Example: We will make use of **pseudo-code** to keep all audiences engaged.

Taking our previous example of Yoda quotes, let us assume we have a function that looks something like these lines:

```
1. def yoda_motivational_quote(quote):
2.     print("Yoda: " + quote)
```

This is a very straightforward example, and one could argue that there is nothing worth testing here, and I agree in the real world. However, to explore this topic and highlight what would have some value vs. no value, let us write a test.

```
1. def Test_yoda_motivational_quote(decorator, quote):
2.     ensure in the output of yoda_motivational_
   quote(quote), the quote is after our expected decorator
```

In this case, since we are using a standard method **print**, we do not have to test that it works. The place where we instructed it what to do is the only place worth validating. In this case, as the function, the testing is ensuring that we are prepending Yoda to whatever the quote is; this is more valuable than asserting that print still works. Someone may decide later to move the decorator to the end. *Yoda speak* typically puts the subject at the beginning and makes use of unconventional grammar in his sentences, so thematically, we could see that changing later. If we rely on this to work the way it is, this test will notify us of future changes.

If we wanted to take this a step further, here is a method we could use to call our generic test function and validate that we are getting what we want:

```
1.  def Run_Test_yoda_motivational_
    quote(decorator="Yoda: ", quote="do or do not, there is no try"):
2.      Test_yoda_motivational_quote(decorator, quote)
```

When writing tests, we should remember our *Code for 3 AM mantra* from the previous chapter. As we will soon be running our tests all the time, it is inevitable that this test will eventually fail for some reason(s) (such as refactoring). If the test is not understandable, a developer will likely simply comment it out and see if anything else breaks before attempting to troubleshoot it.

The value

We can ensure that these small critical aspects of our applications do exactly what we want them to. Instead of a generic *something is not right* we get a specific error that the developer can review to determine if the test is correct or if the code is broken and needs to be fixed.

Integration

Not everyone agrees on what an integration test is and is not. To keep things simple, I will say that integration tests are used to test multiple concerns of a program together. These are typically against the public interfaces or methods that can be called from outside of the program.

Example

Let us assume that we are working on the infrastructure automation for deploying a web application. What is the single most useful integration test? Trying to hit the App! Even something as simple as an HTTP request (opening a URL) tests multiple components. At the end of the day, even if everything is correct on the application side, misconfigurations in our web server, for example, can still take us down.

Again, we will be using **pseudo-code** for readability and to keep everyone engaged:

```
1.  describe http('localhost/maytheforcebewithyou')
2.      its('status') should = 200
3.      its('body') should = 'always'
4.  end
```

In other words, when sending the HTTP request of **/maytheforcebewithyou** to our local system, we expect to receive a successful response back of **always**. This tests that our app is functional at some fundamental level, monitoring a specific endpoint to ensure it responds as expected. Common examples include **/ping**, **/health**, **/healthcheck**, **/ healthz**, etc. They are used to determine when a resource is ready to start receiving user traffic and providing additional diagnostic capabilities to developers and operators.

For many data use cases, running the pipeline and simply reporting back if there are errors is very similar to the health checks we just discussed. We get a lot of bang for our buck. If the data structure or expected fields change, that can affect our pipeline, and we want to know about it without having to query our job scheduler manually.

Value

Many times, problems arise when we integrate two or more components together. Integration testing allows us to inspect single or multiple interfaces to ensure they are working. Generally, I prefer integration tests to all other forms of testing as they most closely resemble real-world problems and, therefore, realize the most value. In fact, you may notice that my unit test kind of feels like an integration test. Based on my experiences, I would say it is harder to write a useless integration test, and more likely to add value with them over its unit counterpart.

Code coverage

Let us take a moment to touch on code coverage reporting, which is commonly used to help teams understand test suite deficiencies. We will also discuss this in *Chapter 10, Trusting Our Metrics, Finding valuable metrics and KPIs*. Now, conventional thinking suggests that the more tests we write, the greater the *code coverage* percentage we will see in our report. Developers and managers alike love these reports and their linear nature due to how they translate test suite improvement efforts into measurable outcomes (at least in writing). What these developers and managers *want*, however, is a *certainty of behavior*, when in reality, the report provides them insight into only one of many layers. Another so-called layer could be how truthful our tests exercise intended behavior - does every test contain relevant assertions, or the number of relevant negative path tests there? Similar to installing a security camera at a busy intersection and claiming the street is now 10% safer, a coverage report is deceptive when presented in such absolute terms. Consider a report that *claims 100% test coverage*. Let us set aside what we desire that to mean, and instead focus on what it represents in its most basic and raw form. It simply means 10 out of 10 lines of code were exercised when running our tests. It does *not* mean our tests have meaningful assertions that catch unexpected behavior. It does *not* mean all of our logical branches and loops were passed the full set of possible values and iterated the correct number of times in the correct order. And it certainly does not indicate any negative path testing has been written at all!

Gaming coverage

Getting back to the integration tests we have already discussed, they have the advantage over unit tests in being less prone to gamify due to their increased level of effort, and broader impact on exercising system behavior. Consider the situation where a manager sets a team's code coverage target to 90%. It is Friday, the deadline is soon, and the coverage stands 1% short of that goal. A developer seeking to satisfy that metric might be tempted to prioritize meeting *the letter* of the team's goal with a simple unit test above the *spirit of quality that the goal seeks to promote*. Encourage your team to focus their testing efforts on multiple layers beyond the coverage report. Favor an explanation from your team as to how these efforts improved coverage quality, over such one-dimensional metrics like the 90% target in our example.

Reduce maintenance cost

Tests can be time-consuming to maintain. If our application or system behavior needs to change, then it stands to reason that our tests (which confirm this changed behavior) also need to change. This type of maintenance is a fact of life, but it is possible to reduce the maintenance burden by keeping a couple of principles in mind.

First, keep your tests as flexible and generic as possible. For example, do not set test expectations based on specific text but rather on whether a text element exists. The Page Object Model can help web applications by providing a technique of marshaling all element references into one place. Then, if that element needs to change, the update for tests also happens in one place, as opposed to being spread across the whole suite.

Second, only test the public interface; think of methods that respond to calls outside their immediate file. The public interface represents the application or system behavior, while the private interface represents the implementation or *the way in which* an application facilitates that behavior. The private interface is only accessible within a module or methods that can only be called from within their class. These private methods perform tasks that provide public methods with the information they need to respond to calls external to the class or module. Behavior can be *implemented* in many ways, but it should respond consistently and in only one predictable way. A test that ensures correct behavior should not care how information gets processed, but rather that the behavior meets expectations. This approach greatly reduces the test suite maintenance burden when optimized and refactored private methods.

End to end

Lastly, **end to end** (**E2E**) tests can be considered a more specialized and in-depth form of integration test. The goal is to increase the coverage and confidence of our suite by exercising all parts of the app together in the context of a complete feature. This then simulates the end-user experience and leverages even more of the program's underlying functionality. Additional components are typically required to run the entire system and often require limited amounts of mocked data, services, or responses. Those familiar with microservice development may find that, like infrastructure development, it typically requires setting up many of the dependencies to have meaningful integration tests, very much blurring the lines between integration and E2E testing. Think of integration testing scope as covering small *overlapping pieces* of functionality, while E2E testing scope should capture the functionality required to provide a complete feature intended for the end user. The scope of E2E tests can overlap with application behavior and its underlying infrastructure.

Regarding testing our service, a production-like environment is often used to test out features whose behavior changes with the infrastructure. Common examples of this could include **content distribution networks** (**CDNs**) for sharing media and determining the IP address of a client request. We certainly do not want to ban our load balancer from legitimate logins because of one bad actor.

Example

As these inherently require a lot of setup work, we are going to focus on the anatomy of an E2E test rather than working with **pseudo-code**. We will focus on the goals and outline the necessary steps to achieve them. You will see that in this case, we do not have any instructions on how to get the necessary dependencies in place.

Scenario: For many applications, a user is required to register with a system and perform some validation that they own the account.

Dependencies that need to be brought up are:

- Email system: working outbound sending from our application
- Website(s)/application(s)
- Databases
- Web servers
- Email system: working inbound email on our test user.

The testing steps are as follows:

1. Launch a browser.
2. Navigate to the site.
3. Click the registration button from the navigation.
4. Supply inputs to any required and optional fields we wish to leverage.
5. Submit the form.
6. Click an email sent from the platform to the registered email address to ensure that the registered user controls it.
7. Log in with credentials.
8. We can optionally go to a user's profile to update required fields, set up MFA, etc.
9. Log out of the application.
10. Attempt to log in with the same credentials.

11. An optional validation that the account is still considered registered as far as the application is concerned.

Test priorities first

Before writing a test, consider how the business would be impacted if this process fails. We should decide if it is worth writing a test depending on this answer. At the end of the day, we are looking to ensure that the most critical aspects of our applications are working as intended.

Let us say for a moment that we are building a *typical e-commerce platform*. What are the most important areas to test? How can we possibly know this without really knowing the business? Due to the wide variety of businesses and organizations, we cannot outline everything worth testing, but we can start with a very clear example of adding value. We do this by tracing the path of revenue and then working our way back into our system. For example, we know that e-commerce companies make money by selling goods. As simple as a test may seem on the surface, once a developer sits down to write, they realize how much complexity there actually is beneath the surface.

Assuming profitability is one of the most critical business concerns, we should verify that the following code permits a user to give us their money. The following is a relatively straightforward workflow for a generic e-commerce company:

1. Optional: The user attempts to log in.

2. The user finds a product, either from the home page, navigation, searching, or direct link (referral?).

3. The user adds the product to the shopping cart.

4. The user optionally repeats steps 2-3 as many times as necessary.

5. The user wants to check out.

     a. Optionally log in to retrieve saved information:

          i.   Login.

          ii. Get customer data.

          iii. Prepopulate form.

          iv. Adds / Updates Payment Information.

          v.   Get Confirmation.

     b. The user wants to check out regardless of login status.

          i.   Goes to checkout:

               • Review quantity.

               • Possibly update Qty.

- Adds / Updates payment.
- Get confirmation.

Instead of outlining which functions or methods need testing, we started by identifying the critical business workflows in the organization. We can then prioritize tests to ensure that these are always working. We know what MUST be tested by starting with the most business or organizationally critical workflows, which will then serve as our minimum set of tests. We can improve upon this, but only after covering the basics. In the context of our app testing code, we want to test all these functions' interfaces. Later, we will use these same tests in a broader observability context in *Chapter 12, Observability.*

I think it is essential to bring forward the idea that the purpose of tests is to gain confidence that our systems are working as intended. I have seen useless tests that bring no value; their only purpose is to claim they have done testing. We should skip writing tests that do not increase our confidence. Some people write *meaningless* tests; they are not *useless,* but *harmful,* as they create a false sense of trust.

When do tests cause harm?

We need to set aside a minute to address an example wherein Volkswagen, a car manufacturer, acted in bad faith with their emissions testing. Putting politics aside, we need to respect the rule of law in the countries we operate in. The Clean Air Act[1] required all vehicle manufacturers selling in the United States to meet certain criteria. In 2015, the United States of America's *Environmental Protection Agency (EPA)* announced[2] that **Volkswagen (VW)** had installed *cheat codes* to deceive customers and regulators. In a nutshell, what this means is that the vehicle was aware of when it was being tested in a lab and would alter the functionality of the car when it was in testing mode to produce better results that did not represent reality. While VW initially denied it, they eventually confessed. When entities we are supposed to trust engage in such practices, it shakes our confidence; if they did it with environmental concerns, would they also do the same with more critical safety tests?

Before someone can say, *a respectable company would never put safety over profits,* I submit the *Boeing 737 Max* incident(s)[3]. These tragedies were caused by an automated process that relied on a single sensor, which gave bad data and forced the plane down, killing all on board. In this new plane, Boeing introduced a new automated system called **Maneuvering Characteristics Augmentation System (MCAS)**. Boeing intentionally misled customers and regulators, not explaining the significance of this system, primarily to avoid the need to retrain or certify pilots on the aircraft. This system was designed to help the plane regain control in situations where the engines may stall. Boeing sold the *extra* sensor as an *upgrade* rather than a **core safety requirement!** To anyone who is familiar with the risks of aviation, this was reckless and grossly negligent. Commercial airplanes are built

---

1 (Summary of the Clean Air Act, 2023)
2 (Volkswagen Diesel Emissions Scandal (DieselGate), 2015)
3 (Boeing 737 Max Groundings, n.d.)

around the requirement that critical functions need to be redundant. We have a near-zero possibility of getting a faulty part or system replaced mid-flight; it must be there before it takes off. Unfortunately, this tragedy was not isolated to a single instance. It repeated a second time, after which various countries' aviation regulators stepped in and grounded the fleets. While each country has its own standards, many relied on the United States of America's *Federal Aviation Administration's (FAA's)* certification in the past. Its willingness to allow Boeing to self-certify safety was a stain on its record, as it allowed an obvious conflict of interest. Many countries' aviation authorities required their own processes to ground the planes once they had been retrofitted. As of July 7th, 2024, Boeing pleaded guilty to *defrauding the FAA during the certification process of the 737 Max*. In addition to the criminal and civil liability here, we are seeing senators hold the FAA's feet to the fire, which has led to the FAA strengthening its oversight and demanding improvements from Boeing.

If we want another example, we can discuss the tragedy with OceanGate, a company that took customers to the bottom of the ocean in a poorly designed and experimental submarine that imploded[4]. According to its waiver[5] that passengers had to sign, they admit they only reached the depths of the Titanic 13/90 dives, or 14% success! In this case, the CEO put Innovation over safety, and he repeatedly ignored the concerns of experts in the field, believing that it was more important to innovate than be safe. It is worth highlighting a particularly telling quote, *You know, at some point, safety is a pure waste. I mean if you want to be safe, don't get out of bed. At some point, you're going to take some risk, and it really is a risk/reward question. I think I can do this just as safely by breaking the rules*. While there is a nugget of truth to what he says, we need to take that with a heavy grain of salt. His statement implies no risk to living one's life in bed. There are always risks, and we need to weigh them appropriately. Equating the risk management required to build a submarine and getting out of bed shows a severe detachment from reality. Many C-Suite executives are failing us as customers, investors, and employees in their fiduciary responsibilities to perform reasonable risk management. We will discuss this further in *Chapter 5, Security, Everyone contributes to security!* Regardless of your specific industry, it is important that tests remain truthful to the intended behavior of the system in question.

Examples

[NOTE: **GOTO X-driven development**] The rest of this chapter, until the *X-driven development*, is geared towards the engineering audience. It is accessible to all but may not be of as much interest to other personas.

Bad tests

There are many characteristics of bad testing. We will discuss several examples of anti-patterns.

---

4 (Titan Submersible Implosion, 2023)
5 (Mann, 2023)

- **Defeat devices / Sabotage:** Defeat devices and Sabotage: While I love the tongue-in-cheek that **https://github.com/auchenberg/volkswagen** brings to the table, this does concern me:

  If you want your software to be adopted by Americans, good test scores from the CI server are very important. Volkswagen uses a defeat device to detect when it's being tested in a CI server and will automatically reduce errors to an acceptable level for the tests to pass. This will allow you to spend less time worrying about testing and more time enjoying the good life as a trustworthy software developer.

  If we engage in these practices (not in jest), then we will erode confidence, and when it comes to light, it will be worse. Very few secrets ever stay that way. Conway's Law guides us to consider that organizations that design systems are constrained to produce designs that mirror the communication structures of that organization. Nothing is covered up that will not be revealed or hidden that will not be known.[6]

- **Fragile tests and edge cases:** The following is a snippet of **pseudo-code** that we will test:

```
1.  def avgStormTrooperPayStub(stubs=[1000,2000,3000]):
2.      total = 0
3.      for stub in stubs:
4.          total = total + stubs[stub]
5.      avg_pay = total / length(stubs)
```

  In this case, we have specifically written some bugs, which we will use later to write a good test that asserts things we clearly should be checking.

  Here, we have written a fragile test:

```
1.  def testBadAvgStormTrooperPayStub(stubs = [1,2,3]):
2.      ensure that avgStormTrooperPayStub(stubs) = 2 # too fragile!
```

  Our test case takes in a static array of numbers and asserts that it should have an average. This is not a good test, as it will easily fail on changes concerning the input array. The developer must then manually update the average every time this happens. Repeated updates to a test are the hallmark of a brittle, fragile test. When we add, remove, or change any numbers in the array, the test needs to be updated.

  Bugs often exist in what we consider *edge cases*; we should always test viable scenarios, no matter how unlikely our opinions dictate that a customer will or will never do something. I assure you if our customers do not *accidentally* find them first, hackers will find them as they are *actively* hunting.

- **Useless tests:** If we are working in any mature programming language, we should assume that the language and its standard libraries are already tested in their own development and are not what needs to be tested, it may seem obvious, but we should be testing our custom code.

---

6 Luke 12:2

Here is an example where we can write a test that may appear valid on the surface; however, it is not testing that we should be concerned with while building our applications:

```
1. describe file('/dev/null/') do
2.   its('contents') { should eq nil }
3. end
```

For anyone unfamiliar with Unix or Linux systems, the operating system creates a special *file* that contains nothing, which is commonly referred to as **"NULL"** or **"NIL,"** depending on the language or system. While the test itself is valid, even from the perspective of the OS developers, most of us will only need to test the system features required for our integrations. To be clear, we should run our suite of tests against all supported operating systems; however, we should only test the direct interfaces (APIs) that we explicitly rely on and should mostly focus on testing our custom logic.

Good tests

Good tests typically focus on critical aspects of functionality, highlight edge cases, and ensure that our interfaces account for unexpected or unsafe input.

- **Finding bugs:** We will spend some time talking about edge cases and bug hunting very briefly.

  For example, using our existing function, I can come up with a couple of things I would want to test, which would likely highlight some logic flaws. For example, I might want to raise an exception if I did not pass any stubs:

  ```
  1. def betterAvgStormTrooeprPayStubZero(stubs=[]):
  2.   raise error(CannotAcceptZeroTroopers) if we have zero stubs
  ```

  In this case, *line 5* in our original example would evaluate as "0/0," which is obviously not going to work.

  Here is another example where our original logic would fail. In our first example, on line 4, it would error out because it cannot add a string of **one** and the numerical value **zero**. We should check the type at play, especially when it is passed directly. Even in a dynamically typed language, what if I mistype something and add **"one1"**? What does that mean? Is that **11**, two values of **1**, or a single **1**? Are we OK with such critical logic switching out underneath us at the mercy of the language? I prefer to be explicit rather than implicit with critical behavior. What if we never passed in an array in the first place? Good programming does not trust data input; it validates what is being passed in before it attempts to perform operations.

  ```
  1. def testBetterAvgStormTrooperPay(stubs=['notANumber', 'two', -66]):
  2.   ensure that stubs is not an empty array
  3.   ensure each element is a number before assuming we can do math
  4.   ensure that each trooper is paid at least one credit
  ```

There is nothing revolutionary about an average. This makes it an excellent candidate for exploration. It requires a very minimal understanding of math, and it allows us to write (intentionally) bad code, write tests that highlight the buggy code, and translate those tests back into safer code.

Now that we have some tests that would fail, how could we modify the code to meet those edge cases?

- **Fixing bugs:** Now that we have highlighted some bugs, let us explore how to fix them.

The highlighted lines indicate new or updated code:

```
1.  def avgStormTrooperPayStubFixed(stubs=[1000,2000,3000]):
2.      if stubs.class not array:
3.          raise error(StubsNotArray)
4.      else if length(stubs) == 0:
5.          raise error(StubsMissing)
6.      total = 0
7.      for stub in stubs:
8.          if not stub.class == Number:
9.              raise error(StubNotANumber, stubs[stub])
10.         total = total + stubs[stub]
11.     avg_pay = total / length(stubs)
```

While this is not the cleanest code, it was a quick and dirty improvement to what was already there. Now that we are raising errors, we do not have to duplicate their logic within our tests. We can simply ask if it raised the expected error given the requested input.

Test files vs. test examples

A quick note on terms, it is important to distinguish between a *test file* and the individual methods that exercise behavior within the file, also known as *test examples*. Each discrete expectation is an indicator of a test example.

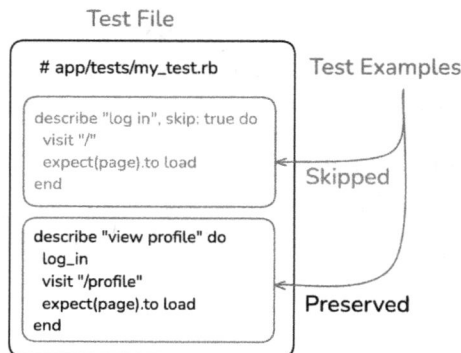

Test File

app/tests/my_test.rb

Test Examples

```
describe "log in", skip: true do
  visit "/"
  expect(page).to load
end
```

Skipped

```
describe "view profile" do
  log_in
  visit "/profile"
  expect(page).to load
end
```

Preserved

Figure 4.1: Here, we see two test examples contained in a single test file

Sometimes tests can block critical workflows and we are forced with tough choices, which may include skipping tests. We generally recommend against it but there are perfectly valid reasons to do so in specific use cases. We can skip the whole file or a specific example within a file. Skipping individual test examples is a much more precise way to preserve the test file's value.

X-driven development

We use many models to help us improve our development processes. The most common ones, which we will discuss, are related to testing, while the other is a bit unique.

Test-driven development

Test-driven development (**TDD**) is a generalized approach to writing our tests that validates functionality before we write our required code.

What would that look like?

Let us pretend that we are working for a film production company on writing a new movie. When entering a new or existing universe, it would be extremely useful to create a series of automatic tests, that could be run constantly as I work on my script; this ensures that if there are any *universe breaking* decisions I attempt to make, we can catch them earlier in the process and address the discrepancies with smaller updates, minimizing the cost of rewrites later.

Aside from attempting to deeply immerse myself in the content, I can probably ask some form of *loremaster*, or the person who is responsible for keeping track of all the rules, lore, etc., to ensure continuity. In the context of engineering, this would be a product owner. Armed with a new set of rules, we could write some tests before ever writing our script. When we do that, we can start with a *clean* build, and as soon as we draft up something that needs addressing, it can be taken care of sooner rather than later. It is interesting that I normally start with writing my tests leaving me with a failing build and I work towards green. However, that makes more sense when we know where we are going, and typically, as programmers, we do know; however, when I put myself in the shoes of a scriptwriter for movies, I decided I needed to adopt the model a little bit to accomplish the same types of goals.

Behavior-driven development

In **behavior-driven development** (**BDD**), we emphasize in our testing the function's behavior from the user's perspective rather than the developer's. While I am sure people will tell you that these are somehow distinct from TDD in ways outside of implementation details, I disagree. In my opinion, this was always something that developers who embraced TDD implemented, as opposed to ones who felt forced to write tests without thinking about their users. At the end of the day, we can align with TDD and BDD; they are not mutually exclusive and are no different than the typical *religious wars* (such as *emacs* vs. *vim*) we have in tech that I would personally rather avoid.

Pain-driven development

Pain-driven development (**PDD**) is not strictly specific to testing and can be applied more broadly. It is a way of prioritizing and motivating efforts based on pain.

In my opinion, there are two sides to the PDD coin. Both methods can make sense in specific contexts, but they are typically mutually exclusive. They stem from the same root desire, but they are completely different when we apply them and how we go about them.

The first form focuses on identifying the customers' pain and using that to prioritize what we work on. After delivering new relief, we interview our customers to see if more is needed or if we can move on. This is very effective in a lot of ways; we can directly see the impact of our efforts when the customers are happier. This is often employed when joining a new project or organization; being new, we need to rely on our customers to inform us where our efforts are needed. Anyone who has worked with a pain specialist in the medical field can relate to this. We have patients who are in pain, and we can observe certain things externally, but at the end of the day, the goal is to get the patient into the most comfortable state possible, given all the constraints. This is typically what we commonly hear folks referring to when talking about pain-driven development.

This next form of pain-driven development should only be considered by experienced practitioners.

This is a last resort when we must introduce a change, and other methods have failed to motivate the transition. As opposed to the previous form, where we use the customers' existing pain to determine our priorities, here we look to introduce pain to motivate our customers to align with a strategic goal. Oftentimes, we create our new path(s), making it painless, while intentionally injecting pain or choosing not to mitigate pain into the old path. As we are about to ruffle some feathers, we will want or need executives or key stakeholder(s) to buy in that the short-term pain is acceptable to achieve strategic victory. It is important to remember that pain is the change agent to introduce a better outcome, not the goal. In a sense, it is like antibiotics cleaning house and forcing the immune system to restart.

A common example where we may need to rely on injecting pain is (tool) consolidation. When we maintain multiple ways of accomplishing the same thing, there is a cost to maintaining each. Oftentimes, we can gain efficiency by standardizing a single solution. However, not everyone is always on board with the changes. Perhaps the efficiency gains only positively impact one team but require effort from many teams. They may see only disruption, even if all things are considered equal. Here is a story from my career where I saw this play out.

Story time, PDD

I worked for a company where we had multiple solutions that accomplished the same things. The teams responsible for maintaining these systems wanted to consolidate, however, there was resistance from their customers. We went around many times in circles, trying to understand what use cases existed. However, some of these customers were intentionally not sharing the information that was necessary to facilitate smooth processing. One day, there was a security issue with the product in question, and it was brought to our attention that the maintainers were previously made aware of the issue and had ignored it. We had our reason that the service needed to die; it allowed us to introduce a certain amount of pain and additional tracking around the use cases that had yet to be migrated.

During this time period, we worked very closely with teams to help them migrate their use cases. From the start of our real effort to kill this service, every week, we would reset the IP allowlist and group membership, forcing users to keep justifying their continued usage. After some time, we had finally identified all the use cases, created solutions to ease the pain once the migration was completed, and motivated the customers to the new system. Once everything had been migrated, we were able to spin down the old service and move on to other challenges to solve.

Functional

In functional testing, we focus on verifying the desired functionality of the application or system. This is made up of unit, integration, and other forms of testing.

Smoke test

What is a smoke test? You might have heard this term before, but it is rife with subtle differences in meaning between organizations and teams. Originally, the term came from hardware testing, where if someone turns on the power on a device and it starts smoking, it is turned off because the test is complete.

In a software testing context, *smoke testing* can be referred to as a minimum set of tests that ensure essential functionality. Common examples of these checks include if a landing page loads, the user can log in, add an item to a cart, and submit a payment. These kinds of tests can be performed manually after a deployment or exist as automated tests, ideally run at the beginning of a test suite. Less commonly, smoke tests might even be performed automatically after deployment, and this could take the shape of a script that crawls the live website, validating what it finds. This methodology is employed in our canary releases deployment pattern, which we will discuss in *Chapter 8, Continuous Delivery, Understanding common deployment patterns, Canary deploys*.

Smoke testing is best thought of as an essential set of end-to-end tests, that can be performed in a variety of ways, in a variety of environments. When quality assurance checking is performed, this may also technically be considered smoke testing if the checks exercise the most essential behavior of an application as a matter of course.

Non-functional testing

OK, so now that we have tested that our code works as expected, we are done with testing, right? Not quite. Once we have validated that we met the feature requirements, we need to ask ourselves if we need to do any performance or stability-type testing.

Load, performance, and scalability

Depending on the size of the organization, userbase, etc., we need to look at ensuring that we can scale to meet the demands. This is typically performed using load tests or simulated user traffic meant to mimic real behavior and test the system. There are many load-testing frameworks out there, with new ones coming out regularly. While we can do this kind of testing in production, it is more common to do it in a non-production environment to better isolate what is happening, as well as to ensure that our testing does not impact real user traffic. This helps us also establish a performance baseline, which we will discuss in *Chapter 10, Trusting Our Metrics,* how we can take the performance testing and apply it to larger numbers.

One thing worth noting is that while we have been discussing this in the context of legitimate traffic, we must also acknowledge that there are bad actors. We need to think about **denial of service** (**DoS**) protection in a layered approach. While some of the solutions may come from the security team(s), we still need to ensure that the systems are able to soak up initial traffic spikes; in parallel, security teams will spin up their investigation and start deploying mitigations.

Security, vulnerabilities, compliance

Good developers recognize that security and compliance can be just as important as other business requirements. We will discuss this quite a bit in *Chapter 5, Security* and *Chapter 9, Pipeline Mastery, Security and Compliance Stages.* By automating the testing to ensure that we meet our security and compliance needs, we can gain confidence that we are meeting our stated goals.

This can include posture management, or the generalized configuration of resources that could introduce a vulnerability; known vulnerability dependency scanning; static code analysis, where we attempt to find vulnerabilities by looking at but not executing the code; dynamic security testing, where we run automated tests against a running application, etc.

Usability

The last form of testing we are going to mention is not about automated testing. Usability testing focuses on evaluating the ease of using the system or product. We do this by creating real-world scenarios and asking users to perform a set of tasks. By observing user behavior, we can counter the bias that we might have about whether a customer will or will not figure out **X** or **Y** easily. This is very important in the context of self-service.

Accessibility

This type of testing concerns users with disabilities. It is commonly referred to as *a11y*, which is a condensed version of *accessibility* in which the number 11 stands in for the remaining middle characters.

The importance of this testing is based on the fact that applications often serve incredibly wide demographics. These demographics are not restricted to race and gender but also ability. Not everyone has the same ability to perceive and use an application. Design patterns that neglect users with color blindness, Parkinson's disease, and poor contrast perception, among other challenges, benefit from clear accessibility standards. Not all *a11y* tests need to be built from scratch since several scanners are available to do most of the job.

I have watched a college professor with mild Parkinson's disease attempt to navigate a drop-down menu, where one mouse shake undoes every carefully hovered-over item. A natural tab order for that page could have spared the frustration of one professor and the time of an entire auditorium full of students.

Fuzz testing

Also known as *Fuzzing* is the practice of feeding unexpected input data to a program to uncover bugs, crashes, and unexpected behavior. This type of testing fits into CI perfectly, and sometimes, it accidentally finds its way into our regular test suite when we leverage fake data generators.

From the perspective of prioritizing work and achieving goals, it is important to separate *fuzz* testing from behavior validation testing (that is, the standard test suite). This is due to the unpredictable nature of the *random* data that constitutes fuzz testing. Tests that fail behavior validation should block a change from being merged because it is related to the change in question. This is not the same for *fuzz* testing because the unexpected behavior that surfaced through fuzz testing may have been present for months! Why should the poor developer who stumbled upon a failed fuzz test put their goals on hold to figure out a fix? Instead, it would be best to think of fuzz testing as a method of *automated exploratory* testing. When a fuzz test failure is discovered, it should be non-blocking to a CI pipeline but rather tracked, reviewed, and prioritized. Fixing fuzz tests should be done relatively quickly, otherwise alarm fatigue will render them useless. We will discuss alarm fatigue in depth in *Chapter 12, Observability, Taming monitoring, alerting, and on-call demons, Identifying and combatting alert fatigue.*

Mutation testing

Mutation testing is useful for surfacing areas of your codebase that are under-covered by your tests. While code coverage reporting exposes lines that are not exercised at all, mutation testing makes deliberate changes to your source code to verify your test suite detected the changes. In other words, it is a way of alerting developers to code that may have been exercised during a test but remains unverified in terms of app behavior. A word of caution: although this can be an effective way to find bugs before your users do, the time and place to perform this check are not on every (attempted) merge to the default branch during normal work hours. A test that matters should block the deployment pipeline when it fails, and since we are not in the business of writing tests that do not matter— there had better be a good reason for blocking the pipeline. Be warned: many of your developer teammates will not consider a library that randomly modifies the codebase as a justification for blocking their feature release. We need some diplomacy and tact to pull this off, and this is where *test frequency* comes into play.

Test frequency

Not all tests should be run at all times. For example, a non-critical, long-running test (typically 5 minutes or more for a single test assertion) should be run at night, after business hours[7]. In addition, the test should be run separately from those run on every merge to our default branch, and not block the release pipeline. If a failure is found, the associated developer should be notified, and time set aside to address the issue should be captured and prioritized. Mutation testing falls into this same category and should be treated similarly. Run your mutation tests in a non-blocking place at a regular frequency. If issues are found, notify the associated individuals so that they can prioritize their work accordingly. They will thank you for giving them insight and appreciate your attention to their priorities. If you have a strong opinion on when that item should be addressed, we can always ask the team to tackle it ourselves!

Test data management

Since our tests should be focused on validating logic, we should not embed our data directly. As we mentioned before, we encourage the usage of scripts that can set up the schema of the datastore and populate it with some non-real data. How do we go about that? When do we choose generation vs. masking and redacting?

Generation

There are two types of data we will focus on in the context of generating data for local development and testing purposes. The first is something we have already mentioned in passing. That is generating and updating the schema through migration tasks. The second is the sample data that we need to have a functional application to work on and test against. Depending on our language, our options vary; however, every major programming

7 Excluding the rare team spread across many time zones

language has tools such as the *faker*[8] Ruby project, which is fantastic at generating different types of data, such as names, addresses, etc.

Tips from Sean: Be careful when arranging a test, to not conflate the need for random data with the need for unique data. Many broken tests have been the victim of generating the same data twice, when it was assumed that random data would always be unique. If you use a library for generating random inputs (like Ruby's Faker) be sure to check if there is a uniqueness option, and apply it by default. Our tests should be very purposefully written, and the example data used within should be no exception.

When working on integration tests, we generally require data that represents the external system. This can be programmatically contrived or it can be done manually by capturing a real API response. As a bonus, example payloads are sometimes included as part of our developer API documentation.

Masking and redaction

Sometimes, our applications need sensitive information, even for testing or data analysis. In some cases, generating some of the necessary data with assistance from production may only be feasible. In these cases, we need to rely on techniques to protect the sensitive aspects before importing them into less sensitive and protected environments. This is done through redaction techniques, where we remove or change the sensitive elements so that they are no longer sensitive.

When using redaction, we need to ask ourselves whether we can always use the same value (for example, **"[REDACTED]"**) or if we want to have unique values for each without exposing the original value. In the first use case, it can be straightforward. We define some patterns and perform a *search and replace* against the data set using whatever the static token is in real-time. When we care about having unique values, we can use a hashing algorithm, which will allow our internal developers to analyze a unique user behavior pattern without knowing the identity of the user the behavior represents.

Data analyst and engineer use cases

There are some interesting nuances involved in data analyst and engineer use cases. While much of what we have covered has been more focused on application and infrastructure, we can apply much of it to these use cases, even if it is not 1:1.

One of the more common data use cases revolves around **export, transport, and load** (ETL). In essence, this is a three-step process to take data from one or more systems (databases, files, APIs, etc.), perform any modifications (such as normalizing field names, changing structures, enriching data, etc.), and then store the resulting transformed data into a new destination. In a sense, when we talk about the output of ETL, this can be the input to our applications. One of the most valuable tests for data use cases is to run our ETL pipeline and report back if there are any errors. This is very similar to our example integration test using a health check.

8 (Faker - Ruby Fake Data, n.d.)

Scaling our testing culture

The value of testing must be internalized and promoted by all leaders involved in the engineering processes at the organizational level. It is important that our leaders communicate and act in a way that will build and maintain the desired culture at an organization. Like a seed crystal, the team's test-centered workflow will only be propagated if leadership understands its value and insists it is implemented. There are often many influential developers who embrace testing, but insistence at the management level is critical for making the practice a cultural facet.

Testing takes time and resources to build a test suite. Even seasoned developers sometimes overlook the value of automated tests when they can retain the (small) system's implementation in their heads. Unfortunately, that does not scale. By automating the tests and their setup, we are relying less on each contributor's understanding of the entire system. As systems grow, it can be hard to understand the impact of a localized change on connected systems. Once we need more than one developer working on a project, it is time to start investing in automated testing to unlock the ability to scale safely.

Tip from Sean: **Beware of lone wolf high-performers who refuse to write tests. Their contributions might seem valuable today, but the projects they support will only scale proportionate to the individual efforts they put forth. This is doubly true for individual contractors, where their incentives are naturally aligned in a way that discourages outside contributions, which keeps their own demand high. If your high performers were to write valuable tests, then your more affordable developers would be free to contribute without fear of breaking the existing system. This should not be too surprising since, after all, our test suite serves to increase developer confidence!**

Conclusion

Automation can add tremendous value, but it comes with its own set of dangers. After exploring the why, we outlined different test types, coverage reporting, and how it can be gamified. We touched on what interfaces to test, and how to reduce maintenance costs. Not all tests are created equally; we discussed what makes a good vs. a useless test. We explored several different development models, such as test-driven and behavior-driven development, which have a heavy emphasis on writing automated testing before the functional code. We touched on the less well-known development models, with the two sides of pain-driven development. We explored why many teams and products need to extend their testing beyond product functionality to include load, performance, scale, security, and compliance concerns. To ensure we do not expose our sensitive data, we explored how best to handle data in the context of testing.

Next, we will be looking at how we will be taking our testing and running it continuously as we integrate code. Doing so will allow us to make it safe to deploy often without sacrificing reliability.

CHAPTER 5
Security

Introduction

Originally, when the internet was first created by the United States **Defense Advanced Research Project Agency (DARPA)**, there was no serious thought of cybersecurity at the time. Their threat model was based on only governments and large universities having the capabilities to connect. Oh, how the times have changed; now we must worry about nation-state actors, professional (financially motivated) hackers, politically motivated activists, and teenagers in their parents' basements from invading our privacy, damaging or stealing digital assets, or causing other harm through cyber and human vulnerabilities. In a perfect world, we would not need to worry about cybersecurity. Unfortunately, there are bad people, and eventually, AI will be out to get us. Just as a criminal would break into a house, car, etc., the same is true for our digital assets. The art form of cybersecurity is determining the appropriate levels of risk management for our engineering and organization processes that impact digital assets or information. Let us take a step back to explain why security is finding the balance between usability and safety. The only completely secure system is one that does not exist; its mere existence is a vulnerability. While our computers are binary, we must take a more pragmatic approach to risk management.

As such, we need to take some time to understand basic security principles, how responsibilities are typically distributed, how we can improve our cybersecurity posture, understanding **security incident response** (SIR), responsible disclosure, threat actors, threat modeling, and collaboration techniques for all audiences. For our engineering-inclined audiences, we will be diving deeper into several of the sections already mentioned, in addition to some more advanced topics.

Security teams should embrace the ethos of a DevOps culture, which is one that focuses on bringing multiple groups together to build and protect an organization's value.

The security of a system is only as strong as its weakest link. Everyone plays a role in security. Security teams should empower infrastructure, application, SRE, IT, etc. teams; for example we can reduce complexity for these various groups by providing self-service modules. Unfortunately, some organizations may not have any security team(s), or their security team(s) lack deep engineering expertise. In these cases, we will explore how to fill these gaps and engage with our security team(s) to translate requirements into modules. By reviewing security reports together as opposed to simply throwing them over the fence, we can leverage our combined skillsets rather than working in isolation. For example, our security engineer could give pseudo code of what needs to happen, which generally can be reasonable for an operations or application engineer to translate.

Objectives

To understand the following:

- What is cybersecurity?
- What is the CIA triad and how does it help guide us?
- Whose responsibility is cybersecurity?
- What is ethical hacking?
- How do we insert cybersecurity into shifting right and left?
- What are the motivations of these cyber threat actors?
- How do we quantify risks and financial losses from cyber incidents?
- Advanced topics:
  - How do we understand and communicate the severity of a vulnerability?
  - How can frameworks help us understand cyber-attacks and risk management?
  - What are some crucial aspects when setting up Security Incident Response processes and procedures?
  - How can threat modeling help us uncover potential vulnerabilities?
  - How do we shrink our attack surface?
  - How do we harden our systems?
  - What is Zero Trust?
  - How do we effectively integrate security teams with the larger organization?

o   How do we reduce complexity for development teams and address cybersecurity concerns at the same time?

o   What are the categories of offensive and defensive tooling?

o   Where do we start our cybersecurity journey?

Cybersecurity in a nutshell

So, what is cybersecurity? It is the engineering discipline in which we look to determine weaknesses in our systems and improve them, in pursuit of better protection of our digital assets. It is important to remember that digital systems that are attacked can have real world impacts. For example, taking down an electrical grid could cause a life support system to fail if there are not appropriate redundancies to mitigate.

Unfortunately, there are many who view cybersecurity as purely a drain on our organization. This is another example of our degrees of separation problems that we discussed in *Chapter 1, Introduction to DevOps, Why is culture everything?, Incentive alignment.* While in some cases we certainly can slow things down for good safety reasons, we are also an enabler. How so?

Would you be willing to enter your **sensitive** information into a service that we **know** is **insecure**? Of course not! In other words, the only reason a customer would do so is if we gave them the impression it is safe; it is a clear unspoken requirement for just about any product that is worth anything. Yet, we often do not think about or discount the risks until we get bitten. In addition to security being an enabler for the entire organization to exist and retain its function; we are also able to speed up engineering teams by providing much needed security libraries that provide features, configuration, automated security testing, automated patch management, etc. to lower the barrier to create secure products and infrastructure. As it does not fit neatly into any single box, we will be discussing this throughout many of our advanced topics sections in this chapter. Near the end of our journey together, we will look to pick this topic back up in *Chapter 11, Valuation, Bridging Management and Engineering,* as it is a subject that requires additional information before we delve deeper.

CIA triad

While there are a great number of concepts the most important is **confidentiality, integrity, and availability (CIA)** which is commonly referred to as the CIA triad. Using this lens, we will explain how to approach security events as they explain the type of impact to our data, systems, or human life. When determining if an event falls under security, we can ask ourselves if it impacted any of these three. It is also worth noting that there are times when there may be a financial or other impact that may not be easily attributed to them; when this is the case, we need to use our best judgment and err on the side of caution.

We shall explore the three pillars (confidentiality, integrity, and availability) of the CIA triad:

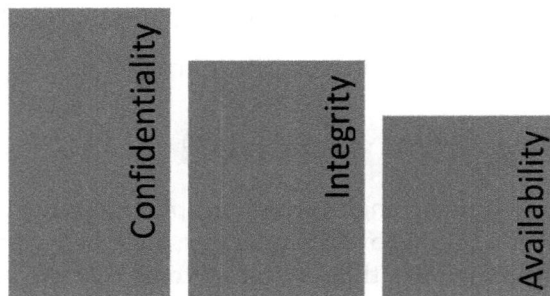

Figure 5.1: Three pillars that act as the foundation to cybersecurity

Confidentiality, integrity, and availability

They are explained as follows:

- **Confidentiality:** Refers to ensuring that only the appropriate or authorized people and systems may access our sensitive data that is relevant to them. In the context of an **Automated Teller System** (**ATM**), a violation of confidentiality would enable an unauthorized user to see information about another person's account.

- **Integrity:** Refers to ensuring that the data (or features) are trustworthy. This means ensuring that it cannot be tampered with at the source or in transit without being able to be detected. In the context of an ATM, a violation of integrity would be an attacker manipulating a transaction to change the requested value or send it to a different account than intended.

- **Availability:** Refers to the ability of authorized users to access their data. In the context of an ATM, a violation of availability would be an attacker denying one or more users access to their funds.

CIA violations

If we want to think of what a CIA triad violation or compromise from an attacker's perspective, any malicious instance of:

- **Disclosure** is a loss of *confidentiality*.
- **Distortion** is a result of loss of *integrity*.
- **Destruction or disruption of access** to a service or resource is a loss of *availability*.

All three of these result in **Distrust** when the triad is violated. We tend to have a higher tolerance for availability violations (with the exceptions where physical safety is a major factor, such as a plane or a life support device), but eventually, persistent problems with this will steer us towards their competitors.

Are the three cybersecurity pillars equal?

First off, we need to recognize that, most of the time, severe exploits will affect more than one pillar of the CIA triad, especially when we consider chains of attacks. When we have systems that have value (which we will discuss in greater depth in *Chapter 11, Valuation, Bridging Management and Engineering*), either in intellectual property, data, trade secrets, etc., we will choose which of the three is most important to our organization or system. While it does depend on the industry, data, and product, we typically will put *confidentiality* and *integrity* over *availability*. The rationale behind this is that once confidentiality is compromised, it is not possible to completely undo the damage; we can prevent further leaks, but the data is out there. If a system's integrity is compromised, if we have appropriate auditing and backup controls, we should be able to reverse the damage done to the system, even if manual intervention is required. Availability, in contrast to the other two, is a point in time view and, with the notable exception of data destruction, which is also an integrity violation (which can be mitigated with backups), is a temporary state. The significance of availability goes up the longer an organization is impacted during an incident. We should refer to our **business impact analysis (BIA)** to help us understand the maximum tolerable downtime for the organization to remain viable in the event of a sustained outage. While going over what a BIA entails is out of scope here, we will summarize it as a process where we critically analyze our organization's important functions, understanding the impact they have on our organization. The BIA is a critical input to our **disaster recovery plan (DRP)** and **business continuity plan (BCP)**.

If we want further confirmation that this default mindset is prevalent, the *Orange Book*[1] is a security document that describes a set of design principles necessary to create a security system for the United States **Department of Defense (DOD)** that could handle both *classified* and *non-classified* data within the same system. The European **Information Technology Security Evaluation Criteria (ITSEC)** is an international model that, among other topics, specifically addresses the lack of focus on integrity and availability in the *Orange Book*, which was written before networking entered the equation.

Going back to our ATM transaction, if an attacker can change (increase) the value being withdrawn from the account, they are also denying our victim's access to those same funds, even if they are later restored by the financial institution.

Everyone contributes to security!

While the security team's primary responsibilities include monitoring security events, giving guidance to engineering, and acting as a rapid response **Special Weapons and Tactics (SWAT)** team of software engineers and operators, they cannot be entirely responsible for all things security. A system's security is typically as vulnerable as its weakest link; we may attempt to layer additional defenses, but there is no guarantee they will be adequate. Most of the time, we, as humans, are the weakest link; we can be tricked into doing something that may harm us or our organization, which is called *social engineering*. Social engineering preys on the human vulnerability of misplaced trust rather than a technical one.

1 (United States Department of Defense, 1985)

We will explore three layers of cybersecurity responsibilities:

- **Personal:** Following the organization's security policies, being aware of danger (in compliance does not mean all risk has been eliminated), and reaching out to specialists. For example, when working in a coffee shop, do not leave your laptop or phone unattended.

- **Producers:** Ensuring that their products are patched with the latest security updates, working through security findings with specialists, and partnering with specialists to ensure that their products are inherently secure. For example, ensuring that only authorized users are allowed to access systems (or data) that they are supposed to.

- **Specialists:** These are our security experts, they will create overall governance of security policies, implement defenses, and such. The higher the budget these specialists are given, the more they can help each of the other personas with the overhead in their respective areas. Risk can never be entirely eliminated, but we can reduce it to a more acceptable level. For example, implementing a spam filter reduces the likelihood that a user will fall victim to a phishing attempt. There will always be someone able to bypass our filters, as we need to enable the mission of whatever the product or service is supporting. If we wanted to entirely reduce cyber threats, we would turn off our computers, but this would simply shift the attacks to other vectors.

To take a step back from securing an organization, let us explore securing our house or apartment to highlight that there is a shared responsibility. Let us say we have engaged with a security consultant or organization to help us design a home security system. The consultants come and observe the property and suggest various solutions to prevent and deter intruders. After reviewing the proposal and making some minor changes, we are feeling quite good about the project. Everything was installed and set up correctly, but one day, we rushed out of the house to run a quick errand. We came back an hour later to discover that someone had robbed the house while we were out.

After reviewing the surveillance footage, it is clear we forgot to lock the door and engage the alarm system. Can we blame the consulting firm, or are we at fault for not using the system correctly? This hypothetical scenario illustrates that everyone plays a part in the security of a system. Coming back to cybersecurity for a minute, it is not uncommon to have no or very limited security-focused staff; we tend to represent only 1-2% of the organization, so it is important that we work as a force multiplier with our partners throughout the organization. This means we need to ensure that our efforts include education and empowerment that enable other developers to move more securely without slowing them down (too much?).

Ethical hacking

Ethical hacking is the process of discovering and reporting vulnerabilities in a system. It is important to note that the term ethical in this context covers both the motivations (to improve the security of the system and not do harm) and expectations around a professional engagement. There is a lot to possibly go into here, so we are going to summarize the practices and processes.

It starts with having effective communication; we need to outline the scope of the engagement, including which techniques may be used, as they may have an impact on users. Once we have our terms of engagement, we can start looking for weaknesses to be exploited, responsibly reporting any discovered vulnerabilities within scope.

These *ethical hackers* are also commonly referred to as *white hats*. In contrast, *black hats* perform exploits with malicious intent. While machines may be binary, we are not; the third category of the attacker's motivation, as crazy as it might sound, is *for fun*. We call these folks *grey hats*, who do not obtain permission from organizations to perform exploits. It is illegal to engage in cyber activities without consent or a warrant, whether we are talking about *grey* or *black* hats.

We will leverage these *ethical hackers* to perform *penetration tests* or attempts to break into our systems and demonstrate how they can exploit the vulnerabilities. The scope, reporting, methods, and such are outlined prior to a penetration testing engagement. These vulnerability reports include a **proof of exploit** (**POE**) to be reviewed and verified; the goal is to deliver a list of the vulnerabilities to the organization and determine appropriate remediation steps. For many organizations, we do these on a regular basis by internal and external security engineers. Many external penetration test results are shared with regulators, customers, etc., to build trust. When we are ready to take this to the next level, we can implement a *bug bounty program*, which we will discuss shortly in the context of *responsible disclosure*.

Shifting right and left

The phrases *shifting right* or *shifting left* are used with the mental model that our developers are writing code on the left and moving right as it reaches our production systems. It becomes more expensive to rectify a defect in production. When we do not have any emphasis on proactive security engineering during development, it is natural that all our issues are discovered and addressed once they reach the *right*. Obviously, this is not ideal, so there has been a push in the industry to *shift left*, meaning that we should catch our security risks in our earlier phases of development, where it is easier and cheaper to fix. That sounds good, but at the end of the day, as much as we want to prevent every risk from being realized, that is not reasonable. While we should look to proactively eliminate and mitigate risk prior to it being exploited, we must accept that exploits will be realized and that we must plan for them, meaning that we need to balance pushing left and right topics. We will focus on several critical aspects of shifting right, as that is where threats are realized. Afterwards, we will focus on shifting left.

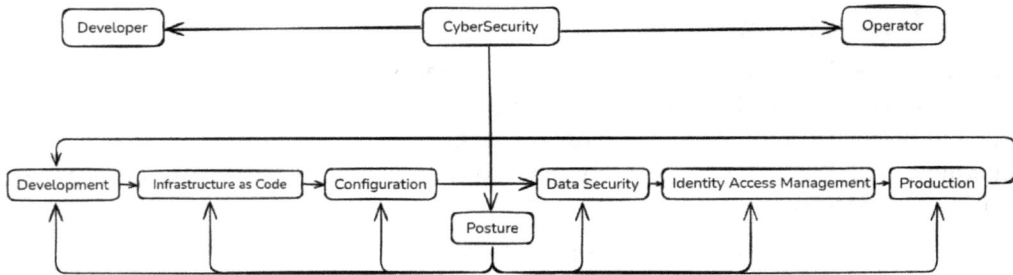

Figure 5.2: *Relationship of cybersecurity policy to shifting right and left*

In the figure above, we have the concept of two personas, one responsible for developing the product and one responsible for operating the product, these could be the same person. Both of these personas need to think about cybersecurity. The cybersecurity mindset helps both of these meet their goals while ensuring that our customers are safe and secure.

Security posture, as depicted by *Figure 5.2*, sits in the *middle* but has the impact of shifting both *right* and *left*. Posture affects how we think about each of the other boxes, including any not represented here. To say it in another way, while there are many benefits of IaC, there are four core reasons to invest in it from a cybersecurity lens. The first two are **disaster recovery planning** (**DRP**) and *scalability*. These both directly correlate to the *availability pillar* of the *CIA triad*. The third reason is to ensure that the system has not been tampered with, which corresponds to the *integrity pillar*. When we have automated a desired state, it is possible to perform drift detection (a deviation from the expected baseline), automated remediation, and alerting when something is modified outside of the accepted processes. If a hacker successfully turns off logging (which is common) to hide their tracks and evade detection mechanisms, we can have it automatically remediated and alerted on. The fourth reason is that if our configurations are in code, we can leverage automated scanning (such as static code analysis) and manual review (such as a pull request) to catch issues that would put our consumers at risk, which primarily corresponds to the *confidentiality pillar*.

An example of attempting to shift left would be to hook up our automated security testing discussed in *Chapter 4, Importance of Automated Testing, Non-Functional Testing, Security, vulnerability, compliance;* into our CI and CD pipelines to discover potential vulnerabilities before they are deployed, something we will be discussing in *Chapter 9, Pipeline Mastery, Optimizing Pipelines, Security and compliance stages.*

An example of shifting right would be to create a **security incident response** (**SIR**) process to help us handle our most critical threats to our organization. This is critical enough that we will have a basic and a more advanced section in this chapter dedicated to SIR for engineering and other audiences.

Artificial intelligence (**AI**) can be used by malicious actors and ethical hackers alike, thus bringing down the barrier to finding, exploiting, and addressing vulnerabilities for attackers and defenders. This will affect how we weigh the probability and overall risk of a particular vulnerability to an organization. A common example of attacker activities could include having it write portions or complete malware, phishing text, etc. On the defender side, this could be analyzing traffic patterns in detection and prevention systems and understanding the threat landscape. We will talk more about attacker and defender tooling shortly in *Advanced Topics, Categories of security tooling.*

Why security teams should embrace DevOps

While some challenges are unique to the security discipline, many of the challenges we face are also present in many engineering groups. By learning how the culture (not tooling, teams, or role) of DevOps brings developers and operators together to provide better business outcomes, we can apply this learning to our domain and bring security teams and other engineering groups closer together. This can be adding automated security testing, code review, architecture review, threat modeling sessions, etc., and will be something we discuss in further depth throughout our advanced section and in our pipeline chapters.

Improving collaboration and communication with different groups reduces our likelihood of creating a silo. The security team should never be described as an ivory tower architecture team, detached from the realities of the organization.

Where does security fit into DevOps?

This is a loaded question to which there are at least two embedded questions that each have multiple answers:

1. Beyond basic security responsibilities, what is my role as a developer or operator?
2. What are the responsibilities of security teams as opposed to product, infrastructure, or SRE teams?

What are the responsibilities of a developer and an operator:

- Developing secure solutions using the CIA triad as one of our core guiding principles.
- Collaborating with subject matter experts to ensure that security requirements are met or exceeded.
- Patching security vulnerabilities and working with SMEs where relevant.
- Ensure that we always sanitize inputs.
- Ensuring resources are isolated, following the principles of least privilege, etc.
- Ensure reasonable secret management.
- Highlight security concerns to the product, engineering, and security teams.

What are the responsibilities of the security team(s):

- Handling vulnerability disclosure processes, including bug bounty programs, triage, validation, working with teams to fix their resources, and additional detections.

- Assist teams where needed with remediation guidelines.

- Build security observability, something we will discuss in *Chapter 12, Observability, Taming monitoring, alerting, and on-call demons, What are the important things to monitor, Security Events*.

- Building and maintaining security incident response processes.

- Security incident response leads and SMEs.

- Build proactive defensive mechanisms.

- Find security concerns and address them or find the right person or team to do so.

- Perform auditing to ensure that we meet internal as well as any externally required compliances.

- Provide guidance, education, etc., on emerging cybersecurity threats and techniques they can be aware of to better protect themselves and the organization.

- Privacy advocacy, while privacy and security are not mutually exclusive, they are distinct. Most security folks will advocate for more rather than less privacy. Context is relevant in privacy. Personal vs. organizational privacy is a common point of contention as they are often misunderstood.

- Most of the time, compliance is a separate team in larger organizations. Often, security and compliance can align, but they do not have to; they are simply a set of agreed-upon rules to follow. Many are dictated by our industry and size.

- Governance means creating and enforcing security policies for the organization. This requires working with legal, finance, HR, IT, engineering, etc. teams to identify the necessary controls.

- Risk management helps the organization identify risks to be managed and determine priorities.

While in smaller organizations, security engineers and analysts might be part of other engineering groups, security teams should have different reporting although this should have very little bearing on the day-to-day interactions. Again, we are all part of one team looking to solve a goal; the reason that security teams need to have different teams and reporting structures is that, while we can do enablement, it still comes down to quality and risk management. We need to ensure that we have a proper seat at the table to ensure that our executives, board members, leadership, etc., understand that security is important because our customers and shareholders say so, and that we cannot sacrifice this for the sake of innovation, lacking risk management. The role of a **Chief Information Security Officer (CISO)** is to ensure that security is taken seriously at all levels of the organization, with boots on the ground, executive representation, and reporting to the board of directors.

Right

This is focused on addressing vulnerabilities that have been deployed to production environments. This also includes proactive investigations called threat hunting looking for threats that have already been realized.

Responsible disclosure

Hopefully, we find our issues ourselves before they are deployed, however, we should assume that some portion of these will make their way into production. We should publish on our site ways to get in contact with our engineering and/or security teams when a security researcher finds a vulnerability.

The best approach is to incorporate this need for external disclosure and communication with a bug bounty platform. These platforms connect security researchers to organizations that want to incentivize reporters to responsibly disclose the issues that they find. In addition to this, having a formalized program acts to communicate with our security researchers what kinds of threats we are interested in fixing. We also get to outline the rules or terms of engagement, including the scope as well as helpful information to help our reporters understand the systems, they are auditing, whether it be a production or a specialized testing environment.

After the researcher(s) find a vulnerability, they write up a vulnerability report for each finding. These reports include reproduction steps, understood impact, and more. The organization or an external service will triage the findings. Once we can replicate and analyze the impact, we can decide whether the finding will be covered under the bounty program. When we have successfully verified the report's validity, we need to look at what the impact is; most bounty program payouts are on a tier-based system, proportional to the severity of the report.

The alternative to responsible disclosure is breaches or irresponsible disclosure. While it might not feel the best to pay out for the report, it is a very cheap insurance policy. Typically, the same exploit on the dark web (black market) will pay out significantly higher than an organization pays out in a typical bounty program. This is because we are dealing with ethical security researchers who are looking out for organizations as opposed to criminals looking to harm us.

You might be wondering why I do not have any stories in this chapter; the reason is that security incidents are sensitive in nature and would be an example of irresponsible disclosure.

Security incident response

Security incident response (SIR) is a framework that helps us understand how we should respond to cyber events that threaten our organization. Some might be wondering; *do I need an SIR process; I am a small and uninteresting target*. The reality is that if our organization has value, someone will threaten it at some point. If we do not have a formalized and agreed-upon response process ahead of time, we will have to determine what the process should be while we are handling the incident, thus conflating our problems.

Many SIR practices and processes are taken from existing frameworks for dealing with crisis management, such as the **Incident Command System (ICS)**, which was developed to combat large-scale forest fires across many fire departments. We should build our own processes based on our unique organization and industry needs. One of the most important attributes of ICS is that we designate an **Incident Commander (IC)** who is temporarily in charge of all decision-making related to a particular incident.

One of the most important things to recognize is that during SIR, we must shift our mindset and processes from *peacetime* to *wartime*. During peacetime, we typically require folks from multiple areas of the organization to come together and make decisions, while there are obvious benefits, this democratic process can be time-consuming. During *wartime*, we need clear directions, a chain of command, and efficient decision-making processes.

When we are dealing with imminent threats to our organization, the *correct* answer too late is always the *wrong* answer, where a *non-optimal decision* is almost always a better call than *no decision*. When we are dealing with potentially severe threats to our organization, we should enact SIR to make sure that it is very clear to everyone that *wartime protocols* are in effect. *Incident Commanders* are trained to make tough decisions under stressful situations to avoid *decision paralysis,* that is, being unable to make any decision due to the fear of being incorrect.

While we should strive to make the best decision, we often are forced to operate with limited information available to us, with time as our nemesis; we must accept that we will make non-optimal decisions sometimes.

We will use our knowledge of the cyber kill chain to look for the earliest opportunity for damage control. While it is ideal to take down a small subset of the system, if we must shut down the entire system to protect our customers, employees, and shareholders, we will.

You may be wondering, *I have been looped into an SIR? What do I do?* While it depends on the organization's process, a good SIR process and team will shepherd all the members of an SIR as needed. Let us focus on three rules that apply broadly:

- The first thing to keep in mind is to remain calm, breathe, this too shall pass. When entering an SIR for the first time, the best thing that people can do is to *sit tight and wait for instructions.* We were looped in by someone, so clearly there is a process, and when they need our help, they will ask for it. The *Incident Commander* will be giving specific instructions to specific response members.

- The second most important thing is to *check your title and ego at the door.* During an SIR, the *Incident Commander* is the highest-ranking officer in the incident. Even C-Suite Executives must listen and respect the incident command system, we must avoid confusion and bickering during an incident, as they lead to inefficient and ineffective SIRs.

- Lastly, be conscious of communication expectations; do not discuss any details of the SIR externally from the designated communication channels except where directed by the *Incident Commander*.

We will pick this up shortly in our advanced section with additional information.

Security Incidents are stressful; our Incident Commanders have been specifically trained to make decisions under pressure. No decision is often worse than no decision. We should avoid decision paralysis at all costs. When we join an SIR, we should look to the Incident Commander for our direction, wait for instructions, and check our titles at the door.

Left

This is focused on proactively removing threats before they are deployed to our production systems. While penetration tests or bug bounty programs can be considered shifting left if they target non production code that has not been released, we generally see these come in post deployment to production.

Inventory of critical assets

We need to sit down and interview the various parts of the organization, to understand what assets exist and the sensitivity of them. This allows us to decide where efforts should be spent, as it makes no sense to put a lot of effort into protecting a low value asset when we are not addressing risk on our more valuable ones.

Our inventory depends on our technology stack but typically consists of cloud resources, IaaS, SaaS providers, PaaS providers, physical and virtual hosts, container registries, container images, running containers, applications, etc., and we will often need a solution to help us aggregate our inventory and later vulnerability data. When we combine the two, they act as a risk registrar or a place where we will register all our risks for prioritization of projects based on risk. The more rudimentary forms of this use spreadsheets; however, we recommend using a generic data lake solution or purpose-built software. This is because we need to ensure that we automate the processes around a constantly evolving infrastructure, applications, and organization.

Threat actor personas

Once we have an inventory of our most critical assets, we need to look at who would be motivated to compromise these systems. We start by outlining the personas of our potential threat actors or entities carrying out an attack for themselves or another entity. We should outline their motivations and capabilities next to each persona. Finally, we will want to take a hard look at what our posture should be towards each of these threat actors. Depending on the value, size, or nature of the organization, there will be differences. Here is an example of some high-level examples that we may see in many organizations:

Who	Motivations	Capabilities	Posture
Nation State Actor (NSA) or **Advanced Persistent Threat (APT)**	Data exfiltration, espionage, defense, assisting military operations, trade secrets, destruction or disruption of operations.	Financial budgets are effectively limitless.	For many organizations, their posture will be prayer and engaging the appropriate authorities, others this is the state in which they live, and they must do what they can proactively to mitigate threats and invest in good response capabilities to counter efforts as they are deployed.
Security researchers, bug bounty hunters, red teams, pen testers, etc.	These can range from financially incentivized work to improving the posture and security of the system.	Often financially constrained but sophisticated tactics and techniques.	Create a responsible disclosure process and work with reporters to improve our systems.
Professional hackers	Typically, financially motivated and acting out threats on behalf of their clients. Often using techniques to specifically obfuscate their origin, can be used by nation state.	Their budget is often constrained by the value of the target(s) or at least what someone values the target as, typically highly sophisticated.	Create observability data, analyze, and deploy proactive and reactive responses as necessary.
Script kiddies	Typically, they are financially motivated.	While they do have some capabilities themselves, most come externally from other proof of exploits, libraries, example code, etc.	We should harden our systems, ensure timely patch management, and deploy proactive defensive technologies to defeat them.

Who	Motivations	Capabilities	Posture
Scrapers	Typically, they are financially motivated.	Limited automation capabilities.	This will likely happen, some effort is put forward to prevent large scale scrape attempts, however small-scale scrapes will be an acceptable risk.
Scammers, spammers, hostage takers (ransomware), and fraudsters	Typically, they are financially motivated.	With the notable exceptions of ransomware (which could also be a professional hacker) these tend to have a relatively low level of sophistication of attacks and tend to rely more on social engineering than technical vulnerabilities.	We should proactively educate users on risky behavior, deploy defensive technologies to defeat them, and rely heavily on backups and automation for ransomware.
Internal Threat. This can take the form of espionage, sabotage, or a compromised employee's device.	Typically, this can be revenge, gaining an advantage (business or government), and may employ both carrot and the stick tactics to pressure employees to harm their employers.	Due to the nature of it being an internal employee, the damage that can be done depends on the permissions of the compromised entity.	Follow the principle of least privilege, extensive background checks, initial limited access, zero trust architecture, etc. from the technical perspective. Terminated employees' access is revoked immediately and without notice. Provide wellness programs, anonymous feedback systems, etc. can be used to help employees when they are most vulnerable to external manipulation, an emotional response, etc. as well as provide a bigger picture understanding should the risk factors of an employee go up.

Table 5.1: *A threat actor matrix outlining various attacker personas and how to approach them*

Threat modeling basics

In a nutshell, threat modeling is a brainstorming session where we produce an artifact of an existing or proposed system or change to the system, modeling out how an attacker would attempt to exploit weaknesses in the system and then draw up additional compensating controls, mitigations, or other preventative measures we can deploy until we have accepted the residual or remaining risk that is left after mitigations are deployed. As threat models typically are associated with specific types of threat actor personas, it is valuable but not required to outline our personas. This allows us to ensure that we have a shared understanding of the terminology used when we communicate internally within our teams and externally. This prevents us from spending time outlining attack paths and proactive mitigations that require nation-state capabilities, even though we strategically decided to respond reactively to such attackers. There are many frameworks out there that we can leverage. We will discuss this shortly in our advanced section on threat modeling for the engineering audience.

What is important to understand is that we are taking a proactive approach to identifying how a system works, how it can be exploited, and how we can improve the system by reducing risk.

Increasing collaboration with security teams

While often security teams are distinct from the infrastructure, application, data, etc. teams that generate the resources that need to be protected, we need to ensure that we do not create a silo. We must ensure that we have appropriate communication between these teams. While some of the decision-making may reside with one group on a particular item/topic, we need to function as a unit, bringing forth the organization's goals.

If we do not really understand our users, we will likely create bad policies, which will weaken our systems rather than strengthen them. Want an example?

The United States **National Institute of Standards and Technology (NIST)** gave the following misguided advice for many decades, which stated that organizations should force password rotation on users at regular intervals. This ignores the human side of the equation; what was found is that the complexity of passwords, combined with their need to change frequently, caused users to either write them down or create their own algorithm, which often was little more than shifting numbers around. Obviously, this had the exact opposite effect of what was intended. After many years of research, NIST reversed its stance in a revision in 2017:

Verifiers SHOULD NOT require memorized secrets to be changed arbitrarily (e.g., periodically). However, verifiers SHALL force a change if there is evidence of compromise of the authenticator.[2]

In other words, we should rotate the secret when we know it is compromised, not because some arbitrary period has passed.

---

2 (Grassi, et al., 2017)

If we had better understood our customers, we would not have given the initial guidance that later needed revision.

Security policies and posture

Yes, policies, procedures, and standards shift left! While they are not the first thing we think of as engineers, this is a great place to affect changes long before they are conceived or implemented. These security policies are high-level documents and guidelines that serve to outline the objectives to ensure we meet our security and privacy needs for our internal customers (employees), external customers, and shareholders to create a successful security program. To ensure that these policies are bringing value to the organization, we need to ensure that we are realistic. A policy no one complies with is worse than having no policy. Policies by default are not advisory unless stated as such, meaning that they are compulsory. If any employee, even including executives, does not like the policy, they are welcome to leave the organization. Many security policies come from regulatory requirements for specific industries, such as the **Payment Card Industry (PCI)**, **Health Information Privacy Protection Act (HIPAA)**, **Sarbanes Oxley (SOX)**, or **Systems of Organizational Controls (SOC NUMBER)**, etc. Each policy must clearly outline its purpose, scope, responsibilities, and compliance with it. Why is this shifting left? Rather than waiting for it to be a problem that is caught in production, we outline our requirements or shared expectations, which can be accounted for early in the development process, which keeps our costs down.

The following represents an example flow of the creation of a new policy and the updates to it through its lifecycle:

- **Initiation:** The realization that we need a policy. We may define an initial scope, even if it is subject to change as progress through the process.
- **Refine scope:** Work with our stakeholders to ensure that we understand the problem statement(s) and clearly outline each one and update the scope as necessary.
- **Design:** Define the requirements, including security, functional, operational, etc., that must be incorporated into solutions.
- **Development:** An SME again meets with any necessary stakeholders to get additional context. Drafts the initial version or updates to the policy.
- **Approval:** After senior management reviews and approves the new or updated policy. This ensures that all members of the organization understand the importance and commitment to the policy.
- **Publication:** A versioned copy of the policy is distributed, and users who are affected are notified.
- **Implementation:** We put our security policies into action; when we are rolling out a policy that affects existing systems, we should be conscious of the load we put on other teams within the organization, including their timelines. While we often

need to set a deadline to ensure that it is prioritized in an acceptable timeframe, we should be flexible enough to meet our organization where they are rather than where we need them to be. We need to accept that it will take time for us to

- **Maintenance:** Regular reviews are conducted to ensure that we can highlight updates needed to the policy or our systems due to the changing needs as our technology, organization, etc., grow.

Reviews

There are many ways security engineers can assist our engineering and other teams, and the best way is to get us involved with the software development lifecycle as early as possible. By getting in during the design phase, we can model threats to the decisions we make, which will be combined with existing security policies and standards to ensure we get security requirements into each of our teams' deliverables. Once the project has started, we bring value by being subject matter experts for code review, automated security testing, and architectural decisions.

Balancing reactive and proactive work

The terms *red* and *blue* in the context of cybersecurity teams and operations come from military exercises and wargames. Blue represented friendly forces, while red represented our adversary. Both *red* and *blue* team efforts are always done within the context of *Ethical Hacking*. Our *red* teams assume the mindset of an adversary or attacker, and their efforts are motivated to find new threats that need addressing. Our *blue* teams are our defenders. They are made up of engineers, architects, analysts, etc., who are proactively catching issues pre and post-production deployments. This manifests through automated security testing, architecture review, requirements creation, patching vulnerabilities, and performing Incident Response. When we look to combine expertise, efforts, practices, and more within the cybersecurity community from our *red* and *blue* teams, we get a *purple* team. When our security operations and engineering teams are working together as a single unit, this is called a *cyber fusion center*. These teams work together to ensure that we push both right and left on our security concerns, further blurring the lines between these once-distinct functions.

There are many cybersecurity maturity models out there, some with very specific scopes while others are broader in nature. It does not matter whether we use the **Cybersecurity Capabilities Maturity Model (C2M2)** from the United States **Department of Energy (DOE)** or the **Software Assurance Maturity Model (SAMM)** from the **Open Worldwide Web Application Security Project (OWASP)**, a non-profit foundation improving security in software. The commonality between them is that we outline a number (ranging from dozens to hundreds, thousands, etc.) of cybersecurity best practices in a set of questions and responses. We interview and audit all the relevant items, assigning a predetermined set of values, which are then eventually converted into a number representing the whole. Using a maturity model can help confirm practices that we believe to be strong, highlighting where we need improvement and tracking our progress as we continue to make investments.

While it depends on the nature of the organization, it is most common to focus on initially building out blue team capabilities and teams. We can augment our capabilities and focus with bug bounty programs, external penetration tests, etc., to augment our *red* team discovery while we focus on solving problems with the available resources. These blue, red, or purple teams can be additionally augmented through **managed detection and response (MDR)**, **security operations center (SOC)**, and **digital forensics and incident response (DFIR)** partners.

Quantifying financial risks and losses

We generally use the following formula to determine whether we should address a threat to our organization:

Probability of vulnerability exploited × Damage Impact ≤ Cost of protections, preventions, and response

We refer to this as a **single loss expectancy (SLE)**, which consists of **asset value (AV)** and **exposure factor (EF)**; it is the monetary loss that would be realized if a threat is exploited. We can generally calculate the **annual loss expectancy (ALE)** as the **annualized rate of occurrence (ARO)** within a year, which is represented by:

$$ALE = SLE \times ARO$$

We need to ensure that the cost of prevention is less than or equal to the loss incurred by the realization of the threat.

One of the biggest challenges is that it can be hard to quantify the rate or probability of a threat being realized, as we do not control that. A vulnerable system with a motivated attacker has a 100% probability of the threat being exploited. Likewise, estimating the damages can be difficult, as it includes factors beyond fines, fees, hours spent remediating, etc., such as reputational damage, which is often unclear to engineering and the organization's leadership. Many times, these are not included in cyber loss calculations under quantitative analysis; while some are convinced that this is a separate type of valuation, such as qualitative analysis, we disagree as reputational damage is, in most cases, the largest factor in terms of affecting the value of an organization rather than the cost of responding to breaches or lost revenue during the attack and response, even if it can be hard to calculate. If there is no quality in our analysis, it is pointless to quantify a number that does not match the actual risk; the potentially projected losses will always be skewed towards not deploying appropriate resources and shortchanging our organization's value.

We recommend that you rely on experts who typically have access to more data, can approach it more objectively, and understand the nuances involved. Many organizations, subconsciously or consciously, discount the impact and importance of factors such as brand reputation, trust, etc. We will be diving into this further in *Chapter 11, Valuation,*

Bridging Management and Engineering, where we will be joined by a professional business appraiser, Jay Abrams, to wade into this messy topic.

Advanced topics

The rest of this chapter, until the specified section, is geared towards our engineering audiences. It will be accessible to all, but we will be diving deeper and will not stop to explain certain topics that are expected to be understood. If you would like to skip ahead, please **[GOTO Where do we start?]**.

How do we communicate the severity of a vulnerability?

While there are several models out there, we will explore the **Common Vulnerability Scoring System** (**CVSS**), at the time of writing, the most recently published specification is **4.0**. We will not be doing a deep dive into all the metrics; this is well documented. We are going to list the type of metrics and why they are important for contributing to a vulnerability rating.

CVSS criteria

As of **CVSS 4.0**, there are several core areas that contribute to an overall score.

Base metrics

These are battle tested metrics that have come from earlier versions of the spec, even if we have had some slight updates. These metrics focus on the CIA triad impact and some specific aspects of *how hard it is to exploit*.

The exploitability characteristics are as follows:

- **Attack vector (AV):** Where can we exploit the attack from? Do we require physical access, network access, etc.

- **Attack complexity (AC):** How hard is it to perform the attack?

- **Attack requirements (AR):** Are there specialized requirements to perform the attack that do not include bypassing mitigation techniques?

- **Privileges required (PR):** What types of permissions are needed in a system to exploit a vulnerability? This can include None, limited, full, or administrative access.

- **User interaction (UI):** There is either no interaction, some interaction, or heavy interaction required to successfully exploit.

The impact characteristics are:

- **Confidentiality:** There is either no impact, partial impact, or full loss of confidentiality.

- **Integrity:** There is either no impact, partial impact, or full loss of integrity.

- **Availability:** There is either no impact, partial impact, or full loss of availability to a single user, or full loss of availability for all users.

- **Subsequent systems:** These are downstream impacts or the ability to affect a dependency.

    o **Confidentiality**: There is either none, some, or complete loss of confidentiality in a downstream system.

    o **Integrity**: There is either none, some, or complete loss of integrity in a downstream system.

    o **Availability**: There is either none, some, or complete loss of availability in a downstream system.

To enable our communication of the impact of a vulnerability to our organization, we can use CVSS or something similar. By having a common language of talking about how severe it is to our organization, we can empower prioritization.

Threat metrics

Currently, the only metric within this category is exploit maturity; we should expect this to be expanded in the future:

- **Exploit maturity (EM):** This speaks to how likely a threat is to materialize, whether we have been attacked, proof of concept is available, and unreported.

Environmental metrics

Whenever we try to compress data, there is always some loss (even if it is not noticeable). As such, the base CVSS metrics are not always sufficient to address the real world. By adding these additional modifiers to our base CVSS scores, we can better represent the dangers to the specific assets in specific deployments; for example, compromising a production cluster is typically not equal to a development one, at least when we assume there is no real customer data in development.

- **CIA:** These are metrics that we use to modify our scores based on the CIA requirements for an environment. For example, we should not have any real customer data in pre-production environments; hence, we could say that the impact is reduced if it can only be affected by those environments. Conversely, if human life is on the line, we must elevate the impact.

    o **High**: Loss of *Confidentiality, Integrity, or Availability* is likely to have **a catastrophic adverse effect** on the organization or individuals associated with the organization (e.g., employees, customers).

- o **Medium**: Loss of *Confidentiality, Integrity, or Availability* is likely to have **a serious adverse effect** on the organization or individuals associated with the organization (e.g., employees, customers).

- o **Low**: Loss of *Confidentiality, Integrity, or Availability* is likely to have **only a limited adverse effect** on the organization or individuals associated with the organization (e.g., employees, customers).

- **Modified base metrics:** Not all systems are considered equal and, therefore, do not have the same requirements in all deployments. As such, we can modify the base metrics. To avoid repeating definitions, we will simply note that they are modified:

  - o **Modified Attack Vector (MAV)**
  - o **Modified Attack Complexity (MAC)**
  - o **Modified Attack Requirements (MAR)**
  - o **Modified Privileges Required (MPR)**
  - o **Modified User Interaction (MUI)**
  - o **Modified Subsequent Systems (MSS)**

- **Supplemental metrics:** Context is king, and these metrics allow us to add more nuance to our vulnerability score. As these are added to the base metrics to modify the outcome, they will either be impacted or undefined:

  - o **Safety**: When a compromised component represents a safety risk based on the definitions of `IEC 61508` (negligible, marginal, critical, or catastrophic).

  - o **Automatable**: Can our attacker automate a significant portion of the attack? (specifically, we are looking for stages 1-4 in the cyber kill chain (recon, weaponization, delivery, and exploitation), which we will discuss shortly.

  - o **Provider urgency (PU)**: The producer, maintainer, or distributors of a software may be best suited to evaluate the severity as it could be dependent on how it has been configured separate from its capabilities.

  - o **Recovery**: How resilient are our systems? Do our systems automatically recover after an attack, are our users or admins able to recover manually, or is recovery impossible for the user after an attack?

  - o **Value density (VD)**: Refers to what resources an attacker will gain access to after a single exploitation. Does it only affect a limited system (such as an email client) or does it affect the entire system (such as an email server).

  - o **Vulnerability response effort (VRE)**: How much effort is it to remediate a vulnerability from a user perspective?

    - ▪ **Low**: Changes that **do not require an immediate update** and can be accomplished with communication, configuration workarounds, etc.

- **Medium**: Requires immediate update and has **the risk of a short disruption to our users** when rolling out the changes. This could be remote updates, one-click installs, etc.

- **High**: Requires immediate update and/or the update has **the risk of incurring significant disruption to our users** when rolling out the changes. Low-level changes, such as networking, firmware, etc., should all fall into this category.

- **Qualitative severity rating and vector strings:** Each of these criteria is combined, allowing us to create a representation of the threat, including a score:

Severity rating	Score range
None	0.0
Low	0.1 – 3.9
Medium	4.0 – 6.9
High	7.0 – 8.9
Critical	9.0 – 10.0

Table 5.2: *A defined set of ranges that takes a numeric value and associates it with a severity rating*

We used all these inputs to create a function that splits out a severity rating into short strings and a number. We can use this number to ensure that we do not push something to production higher than a certain value, which is commonly referred to as a quality gate, which we will discuss in *Chapter 6, Understanding Pipelines, What does a CI/CD pipeline look like?, Quality Gates*, and again in *Chapter 9, Pipeline Mastery, Optimizing pipelines, Quality Gates*.

Frameworks for understanding cyber attacks

Whether we use *MITRE's ATT&CK* (Attack) framework or the *Cyber Kill Chain*, the goal is the same: to help us map events to various stages of exploitation. As the *MITRE* framework is a bit more extensive and frequently changing, we will focus on the cyber kill chain, which was developed by Lockheed Martin and released in 2011. This framework defines stages of an attack's progression, giving us a stage where we can act appropriately and break the right link to regain maximum control of our systems and prevent further damage.

Cyber kill chain

For those who come from a military background, you have likely guessed correctly the *cyber kill chain* was based on the *kill chain*. The military kill chain consists of four concepts when attempting to map out the phases of an attack:

1. Identification of target(s)
2. Dispatching forces to target(s)

3. Initiating combat with target(s)

4. Destruction of target(s)

These concepts are more cleanly translated as:

1. **Find:** Identify the target through recon or surveillance data, intelligence teams, etc.

2. **Fix:** Pinpoint targets specific locations through existing or additionally collected data.

3. **Track:** Monitor the target's movements until decisions to engage are made or you have successfully executed engagement.

4. **Engage:** Application of force with the target(s)

5. **Assess:** Evaluate the effects of the force applied and decide whether to re-engage as necessary, escalate, or stand down.

Both the *kill chain* and its cyber variant are designed to inherently map out the anatomy of an attack and identify the earliest possible stage of disruption, as well as further stages, should prior attempts be insufficient or go unnoticed.

The cyber kill chain [3]consists of several stages:

- **Reconnaissance:** Research, identification, and selection of targets, often represented as crawling Internet websites such as conference proceedings and mailing lists for email addresses, social relationships, product releases, or information on specific Intellectual Property and technologies. This also includes software that helps with creating an inventory of what targets exist. Such as network scanners, fingerprinting software, etc.

- **Weaponization:** Coupling a remote access such as a trojan with another exploit into a complete deliverable payload, typically by means of an automated tool (weaponizer). Increasingly, client application data files such as **Portable Document Format (PDF)** or Microsoft Office documents serve as the weaponized deliverable due to their ubiquity.

- **Delivery:** Transmission of the weapon to the targeted environment. The three most prevalent delivery vectors for weaponized payloads by APT actors, as observed by the **Lockheed Martin Computer Incident Response Team (LM-CIRT)** for the years 2004-2010, are email attachments, websites, and USB removable media.

- **Exploitation:** After the weapon is delivered to the victim's host, exploitation triggers the attacker's code. Most often, exploitation targets an application or operating system vulnerability, but it could also simply exploit the users themselves or leverage an operating system feature that auto-executes code.

- **Installation:** Installation of a remote access trojan or backdoor on the victim system allows the adversary to maintain persistence inside the environment.

---

3 (Hutchins, Cloppert, Amin, & Lockhead Martin Corporation, 2011)

- **Command and control (C2) (C&C):** Typically, compromised hosts must reach outbound to an Internet controller server to establish a C2 channel. APT malware especially requires manual interaction rather than conducting activity automatically. Once the C2 channel is established, intruders have *hands on the keyboard* access inside the target environment follow-up actions.

- **Actions on objectives:** Only now, after progressing through the first six phases, can intruders take actions to achieve their original objectives. The most common objectives are data exfiltration, which involves collecting, encrypting, and extracting information from the victim environment; violations of data integrity or availability are potential objectives as well. Alternatively, these intruders may only desire access to the initial victim box for use as a hop point to compromise additional systems and move laterally inside the network.

Our kill chain tells us how we should respond technologically to an attack; however, we still need a process, which we previously touched on and will discuss in further depth shortly called **security incident response (SIR)**, which is more focused on our organizational specific processes and will account for concerns such as legal, compliance, etc. that are out of scope for this topic.

In cybersecurity, we are looking at managing threats to our digital systems. We take a lot from our militaries which have had to solve many of the same challenges. With a cybersecurity attack (and defense) framework, we map events to the stages of an attack and look for opportunities to disrupt our attackers.

Risk management frameworks

Like our frameworks for understanding the anatomy of an attack, risk management frameworks such as **Operationally Critical Threat, Asset, and Vulnerability Evaluation (OCTAVE)**[4] from Carnegie Mellon or the ISO 27000 series from the Institute of International Organization for Standardization help us bring some uniformity to how we address risk management.

OCTAVE focuses on a three-phase approach:

1. Identify knowledge within the organization, operation, and personnel to build an organization-wide set of security requirements. This should include classification of assets based on impact on the organization.

2. Identify vulnerabilities using the output from the previous phase, as well as additional efforts to identify high priority threats to the organization.

3. Determine a risk management strategy, having identified our assets and threats, including probability and impact, we can look to come up with a strategy for detection, prevention, mitigation, etc. based on our needs.

---

4 (Alberts, Beherens, Pethia, & Wilson, 1999)

Security incident response

With a foundation of why we need SIR taken care of, we can dive a little deeper into some of the practices at play.

Roles

It is important that we keep in mind that these are roles or hats that we choose to wear. Especially in smaller organizations or ones just starting out on their cybersecurity journey, we typically will need to wear more than one hat. In some cases, it may not be feasible to have a person for each of these specific roles; however, we need to ensure that each of these roles is assumed by someone during SIR, even if they are wearing multiple hats. Some roles require additional training and qualifications before being able to be assumed.

- **Incident Commander:** We already discussed the Incident Commander role previously. Due to the sensitivity of this role, it requires extensive training, knowledge of the organization, etc. Many organizations restrict who is considered a qualified Incident Commander until certain criteria have been met. Some examples include organization tenure, certification, or other training, having shadowed an Incident Commander, having been vouched for by other qualified Incident Commanders, having participated in a large-scale incident at the organization, etc. There are very good reasons to pass the role around. Ideally, the Incident Commander is focused on understanding what is happening and making decisions rather than being directly involved in performing the remediation.

  Some common examples where this makes sense:

  o Long incidents and need to keep a rotation of Incident Command as well as responders.

  o Allowing a **subject matter expert** (**SME**), which will discuss shortly, to *get hands on keyboard if necessary*. This typically happens when there is a shortage of available resources to respond to an incident, make sure to staff our teams to handle people going on vacation, being sick, unavailable, etc. Other times it allows us to allow a specialist to handle a specific problem while having a generalist take over command.

  o After technical questions have been answered, we may have business concerns requiring an engineering executive to take over a portion of the process while keeping it under the SIR umbrella.

  Many times, as responders for many years, we have a natural tendency to want to jump in and assist. However, this is not where we can bring the most value in the chaos; when we are *Incident Commanders*, we are the calming force in the room. Everyone else might be freaking out, we are firefighters, and this is our Tuesday.

  While *Incident Commanders* often seek to build some kind of consensus where possible, they recognize that this is something that is not reasonable in all cases.

Phrases such as *is there any strong objection to the following?* are encouraged. Using clear language removes ambiguity and reinforces the *peacetime* vs. *wartime* transition; we are not looking for a congress, jury, committee, etc., to unanimously make decisions; we have an Incident Commander for a reason. An *Incident Commander* is specifically looking for any good reason that they may not have thought through before making the call.

It is important to keep in mind that the *Incident Commander's* role is stressful. They are under a lot of pressure, and in some cases, we may be in a situation fighting for our organization's survival, even if that may not be apparent to everyone else. While we look to find the smallest impact that addresses our concerns, our priority lens is that of the *CIA triad* and our mission statements. If the only way we can temporarily protect confidentiality or integrity (in addition to physical safety) is by taking down availability, we will. Such decisions should be made with great care and consideration for the impact on the organization. This is one of the primary reasons being an Incident Commander is typically restricted to specific individuals in the organization who have the appropriate training to handle these situations, making the toughest calls of their career with very little time to react. When such a call has been made, it is no longer time to discuss it; we must proceed as directed by the *Incident Commander*.

- **Scribe:** The Scribe has an incredibly important responsibility. When we deal with SIR, we need to provide documentation on what happened, how we responded, and what we could do to improve next time. The *scribe* is the one who monitors all the SIR communications, taking notes of decisions, times, etc., as we progress through the incident. Finally, they are responsible for working with the *Incident Commander* to produce a blameless postmortem document to be reviewed with the core response team and any necessary external parties. Keep in mind that when we are a publicly traded company or are in certain industries, we have regulatory and contractual obligations to report significant cyber incidents. This can manifest in a SOC2 report or a public filing *of* an 8-K with the United States **Securities and Exchange Commission** (**SEC**) within four days of establishing a cyber incident to be material, which essentially means it is critical to inform our investors of the impact. Otherwise, the stock price will not accurately reflect the value of the organization, as the market will not have been able to price in the discounted risk. This is something we will explore further in *Chapter 11, Valuation, Bridging Management and Engineering*.

In some cases, when we are lacking human resources, we can look to use technology to augment as best we can. In such cases, the *Incident Commander* will typically opt for relying on automatically recording their thoughts, decisions, etc. during the incident in the approved communications channel so they can reference it later when they are having to build the postmortem document.

- **Deputy:** In large-scale incidents, *Incident Commanders* can be overwhelmed with all the responsibilities. When this happens, we can look to adopt a *deputy* who will serve the *Incident Commander* to allow them to remain focused on what is most important. While this can differ depending on the organization and scale of the incident, common examples of ways a deputy assists their Incident Commander:

    o **Keep track of time**: Time is of the essence, the *Incident Commander* may be asking multiple response members to perform individual tasks, some of which are time-boxed. The deputy becomes responsible for following up with each of the members and getting status updates, then looping in the *Incident Commander*.

    o **Communications bouncer**: Track down, add, and remove people during an incident as requested by the *Incident Commander*.

    o **Incident Command backup**: Be ready to jump in and take over when requested by the *Incident Commander* or communications with our current *Incident Commander* have been disrupted and cannot be immediately reestablished.

- **Subject matter experts (SME):** are folks who we have brought into the response to either answer specialized knowledge or address the response in some manner. This includes core response team members as well as those brought in to augment the current response team. All subject matter experts are there to provide something valuable to the response effort itself. This could be explaining aspects of entire or sub-systems, providing opinions and options when requested by the *Incident Commander*; if anyone gets in the way of our response efforts (such as being disruptive), they will be ejected from the *war room*.

- **Legal:** Many in engineering are often surprised when they are first looped into a security incident, and they see a *General Council (GC)* or similar. Why would we need a lawyer in our *security incident*? Depending on the organization we work for, we will have different needs. In some cases, we have legal obligations to our customers, shareholders, etc. Security teams are more *technical experts*; we need input from *legal experts* to help us with decisions in terms of what types of evidence may need to be preserved, customers notified, etc. The *Incident Commander* needs to be aware of when decisions are needed from the GC to proceed.

  Another reason to include our GC in our SIR is that it can sometimes make our communications have attorney-client confidentiality applied to them as long as we do not invite a third party into our channel with legal. This can make it safer to discuss issues accurately without fear of retribution for speaking the truth; it could, in some cases, remain out of the courts should we get a subpoena.

Process/Flow

Essentially, we start with some trigger for the creation of an incident; it could be an automated system or someone manually declaring SIR. From there, we organize a response and keep at it until we are out of immediate danger, which allows us to start closing the incident out, preparing documentation, and learning to improve. The process looks something like these lines:

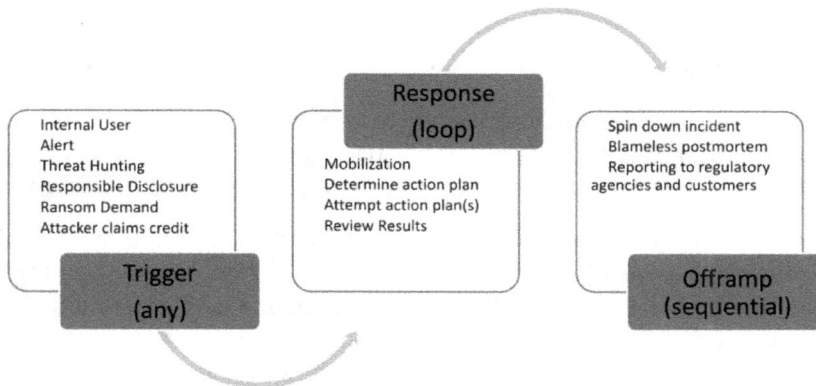

Figure 5.3: An incident has a start and end, the middle loops until we are ready to step down

- **Trigger:** We start with an alert of some kind, whether it be from an automated system, user report, or through various threat hunting exercises.

- **Response loop:**

  - **Mobilization and organization**: The *Incident Commander* declares SIR and sets up communication channels, and our response team will be assembled.

  - **Understand the problem sets**: Most of the time, we have no idea what we are walking into. *Incident Commanders* initially lack a lot of valuable context, which is their first order of business to address the gap.

  - **Determine action plan(s)**: Once we understand the problem sets, the *Incident Commander* needs to decide what course of action(s) we wish to take. These tasks will be directed at specific individuals rather than asking if someone from the group can do it. This is to optimize our efficiency in these situations, we do not want to waste time trying to figure out, am I best the responder for this?

  - **Attempt action plan**: SMEs take response plans.

  - **Review results**: Loop through these steps in our process until we are at an acceptable offramp. Until we get there, we should determine if it is appropriate to restart the cycle with steps A, B, or C.

- **Spin down incident:** let people leave the call, coordinate documentation, perform a postmortem, and potentially notify customers or regulators.

While many operations and **site reliability engineering (SRE)** teams use a structured *Incident Response*, they are typically less severe in nature, have different needs, etc. One of the most important differences comes from the mindset between security and these groups. Typically, these operations teams are tasked with *keeping the site online*, however, the mindset of a security engineer in SIR is perhaps the opposite, instead, they are asking *should I take the site down?*

Creating our process

While there are many good resources out there to help build our SIR process, it is important to customize these frameworks to the needs of our organization. This includes getting buy-in from executives, processes, compliance, contractual or regulatory concerns, and more.

Once we have an initial version of the process, we need to ensure that our core response team, which always consists of an *Incident Commander, Scribe, General Council*, and *Subject Matter Experts*. It is important to note that in smaller teams and organizations, we will be required to wear multiple hats or roles as we scale out our teams to meet the needs. We will want to do training through tabletop simulations, with cyber ranges, or solutions that allow us to train on an incident as if it were the real thing. As these incidents are stressful, training regularly is important. We need to be familiar with the processes enough that we can walk through them at 3 AM with our eyes closed.

Once we have our team feeling confident in their ability to handle what is thrown at them, we should communicate with other groups of people who are likely to get looped into incidents. The more we can prepare people prior to being thrown into an incident, the better the outcome. It is always the responsibility of the *Incident Commander* or *deputy*, if applicable, to ensure that as new people enter the Incident, we establish expectations on what they should (and should not) do and the status of the situation, although the latter might not be immediate. Ideally, we would even, at some point, want to include non-core response team members in our *tabletop exercises*.

SIR frameworks help us achieve better and more consistent outcomes. By having an agreed upon process and roles ahead of time, we can avoid debate during the incident on what the process is, rather than what is the best response option in front of us.

Threat modeling

Let us take a quick look at three common threat models.

STRIDE

Stride was developed by Microsoft and focuses on surfacing vulnerabilities during the software development live cycle through the lenses of:

- **Spoofing:** Pretending to be someone else.
- **Tampering:** Affecting the data either in the target system or locally for the victim(s).
- **Repudiation:** Verification of events.

- **Information disclosure:** Sensitive information was made available to parties other than the intended authorized personnel.

- **Denial of service (DoS):** Preventing authorized personnel access to their data or service. This is typically accomplished through resource exhaustion, shutting down systems once access is obtained, or encrypting or destroying data in a *wiper* or *ransomware* style attack.

- **Elevation of privileges:** Performing an action we are not authorized to do. There is a common need to install and establish command and control. Attackers typically need to obtain high levels of access to set that up.

DREAD

Dread was also developed by Microsoft, it focuses on risk and impact assessment:

- **Damage:** How much damage would be done in an attack?

- **Reproducibility:** How much effort is it to reproduce the exploit?

- **Exploitability:** How much effort is it to exploit once discovered?

- **Affected users:** How many users are impacted?

- **Discoverability:** How much effort is it to discover the exploit?

PASTA

Process for Attack Simulation and Threat Analysis (PASTA) is an attacker-centric model and puts emphasis on risk management and organization context in our threat modeling process, unlike STRIDE.

PASTA uses a seven-stage model to guide us:

- **Define objectives:** This includes organization, functional, security, and operational requirements for the assets within scope.

- **Define scope:** This includes which assets we are looking to review; this includes any dependencies we want, such as infrastructure.

- **Decompose system:** We look to understand how the application works under the hood, identifying possible weaknesses to be exploited.

- **Analyze threats:** Identification and analysis of possible threats to our assets.

- **Vulnerability analysis:** We will look to correlate vulnerabilities with the associated assets. While we may have found it on a specific asset, does it apply to other assets as well?

- **Attack analysis:** We will take the previous threats and vulnerability analysis to create *attack trees,* or conceptual diagrams showing us how simulated attacks would play out.

- **Risk and impact analysis:** Work with our partners across the organization to understand the impact that it would have on our organization, look at the probabilities of this, etc. Once we have all of this, we look to outline mitigations.

Threat modeling is a specialized brainstorming session. We map the system of interest (including any potential lateral movements), identify weaknesses, and design countermeasures for defending against an attacker. Whether we use STRIDE, DREAD, or PASTA, the goal is the same.

Shrinking our attack surface

When defending a system, especially with finite resources, one of the most effective investments in cybersecurity is shrinking our attack surface. This can take many forms; examples include taking services off the public internet, switching public APIs to private, following the principle of least privilege, etc. By moving potentially vulnerable systems *out of the line of fire*, it is no longer possible to attack them directly; an attacker would need to compromise another system, increasing their complexity and affecting their ROI.

Removing public interfaces: within applications, we can move APIs to be marked as public or private. This affects whether the functionality can be called externally or only within the program itself. Often, we want to make critical systems accessible through a **local area network (LAN)**, **virtual private network (VPN)**, Proxy solutions, **Zero Trust Network Broker (ZTNB)**, etc.

Principle of least privilege: Systems and users should be given the minimum set of permissions that enable them to perform their work or function. This is a manifestation of our separation of duties concept that is applied to permissions and limits the damage that can be done to a compromised user or system.

This comes into play when evaluating *CVSS* with *subsequent systems* and *privilege escalation*.

Hardening systems

While we recognize that all systems that exist are vulnerable to attack, not all are equal. While it might sound counterintuitive, many criminals do some kind of basic risk management. They are looking for the biggest payouts with the lowest risk and effort. Their mindset is not too different from that of our business executives.

When looking at two houses side by side, one with a large dog and a home security system, and the other without. Which will our attacker focus their efforts on? Obviously, they will look at the house with lower protection.

By making our systems more difficult than our neighbors, we motivate the attacker to move on to easier targets with similar payouts. While this does tend to deter a non-targeted attacker, a motivated attacker will continue to look for vulnerabilities. As we reduce what they can do, they must expend more effort to keep attacking. Dealing with targeted attackers is a more advanced topic than we can cover in this book.

This process involves taking the system and stripping it down to its minimum, ensuring that we perform proper data validation, reduce our attack surface, and deploying deterrents and preventative controls.

Zero Trust

What is *Zero Trust?*

It is an architectural philosophy that states that we should evaluate the request being made and determine if this is something that we should allow. In other words, this is the opposite of *trust but verify*: we verify, then trust if there is no determined risk.

Zero Trust breaks down the perceptions that we can trust the request that comes from *internal* resources when we are evaluating whether to allowing/denying an action on a system. Systems that have implemented a *Zero Trust* model typically have isolated their networks and systems from each other, are aware of identity (not just network location), and perform risk-based checks before granting or denying access.

What are some examples of Zero Trust?

One of the most common examples these days is VPN replacements or solutions that are looking to solve some of the challenges that brought us to VPN without the implicit risk and trust once the connections have been established. A lot of times, they call themselves **Zero Trust Network Access (ZTNA)** Brokers (or Proxies). These systems look to broker specific access as needed rather than putting the user directly on the network, which is how a VPN works. The solution acts as a proxy between the client (user) and the requested service. If the user successfully authenticates, then the system determines if they are authorized to access a particular resource. Before it grants access, it performs a set of risk-based checks to determine if brokering is safe, regardless of the defined **access control lists (ACLs)**. Some examples of risk-based checks include ensuring that the device has full device encryption, has anti-malware software installed and enabled, and has not recently performed impossible travel, or logging in from two locations that are not geographically possible within the time range of the two events with existing technology, as well as other posture-related aspects. For example, while a VPN or compromised credential can facilitate a user's login from multiple locations across the world within minutes, we do not have reasonable transportation to facilitate that, be it teleportation or any vehicle to date. Even if one of our engineers is authorized to perform an expected task, if we know it is compromised, we can provide inline isolation to protect the system. To be clear, *Zero Trust* philosophies can be applied to proxies and other brokering services; while we can install *Zero Trust* features in our products, we cannot buy the philosophy; it must be embraced and implemented.

Within a clustered solution such as Kubernetes, we can use **network policies** or **authorization policies** to define which services can access each other. These can be implemented within k8s directly, through the usage of a service mesh, etc.

When we allow our instances to be able to be accessed by anything other than our load balancers for web traffic, to ensure that even service-to-service calls go through the **web application firewall** (**WAF**), which will look to prevent malicious requests from one compromised service to another if it contains malicious intent.

When sending an email with the contents encrypted by the client rather than the server, this is a manifestation of Zero Trust. Regardless of whatever protections might exist on the email system, we take the stance that only parties with the appropriate decryption keys can access the contents of the message, which keys are shared *out of band*, or outside the message sent. This, for example, protects us from an email administrator at our organization or provider from being able to access our messages.

Our posture improves by adopting a stance of not trusting or allowing clients' requests until we validate that they are not a risk to the organization, regardless of their origin. Isolating our resources has a significant impact on our attacker's ability to move laterally.

Cross-team integration with security teams

In larger organizations, we will have one or more security teams for various functions. Split along various responsibilities and focuses within the organization. For example, *Internal Security* is focused on the organization's security practices, whereas a *Product Security* team is focused on the development and production of security measures for our goods or services. At the end of the day, we must realize we are all partners. By looking to use the same tooling where possible across teams for threat detection, protection layers, change management, etc., we can reduce cross-team friction and costs and improve the outcomes. The same is true when trying to apply this from the security teams to our other engineering counterparts. We will shortly discuss a very common way that we can meet our operational and product teams using the tools they are already leveraging to improve security through creating and updating modules of shared functionality.

Let us acknowledge some of the friction that comes into play when security teams work with engineering teams. Let us start with what the mission statements of the two teams are. Product, site reliability, and other operations engineering teams' mission statements typically include bringing new value to customers, while keeping the system online, serving the customer, some specific purpose, etc. In contrast, the security team's mission statement makes it clear that they are there to ensure that our organization, our employees, and our customers are safe, depending on the appropriate lens. So, we could come in and say, *Hey, I know you had your next two weeks planned out, with marketing and all...could you simply drop everything you are doing and work on the following thing you had no idea of until 10 seconds ago that you probably do not even understand?* That approach does not appear to be effective most of the time. One of the best ways to deal with this is to get engineering and product leadership buy-in that security is important. We can create a set of **service level objectives** (**SLO**), which are metrics that we track in a **service level agreement** (**SLA**) that outlines what thresholds we expect our SLO to meet or exceed and what the consequences are for parties when that does not happen. By creating an SLO for vulnerability patch management, we can at least cut down on a lot of *20 questions*. Essentially, what we agree on ahead of time is how long a typical vulnerability should take to understand and fix based on severity or potential risk to the organization. It is important that we build escape hatches where teams can discuss with the security team if there is a good reason that they cannot make that date. The important thing is having a conversation and keeping people on top of things. In many cases, we can choose to implement the SLO without an SLA as an early step and only create the SLA should we find that the organization is not keeping up with it, and it is a prioritization rather than a resource problem. This also helps translate to better expectations and interactions with *ethical hackers* when dealing with responsible disclosure. While we do not condone this behavior, some security researchers will make their findings publicly available if they feel that the organization is not taking them seriously. When these lines are crossed, they are in *grey hatter* territory, and only a qualified lawyer in this field can tell you what the consequences will be, especially since this is typically explicitly forbidden in the rules of engagement when working with responsible disclosure processes and systems.

Building blocks for reusability and encapsulation

Our infrastructure teams should be creating systems with Infrastructure as code, such as **configuration management** (**CM**) and resource orchestration. This is a great place for security teams to review, provide suggestions, and make modifications that result in providing security improvements. A lot of vendors have defaults that are designed to make it easy for developers to get started, but are expected to be tuned for production use cases. This puts us at risk of a lack of awareness, forgetting, and prioritization concerns to ensure we deploy safely. Using modules or libraries, we can encapsulate the security needs while keeping the interfaces simple for other teams. This is an example of creating a *secure by default* deployment even when the underlying solution defaults are not secure. Instead of asking our developers to fix individual instances, we can tell them to pull a minimum version of our updated module. This is a good way to ensure that our organization has *sane defaults* regardless of what the provider has set.

Key takeaway: **Do not Repeat Yourself** (**DRY**) is an excellent engineering principle to keep in mind when we decide to encapsulate a configuration or change across systems, look to use modules in existing solutions that our teams are already using, such as Terraform.

Categories of security tooling

Often, the differences between defensive and offensive tooling are the context of how they are being used. There are clearly some that are squarely in attacker territory, and we will try to call this out. Before we judge a tool as an *attacker only*, we need to consider that ethical hackers likely are using the same or very similar tools, techniques, etc. The difference lies in the ethical nature of the engagements, that the differences between *malicious actors* and *ethical hackers* are clear.

Offensive

In most cases, defenders need to understand and leverage various attack tooling to understand our adversaries. Many tools can be classified as both, depending on the context.

- **Malware:** In general, we define malware as any software that was maliciously written to harm an end-user, entity, organization, etc. There are many families or similar categories of malware, we will cover the most well-known and common examples.

- **Trojan:** When an application appears to have a legitimate purpose, but under the surface has another purpose.

- **Worms:** Self-replicating malware that discovers devices such as networks, USB storage, etc. to spread to additional victims. The primary uses for worms are either **distributed denial of service** (**DDoS**), which we will cover shortly, or being a delivery mechanism for other malware from various categories.

- **Rootkits:** These programs look to obtain high-level permissions on a system to provide remote access to our attacker. These are very low-level attacks, which target BIOS/UEFI, firmware, drivers, kernel modules, etc. These are typically deployed and remain undetected for a significant amount of time due to the nature of their high-level access. It gives it the ability to evade many detection techniques, such as denying antimalware software from running.

- **Spyware:** This includes any malware that is designed to covertly monitor events on the target's system. This includes subcategories such as keyloggers (which keep a copy of everything typed, including passwords, and could include screenshots or links clicked).

- **Adware:** When undesirable software is installed on systems to track a target's behavior, patterns, etc., to bombard them with popups and other forms of notifications to users, they are typically paid fees for referrals, both on views and actual purchases.

- **Cryptocurrency miners:** When malware is running cryptocurrency mining without the user's knowledge. While this is typically motivated by financial gains, it can also be used to slow down systems. These are often bundled into software that is installed by the user, developer, or operator. In the context of software development, we need to be careful of the modules or packages we install, as they could insert malicious code that includes this and other flavors of malware.

- **Web:** There are many categories of web attacks, and they are ever changing. One of the better places to learn about these is the **Open Web Application Standards** (**OWASP**) organization, which is focused on providing security standards for web application security concerns. They track and compile a yearly list of the top 10 categories based on impact and prevalence. It is important to understand that these attacks typically start manually and then are automated in attack tooling.

This could be either more generic tooling, such as Metasploit, or purpose-specific tooling.

o **Injection**: When user-controlled data is not properly sanitized or filtered to match expected patterns, it can have interesting results. By using *escape characters*, or special characters that change the context and allow us to run arbitrary code or queries that were not intended against the target. As this is a broad category, it can be used to attack databases, operating systems, browsers, etc.

o **Broken or missing authentication and authorization controls**: While these are unique concepts and challenges, they both stem from either missing or invalid checks. Many developers easily confuse the two. Let us take these complex topics and make the distinction between them clear:

  ▪ **Authentication (AuthN)**: Deals with identification. Who is making the request?

  ▪ **Authorization (AuthZ)**: Deals with determining access control. What should the authenticated requester be allowed to perform?

When either of these is in play, it can have serious consequences. As it could affect all three aspects of our *CIA triad*.

o **Insecure design and missing security configuration**: These are broad categories of attacks that state that we are not putting enough effort into building software securely. Through the constant hardening and improvement of systems, we can solve systematic security design flaws that do not have another home.

o **Vulnerable and outdated components**: When we provide software to our users that must be updated in the event of the discovery of a vulnerability, we should create a report in the form of a **Common Vulnerability and Exposure (CVE)** and register it with vulnerability databases. In addition to any customer outreach, we will publish updates to the *CVE* when a patch is made available. When we do not patch our systems quickly, we leave ourselves open to attack. It takes far less effort to exploit a known vulnerability than to write one from scratch. Over several decades, it has remained a core concern and a leading cause of major breaches. The best defense is heavy automation of our patch management and testing processes using pipelines.

o **Software and data integrity failures**: When our software does not perform appropriate integrity checks before trusting infrastructure, this includes calling scripts from public **content delivery networks (CDNs)**, running modules that call arbitrary code, not performing checksum validation, etc.

o **Security logging and monitoring failures**: The lack of adequate security logging, monitoring, and observability is a *bug*, not a *feature!* Many organizations attempt to present it as such, especially when they do not realize the value of the organization is directly tied to the trust that our customers place in us. We will discuss this from a value perspective in *Chapter 11, Valuation, Bridging Management and Engineering.* From the technical side, this is a broad category that we can attribute when we fail to detect a security incident, such as during a penetration test or flaws that prevent us from discovering the breach. We will be discussing this further in *Chapter 12, Observability, Taming monitoring, alerting, and on-call demons, What are the important things to monitor?, Security Events.*

o **Web attack tooling**: There are a lot of projects out there that are designed to help both attackers and ethical hackers streamline their attack workflow and can provide significant capabilities that lower the barrier of attacks. This can include reconnaissance, proxy, interception, brute forcing, dictionary attacks, etc., with the flexibility to be extended with modules to suit our needs.

o **Social engineering**: When an attacker abuses our human trust, attempting to trick us into divulging or performing an action that is not in our best interest. This includes *dumpster diving*; while this initially was considered yes, searching through people's or organizations' trash, we have expanded this to include **Open Source Intelligence** (**OSI**), where we use information that is publicly or semi-publicly available. Examples of this include searching through social media, public records, etc. The goal of this type of reconnaissance is often to help the attacker understand the organization. By providing information that would not be publicly accessible, attackers gain trust that can be exploited. At this point, it is then followed up with other social engineering tactics to gain information or a launch point for a more technological attack.

o **Reconnaissance**: This category of tooling is meant to help an attacker identify which assets the target has so that we can start planning our attack. In most cases, they are looking to essentially ask *which resources exist and what are they?* Moving on to more sophisticated probing of defenses as they better understand what they are looking at. Considering our *cyber kill chain*, this is the first stage of every attack. However, much of this recon activity is hardly discernible from normal usage patterns if done carefully. We will typically need to analyze events from the same entity over a period of time to discern the nature of the activity.

o **Proxy in the Middle (PITM)**: refers to a set of capabilities where we rely on software that is deployed between a user and a target system. The requests from the victim are intercepted by an attacker, who can steal data or modify the original request before it reaches the destination. Such attacks are highly impactful when successfully carried out, as they typically violate confidentiality and integrity and sometimes impact availability as well from our *CIA triad*. As many services these days rely on **Transport Layer Security** (**TLS**), which ensures secure communication between the client and server, we can validate the certificate against a known trusted entity, and it is possible to detect and prevent many *in the middle* attacks from succeeding provided that they have not managed to insert their own malicious certificate into our system. However, that is something we can detect, monitor, audit, and respond to.

While this is primarily used for offensive purposes, we can use it defensively as well. Proxies are not inherently bad; like many tools, the context in which we use them determines if it is for ethical use. If we are using an organization-trusted proxy to perform the inspection on requests, we prevent malware from being downloaded, run, or spread. This is a common pattern when attempting to implement zero trust principles when connecting to the public internet.

o **Denial of service (DoS)**: This is a general category of attack where the sole purpose is to deny legitimate users access to resources that they should have access to through exhaustion or destruction. While there are many approaches, the more common approaches when discussing destructive actions are the use of a *wiper* program that destroys all data on the system, thus taking it offline. We will also explore how some *ransomware* can affect availability shortly.

When talking about resource exhaustion, we need to keep in mind that both sides have resources to deploy. Some of the most resource-based effective *DoS* attacks rely on techniques where the attacker will look to leverage other entities' resources at the lowest cost to themselves. This manifests in several ways; the first is that we can get a lot of victim machines to send requests from multiple locations, typically referred to as DDoS. When we do not have a fleet of already infected victims that we can use the distributed nature to their advantage, they will look for opportunities where there is a disproportionate number of resources being expended by the attacker compared to the target system. These techniques are typically referred to as amplification, reflection, etc., and rely on some logic in a system where one request to a system generates additional requests. Protecting against *DDoS* requires serious planning and a multi-faceted approach. While there are certainly many defensive capabilities to consider, we need to deploy solutions such as a WAF, which seeks to prevent malicious requests from making it to our servers. Our applications and infrastructure will need to be able to handle scaling up these components, the ability to soak traffic spikes on our defensive layers, have a *DDoS* mitigation partner, etc.

Pro tip: **While it is uncommon, there are cases where attackers will perform a DDoS against an organization to act as a smokescreen to hide other actions and tie up our defenders. Make sure we do extensive log, alert, and forensic analysis, followed up with additional threat hunting after such an event, to discover anything that might have snuck past our defenses in the chaos.**

o **Ransomware:** When a malicious actor or some intermediary reaches out to the victim after a system has been compromised, demanding a ransom or payment to either get our data back after it was encrypted or to *guarantee* that they will not disclose the information to an individual, organization, or the public. These people are criminals, and they do not operate in the same field as we do. In many cases, there is no guarantee that they will deliver on their promise after payment has been made. It is not that uncommon for one or more threat actors to work on multiple extortions from the same victim. While it requires a broad set of defensive capabilities to detect and prevent, the most critical is our ability to get back online, which is our backups and automation. If we do have backups, then we can mitigate the undesired encryption of our data. Unfortunately, there is no great answer to the disclosure concern. In general, the advice prevalent in the industry is not engaging. If we pay the target, we have signaled that we are open for business. They will strike again.

- **Footgun:** While we have mostly been discussing DoS as an intentional outcome, it is quite possible for developers or operators to write code or perform some action that results in a limited or complete DoS. Two common examples are running a large query on the production databases and flooding our systems with requests.

  A footgun in development refers to features and designs that are likely to not be used in the correct way, leading to self-inflicted wounds.

  It is important that when we build our software modules, we do it in a way that we think about not accidentally flooding or overloading systems. Do you recall how adding exponential backoffs on a **429** status code was mentioned earlier? We could also apply the same concept to specific error handlers or to additional status codes for different types of disruption.

  A good example of accidentally causing this type of disruption is someone not inspecting all the available options and, more importantly, understanding all the defaults before launching a program, especially when dealing with concurrency. We may be sending a much higher volume than we intended. For example, if we wanted to send 1,500 **Requests Per Second (RPS)**, however, we missed that the number of requests per second we supplied was multiplied by the number of process threads, and it defaults to creating threads for half the number of CPU cores we have on our system. Oops, suddenly, we have gone from the intended 1,500 RPS to 6,000 on an 8-core machine.

- **API rate limits:** Many services, to protect their own availability, impose limits on how we can use their systems. As we discussed previously, we should be conscious when making such requests about what the *budgets* or *quotas* are before we make the call and be prepared to back off. In other words, we knock on their door and ask, *can I send more?* before we decide to send them something that would be rejected. Similarly, we need to handle each exception raised by the response of the exhaustion of our quotas. Typically, APIs will give a response indicating our budget, if we are rate limited, when we reset our budget, etc. so that we can make intelligent client calls that minimize disruption to our partners and customers alike.

Make sure we audit and understand the impact on our customers and organizations of all our critical third-party solutions within our system. If they are unacceptable to us, then we should look for another vendor to use to replace or supplement our needs. Last resort is typically to bring it in-house.

An example of a scenario where a single bad actor in our system is sending too many messages, promoting the API budget exhaustion. As it is most likely to use the same entity to authenticate (user, keypair, etc.) for all users of our systems, it will affect our ability to send messages to all users. This is a good reason that we should always consider whether it is appropriate to rate limit user actions within our system, especially when it relies on a third party, and it is disruption would affect all customers rather than a single one. Having a secondary text message provider could give us the opportunity to fall back in an emergency after someone has tripped the limits.

- **Exfiltration:** It is the sending of data externally from a victim's system to the attacker through the means of a covert channel, or hidden communication. In many cases, exfiltration is a common trait with other categories of malware, such as ransomware, proxy in the middle, spyware, etc. As large data transfers out of the network tend to raise alarms, many attackers will perform exfiltration over an extended period to avoid detection.

Defensive

We consider any software that meaningfully enables an organization to have better security as defensive. This includes the applications themselves that we are trying to protect, as well as any purpose-specific capabilities. This includes encryption, hardening, detection, response, prevention, communication, patch management, configuration management, posture management, etc.

- **Forensic investigation:** We have two primary phases of an investigation. The first is focused on evidence collection and preservation. Once we have forensically sound evidence, we can analyze it with read-only access (ideally of copies) to ensure that we preserve the integrity of the evidence. When we are investigating infrastructure, the types of techniques and tools may vastly differ depending on the infrastructure. For example, in a virtualized environment, we can typically take a byte-level copy of the virtual machine as a read-only disk image. When we are working with physical devices, we will need to have the appropriate equipment, such as hardware write-blockers, which prevent any possible data modification. On the investigative side of the house, we go as deep as we need to prove whatever we need to in an objective manner. This can include analyzing the logs, metrics, data, and metadata of systems in search of clues. Due to the way that data is deleted, it is often possible to recover data from *deleted files*.

- **Detection and prevention:** We can only prevent issues that we discover, so these two types of systems that we shall shortly discuss have a very close relationship. While there are many automated tools out there to help us with detecting vulnerabilities, these systems we are currently discussing are unique in the sense that they are looking not at potential vulnerabilities, but actions in the system to determine if there is an intrusion.

  o **Intrusion detection and prevention**: These are systems that are deployed on systems which inspect requests made (including logs from external systems) and can then alert or take preventive actions to contain the threats. **Intrusion detection systems (IDS)** are characterized as being purely for detection capabilities, while **intrusion prevention systems (IPS)** or **threat detection and response (xDR)** are for preventing threats in real-time without needing to engage a human. These systems have evolved quite a bit from the early days of simple anti-virus. In addition to the obvious technological differences, it is worth asking ourselves why we would NOT want to automatically prevent something bad. There are two compelling arguments around only doing detection; the first is *what if it is not actually bad but looks bad?* We call this a *false positive*. The second is from the principle of least privilege. Perhaps we should have a different system for automated remediation, but it should come from a distinct system to reduce the impact of a compromised service, this is especially true when we discuss vendors hosted applications that have access to our systems. We need to weigh the cost of tuning and maintaining our system to the point where we have an acceptably low false positive rate against the savings in a potential breach scenario where we did not prevent the threat from being exploited.

  o **Web application firewall (WAF):** Is a specialized firewall that operates at the application layer, meaning it is protocol-aware; it uses sets of rules to deny malicious web traffic before it hits our web server. Rules can be pattern-based, rate-based, perform challenges (such as captchas), etc. We can deploy our WAF via based solutions as well as software installed on the systems we control. They both have their benefits, and we can take advantage of the unique characteristics of each to be used together to provide additional security at a combined reduced cost.

  What is the single best reason for a hosted WAF?

  We do not have to scale it, which is very relevant in the context of dealing with malicious traffic. WAFs are typically the primary defensive mechanism to defeat *DDoS* attacks, even if they often use multiple tools together to accomplish the goals.

What is the single best reason for hosting our WAF?

Depending on the topology of our infrastructure and deployments, it may be possible to circumvent going through a hosted *WAF*, where when it is deployed directly on the server, it protects all traffic regardless where the attack comes from.

What would the ideal state look like?

Deploy both and use them for what they are best at. Not all solutions are geared towards solving the same problems; some are better at handling load, bots, etc., while others are more focused on targeted attacks, such as patterns from the OWASP top 10 and more. Deploy your layers of protection at each layer. Combining them from different layers such as **content delivery networks (CDNs)**, **cloud load balancers (LBs)**, and directly on our web servers, service mesh, etc., we can ensure that each layer is focused on protecting specific components and can cover each other's weaknesses. In some cases, *WAFs* give us a unique way to protect against a known *CVE* before we are able to patch our applications and services. We (or our vendors) can deploy rules that block these attempts, which is referred to as virtual patching. Patching it at the source is ideal, but sometimes, we might need to test deployments on many services when a core component is found to be vulnerable, and deploying a patch centrally may buy us time to get through all the validation testing before pushing to production.

- **Posture management:** Whether we are talking about servers, networks, clouds, etc., we need to ensure that we have properly configured our systems to be secure. Generally, when we find issues with our posture, we will reach for automation to solve our problems in a scalable manner. While a security team might be responsible for setting up posture management, we are typically not on the hook to review each report; these are sent to the appropriate resource owners (typically based on tags); if there are questions or concerns, we are of course, there to help.

- **Incident response:** While there are a lot of tools we might use in an SIR, let us focus on the types of tools that facilitate SIR rather than the technical investigations and responses themselves. When we think about SIR tooling, the first thing that comes to mind is establishing communication channels. As these incidents are inherently sensitive, we need to be conscious of restricting who is able to access the system. As scary as it is to think about, we should probably consider what our backup solution is in case our communications platform is a compromised system. This includes systems that we will use during the incident as well as the tools used to trigger the incident itself, such as our on-call management software responsible for waking engineers up at 3 AM. While it depends on the organization and the process we build, SIR does tend to have some manual steps, and we should look to automate away what we can. Good candidates for this include creating war rooms, getting a qualified Incident Commander on the call, data retrieval, tooling around postmortems, and more. Many of these functionalities are either offered directly as part of a **security orchestration automated response** (**SOAR**) or through APIs. Larger organizations that see more security incidents will tend to invest more heavily in automating these steps that speed up our investigation and responses. If we only have a dozen or so incidents a year and they are not severe, our budgets might better be spent elsewhere. Open-source is always an option on a restricted budget.

- **Patch management:** When security defects are found, we need to communicate it to anyone who may need to patch their software. For many software development organizations, this includes operating systems, container image definitions (Dockerfiles), proprietary code and modules, and open-source software. Ideally, these should be communicated to a central vulnerability disclosure database such as the United States **National Vulnerability Database** (**NVD**) hosted by NIST. This allows us to communicate about *CVEs*. It is ideal that we can automate much, if not all, of our patch management processes. There are tools out there, such as *Dependabot, renovate*, etc., that assist us with this for our custom applications and, in some cases, container images. Similarly, configuration management and orchestration engines can be incredibly helpful in automating patch management. In addition, there are specific services that are offered geared entirely at patch management, including live kernels such as *Ubuntu Livepatch, RedHat Satellite*, etc. A key need will be to test the changes to ensure that they do not cause disruptions to our users. We will do this the same way we test all our changes, using automated testing, automated pipelines, etc., which will be discussed shortly.

Keeping software up to date with the latest patches requires effort. Automation and testing will be the way we solve these scale challenges with writing and maintaining software systems. Consider creating an SLO or SLA for vulnerability defects in our organization to reduce friction and increase communication with teams.

Where do we start

So, we want to start building our cybersecurity at our organization; where do we start?

- **Identify our most critical assets:** To effectively prioritize where efforts should be spent, we need to understand the value that each asset provides so we can engineer the appropriate level of security, balancing usability and security needs.

- **Identify threat actor personas:** To better understand who is performing the potential attacks and their motivations, we need to outline these. Often, if we do not take the time to create a clear definition, we realize that we have been talking past someone because we were using the same term with different meanings. I have seen this happen with a product manager who thought I meant a marketing script kiddie when I was referring to a hacker.

- **Create processes for SIR:** As much as we want to put all our efforts into proactive efforts, we must at the same time ensure that we have a process that allows us to deal with threats efficiently and effectively as they present themselves to the organization.

- **Create process for responsible disclosure:** Similarly, we need to ensure that well intentioned ethical hackers have appropriate channels to reach out to discuss discovered security concerns.

- **Create Proactive Engineering efforts:** There are a lot of areas to discuss here, so we will keep this focused on the high level:

  o **Improving observability:** This includes having the appropriate logs, metrics, and other types of data to understand what is happening in our systems.

  o **Reducing risks to systems:** This includes proactively reviewing risks to systems and addressing them.

  o **Defensive and offensive capabilities:** We need to build preventative capabilities such as Firewalls (network firewalls, **web application firewalls (WAF)**, etc.), **intrusion prevention systems (IPS)**, **threat detection and response (XDR)**, etc.

- **Create educational programs:** As we are all part of the larger system, and we know people do not make mistakes intentionally. Typically, security risks come from not understanding the importance of some aspect that seems small or unimportant on the surface but has significant cybersecurity implications. Through improving everyone's cybersecurity awareness and behavior, we will reduce our organization's risk.

- **Address our most critical risks:** While we are often cataloging various levels of cyber threats, it is important that we stop when we come across something that brings unacceptable risks. On the same note, while its often preferable that the engineering team responsible for the resource fix the vulnerability, security teams may in some cases decide to come in and fix the problem due to time sensitivity, bandwidth constraints, etc.

If you are wondering why we are answering *where do we start* at the end of the chapter, the reason is that we needed a foundation of knowledge before we can even start thinking about putting together a game plan.

There are a lot of investments to make when starting to build our security program. We need to learn to crawl before we walk. This is not a prescriptive list of items that need to be addressed; more questions to help us ask our organizations to figure out where the best places to start are.

Conclusion

Cyber security is an important aspect when we build and maintain quality software. While our security engineers and teams are extremely helpful, they are not a magic bullet, as security is everyone's responsibility. We went over some valuable information regardless of personas around the CIA triad, ethical hackers, why we must accept that security requires shifting left and right, as well as some examples. We addressed some of the squishier topics, such as *why security teams should embrace DevOps culture and philosophy,* and how this helps us with both. We discussed how responsible disclosure and SIR are two critical areas that require us to *shift right* to ensure that we can deal with the most sensitive and urgent issues. At the same time, we discussed ways to *shift left* and identified our threat actor personas, threat models, and techniques to increase collaboration between one or more security teams and our partners throughout the organization.

For our engineering personas, we had an advanced topics section. We established some techniques using CVSS to communicate a nuanced but easy-to-understand severity rating that our engineering and product leadership can use to prioritize. We gained insight into how attackers think through ATTACK Framework models such as the cyber kill chain. We delved deeper into SIR topics such as additional roles, the phases of a SIR response, and how to go about making our own process for our organization. While we briefly touched on threat modeling at a higher level in our *Cybersecurity in a nutshell* section, our engineers needed additional exposure to this. From here, we cover several proactive security concepts, such as shrinking our attack surface, hardening systems, Zero Trust architectural principles, patch management, and sane defaults. After all that, we outlined how we can start using a maturity model and what we have learned at this point to put together a plan of action.

Now that we have addressed all the core quality requirements, it is time to explore pipelines, an amazing technological concept that enables us to build quality software faster.

Join our Discord space

Join our Discord workspace for latest updates, offers, tech happenings around the world, new releases, and sessions with the authors:

https://discord.bpbonline.com

CHAPTER 6
Understanding Pipelines

Introduction

Now that we have an automated system and testing, we should consider using pipelines to *level up* our development, build, and release processes. This chapter will serve as a primer for the next three chapters, which delve deeper into continuous integration, continuous delivery, and pipeline mastery.

Developers who are familiar with pipelines may want to skim or skip to the next chapter [NOTE: GOTO Chapter 7, Continuous Integration].

Objectives

The objectives of the chapter are:

- What are pipelines?

- Why do we use pipelines to help us with CI and CD?

- What types of quality controls can we use in a pipeline?

- How can we use pipelines to improve the efficiency and effectiveness of our development processes?

Introduction to pipelines

In a non-technical sense, it is a set of pipes that brings resources (oil, gas, water, coffee beans, etc.) from one place to another. When we talk about pipelines in terms of software engineering, we refer to the process of development, testing, deployment, and maintenance of our production systems that allow our developers to write their changes and watch them as they pass through a delivery process that consistently ensures quality, whether they are external or internal.

If that sounds like nonsense, let me offer a much simpler definition in our context. We simply define a list of actions that happen in a specific order.

Two very common use cases for pipelines are continuous integration and continuous delivery. Understanding the basics of pipelines will provide a foundation for how CI and CD are supported. This will be followed up with some pipeline considerations that will help maximize the value of your CI and CD system.

Pipeline anatomy

It is easy to get confused about terms in this space because various tools have different names for the same thing. We offer a few general terms to capture several key concepts without subscribing to any specific tool:

- **Process:** A set of instructions that are being executed
- **Job:** One-to-many virtual machines or containers that facilitate running a process.
- **Job-stream:** A series of jobs that depend on other jobs. A job-stream made up of a single job is still considered a job-stream, just a very short one. Anything that happens before a point in the job-stream can be considered upstream, while anything occurring after that point can be considered downstream.
- **Pipeline:** The configuration of our CI/CD solution is typically expressed in some configuration file. Our pipeline can have multiple job streams.

Story time

Story time with Sean: In college, I worked on a literal pipeline in the oil industry. Somewhere between Valdez, Alaska, and the Arctic Ocean, I walked the buried sections of the Trans-Alaska pipeline for corrosion testing. Now, years later, I find myself again working on pipelines, this time in the software industry, which I think shows how useful the structure is for getting work done!

What runs a CI/CD pipeline?

Like physical pipelines that need pumps and power, our CI/CD pipelines need something to run them. This will involve a combination of hardware, software, configuration, and engineering hours.

Both hardware and software must be configured to optimize their operational efficiency, which includes blocking a pipeline's execution if certain conditions are not met. The engineering hours involved will include selecting and provisioning our hardware/software combination and continuing maintenance. Maintenance activities can include a wide variety of tasks, but at the very least, a CI/CD system must reflect an application's ever-changing needs and underlying business goals.

What hardware powers a CI/CD pipeline?

Hardware takes the form of one or more servers, which are just specialized computers. We can purchase servers and maintain them ourselves or opt for someone else to host the hardware, which we will discuss shortly, the pros and cons of each. There is a spectrum of options when it comes to server selection. Servers have a combination of CPU, memory, and **input/output (I/O)** capabilities. The performance level each of these aspects provides will constitute our server's overall performance profile. This profile can range from a general balance to more specialized, and as such, the selection should depend on the nature of our pipeline tasks.

Think of our server(s) like a car; if we need to go to the grocery store, we might find a sedan to be a perfect balance of performance, fuel economy, and safety. This would provide a good general use case. Let us say a task our pipeline performs has to do with moving lots of data. When our pipeline needs to crunch lots of data, then we might need the diesel engine of an 18-wheeler as opposed to our sedan to handle that load. All to say, choose what is fit for purpose.

Software powering a CI/CD pipeline

The software that runs a pipeline leverages the underlying hardware we have previously described. This software can be thought of as a tool that defines the pipeline structure and executes its contents. Structures will take shape as a series of stages, each with one or more tasks (also called a *job, action, or instruction set*).

Tasks vary in their duties, but commonly perform the following:

- Cleanup and initialize
- Run tests/Exercise application functionality
- Report on results
- Quality gates[1]
- Build artifacts
- Deployment
- Cleanup

1 While we can implement a quality gate as a single task, it is typically implemented as an overall checkpoint or set of criteria is met before the pipeline can proceed.

Pipelines are often triggered when a change is made to the source code, which then executes each stage in order.

Examples of CI/CD pipeline designs as projects scale

Now that we know what a pipeline is and how we use hardware and software to power it, let us look at what a CI/CD pipeline looks like.

Pipeline A, humble beginnings

Pipelines do not have to be complicated; let us look at what our first pipeline(s) typically resemble when starting out a new project. In this example, *Pipeline A*, we have a configuration that consists of a single *job-stream* containing one job, which has four steps executed in order from top to bottom. For small projects, this is fine since there is presumably one single project with a limited number of tests. In the following figure, we have an example of our simplest pipeline that has not started to deal with increased complexity or scale:

Pipeline A

Job-stream: "Main"

Job: "Build"

- Clone Repo
- Spin up
- Run Tests
- Generate Reports

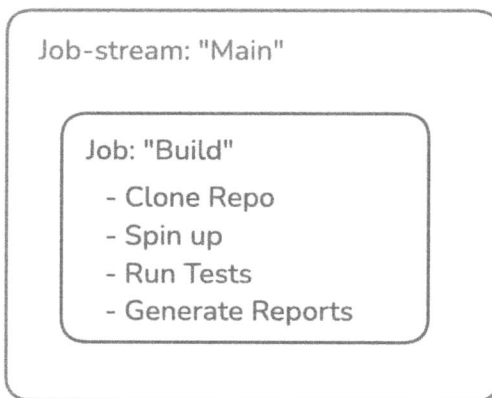

Figure 6.1: *A simple pipeline to run tests in a single job*

Pipeline B, collaboratively preparing for scale

As the teams' needs grow, we will find that intuitive naming (See *Pipeline B* as shown in *Figure 6.2*) and having separation of concerns will make it easier to understand the purpose of our pipeline's *job-streams*, while also reducing the complexity of management. A standard for naming *job-streams* and jobs also helps with collaboration. It should not take a **subject matter expert** (**SME**) to decipher the purpose of a pipeline; it should be understandable at a high level, relying on its high-level labels.

Pipeline B

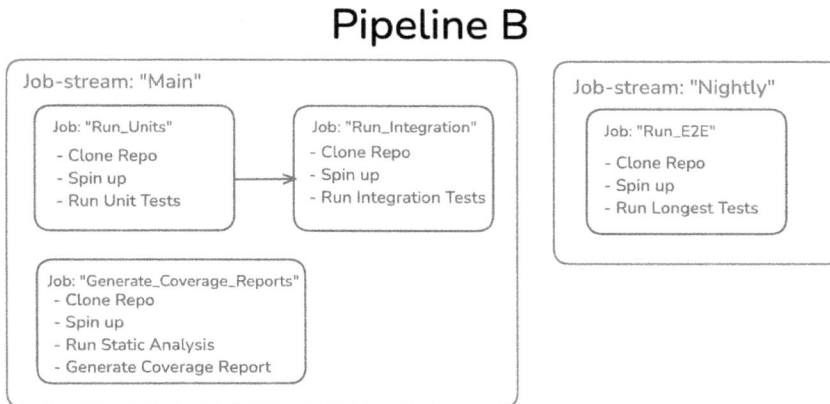

Figure 6.2: *Splitting a single job into multiple with clear labels*

Pipeline C, Intuitive, complex, yet scalable

Pipeline C illustrates how a single *job stream* can become increasingly complex. Beginning with the initial setup, individual flows can split into separate concerns and then converge throughout their execution. If a job cannot run without a previous job's success, we place dependent jobs further along in the *job-stream* sequence. Here is an example of a more complex pipeline that takes effort to name the jobs and split concerns in an intuitive and understandable manner without requiring us to be an SME:

Pipeline C

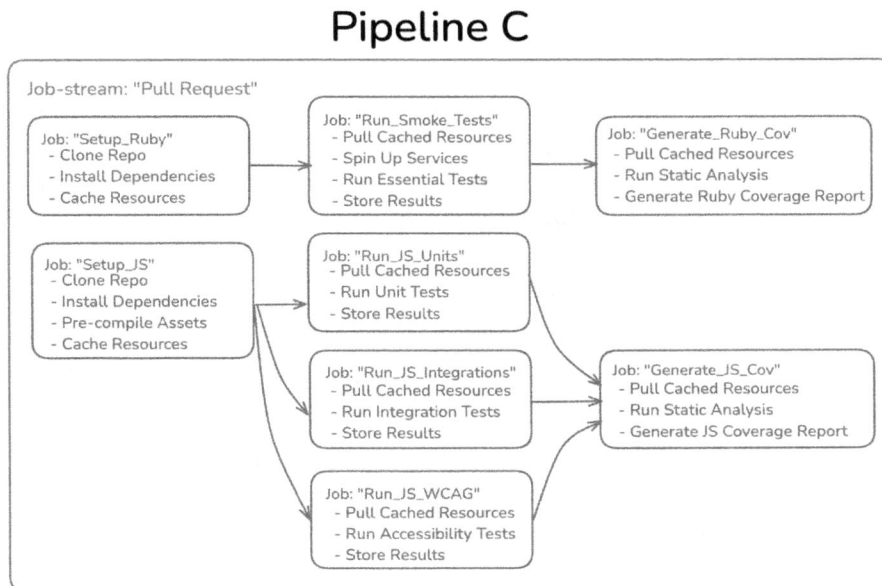

Figure 6.3: *As projects scale, they require breaking up jobs to keep them intuitive and performant*

Quality gates

To ensure the quality of our products and services, we create various types of quality control requirements, also known as *quality gates*. These gates can be anything that limits or prevents an action from happening until another action is successfully performed. All quality gates must eventually pass before a proposed change is merged into our project. Quality gates can take many forms and can be inserted at any point in our development process, including points before, within, and after our CI/CD pipeline.

Admittance or denial through a gate can be determined by the pass/fail result of a test run, manual testing results, or approval from the appropriate people in our process. If these required criteria are not met, we can block merging or deploying until they are addressed. Since the goal is to constantly deliver value, we should strive to automate as many of these as possible.

Soft gates

If a quality gate is identified, but no automated process exists to avoid it being bypassed, the gate can be thought of as a *soft gate*. The mechanism for blocking a change's progression is, by default, entrusted to each developer in the form of a cultural understanding or formal instructions, for e.g., *Changes must be approved by QA before they are merged*. Another example of a soft gate could be the simple need for acknowledging the process should proceed by the click of a button. There is flexibility in this type of gate, but there are also risks of mis-clicks and mistakes. We may find that all soft gates that have proven themselves valuable will eventually need to be automatically enforced as hard gates.

Hard gates

In contrast to *soft gates*, quality gates that are automatically enforced are referred to as *hard gates*. To bypass these checks, the configuration must be changed by an administrator or at least approved by the appropriate team. There is no self-approval option available, or judgment calls to be made for this type of quality gate. By design, bypassing them is difficult and typically requires multiple steps.

Choosing how we build our pipelines

The software and hardware we choose to run our pipelines are motivated by many variables with different weights assigned. The solutions are inevitably intertwined. We can only call them out here; you are the only one who can assign the appropriate values and determine how important they are to your organization. We will explore a few of the many factors that we should consider before choosing a solution; this is not meant to be an exhaustive list.

Hardware: Buy vs. rent

There are advantages to having servers available and maintained on-location (or in-house). Our team(s) will typically have access to the server's full performance capacity and the highest granularity of configuration options. If our team(s) have the skillset for managing a server(s), then the performance-to-cost ratio of ownership can prove significant value compared to a hosted solution. There are other reasons to consider self-hosting, such as security, disaster recovery, business continuity, etc.

On the other hand, hosted solutions that include managed servers offer flexibility that might be very practical. If optimizing the performance of our hardware is not a high priority, our workload requirements vary widely and unpredictably, or our project would benefit most from focusing engineering efforts towards the logic of our application, then consider a hosted solution. Even if we decide we want to buy the hardware, we may consider renting additional capacity on demand beyond a certain threshold or for disaster recovery and business continuity reasons.

There are hybrid *self-hosted* options available, in which servers under our control can be the chosen *runners* of our pipelines, even though they are managed by a paid service. In this case, servers under our control can be in-house or rented from yet another service. Examine the pricing of your paid service runners; you might find a self-hosted option to be more cost-effective.

Open-source vs. proprietary software

Choosing an open-source solution to run our tests could be a good fit if our team's composition includes technical expertise. This can be installed on hardware on location or on paid compute capacity (think rented servers in the cloud, as mentioned above).

Choosing a free solution does not necessarily mean that it is open sourced. Check with our preferred CI service to see if they offer a free or introductory tier. These free tiers can be outgrown somewhat quickly, but a growing project is a cause to celebrate, after all!

We can also pay for support on open-source solutions or for a license to install proprietary software on our own in-house hardware. This could be motivated by an open-source ideology or paid computing capacity. Check to see if your preferred CI solution offers a license to run it in-house.

Many great services easily integrate with your version control system. These services often promote an off-the-shelf experience that can reduce setup and maintenance effort. For a hosted solution, metering typically takes the form of *compute credits,* where we pay only for what we consume. A self-hosted solution typically comes with a licensing fee.

Tightly integrated

There is a lot to be said for CI solution options built directly into SCM. If our project uses a Git repository hosting service, chances are there is an option to leverage this as a natural extension of your existing development workflow. A tightly integrated solution will not require an external integration, typically configured via webhooks, and redirection to a different system. Keep a pulse on our team; a looser integration can be disorienting for some sensitive to changes in their development workflow.

Collaboration techniques

Developers who are familiar with SCM may wish to skim or skip this next section [NOTE: GOTO Security considerations].

Source control management

Before the days of what I consider real **source control management** (**SCM**), we relied on storing our code on a file-sharing server, email, etc., to communicate and collaborate with other developers. Today, we have amazing purpose-built tools such as `Git`, which have some important concepts and features.

Versioning mechanisms within our SCM enable us to keep a historical record of all the changes, allowing us to compare and, if necessary, roll back.

To allow multiple developers to work on different tasks, support different versions of software, etc., we introduce a way for a developer to create a branch, or a copy of the existing code for them to modify without disrupting other developers. This also allows multiple developers to pull and push to the same branches, allowing us to collaborate on larger features more easily. When the changes are ready, they can be merged back into the source branch. Anytime we attempt to parallelize, it introduces complications. While it is safe for multiple developers to work on very related code together, it is not safe to have two developers touching the same code at the same time. At the end of the day, whoever finishes first will end up forcing the other developer to reconcile the merge conflict. Thankfully, we have tooling within our SCM to help us handle this conflict resolution by allowing us to replay history and rewrite it while we are integrating both sets of changes.

The ability to view all the changes is helpful for developers and has a nice side effect: It provides exactly what we need for our auditing and compliance needs, as it keeps a perfect transactional log of all the changes.

Another of my favorite things about good source control is that it is inherently a distributed system. We still require backups in case something bad is pushed, destroying the history on our server. I have recovered data multiple times using a local copy of a user's git history who had not pulled before the corruption and pushed it back to the server. This is possible due to git's distributed nature. Unfortunately, it will be out of scope to go too much into this.

Look at each SCM solution and determine which works better in different use cases. I have maintained projects on teams where different projects had different models, and that was OK because there was fantastic documentation and good workflows that reduced the burden on the developer to figure out what to do. We shoot for a guided experience; the developer should be told by the system what their next steps are.

Branching strategies

To decide what our SCM strategy should be, let us look at common models enabled through branching. Branching is an incredibly flexible concept. This feature enables us to allow many developers to work together in a way that meets their needs. Please adopt the model that makes the most sense to you. As usual, I cannot give you a perfect list, however, these are suggestions for when one model may be more appropriate than another.

The two most common models talked about these days are *GitFlow* and *GitHub Flow*.

GitFlow uses a model where our branches are an integral part of our software development and deployment process. It is most used when long-running branches are desirable and helps us by providing structure for how we introduce *features*, *hotfixes*, and more. Typically, we have a source branch, commonly referred to as *master, main,* or *production*. This is considered the source of truth for what is in production. We create a branch from our source, typically called *development,* to integrate multiple features together before they are tested and released into production. We create a *feature branch* off development to work on our changes until we are ready to integrate them with the rest of the team's codebase. When we run into a scenario where we need to perform a *hotfix,* we create a branch off the original source for production to not try introducing any potentially unvetted development features.

GitHub Flow is a much lighter-weight approach and is favored by teams that want to move quickly. Compared to the previous model, we strive to have short-lived branches and rely heavily on the usage of CI and CD to provide some of the structure being accomplished with the extra branches. I want to be clear, it is not superior; there are distinct advantages to *GitFlow* and longer-running branches. If we must support multiple versions of our product, then it might be a better choice. Anyways, similarly, we have a source branch typically called *master, main,* or *production*. Developers create *feature* and *hotfix* branches off of this, and perform the required development and testing. This supports models where changes are deployed directly from *feature* branches. The important thing is that our source branch should always be considered stable code that represents the last known stable production.

Pull requests

When we are ready to integrate our changes, we need to get a review from one or more people depending on what quality gates are defined. The submitter creates a *pull request,* which is the set of changes between our source and a particular branch as the destination; this is commonly referred to as a target. This is a great place for us to integrate those tests into our process, which we will discuss shortly. Once our tests are run and we have our approvals, we can look to merge the pull request back into the target branch.

Good *pull requests* always contain a detailed description of newly added feature or bug fixed. This should include, external links to issue tracking or other contexts, explain the impact of the change, and most importantly, explain why this makes sense. Especially when we talk about larger organizations, we are often requested to review code we are unfamiliar with. If the submitter wants to ensure that they get a quick review, then they should do everything possible to make it easier for the reviewer. When we take the time to help the reviewer, they can more quickly get to the heart of the matter at hand. This is a natural extension of our *code for the 3 AM mantra*. I regularly go back to pull requests to better understand the context.

While it may not seem like it on the surface, this is a dialogue between our various developers, bots, and systems and is focal to our development and deployment workflows. It comes in the form of comments by the submitter, our CI and CD systems, quality gates, approvals or rejections, statuses of deployments, etc., which ends up creating an extremely valuable audit log when we are trying to understand what happened when troubleshooting an issue or investigating some event.

Communication through integrations

Pipelines are essentially a grouping of tasks; they keep track of overall success and failure and can prevent it from proceeding when a problem is found. Our tasks often need to communicate more information than the outside process can know. As such, we often use APIs to add additional context or hide complex logic behind a much simpler button.

Let us examine the boundaries of our pipelines to highlight what actions happen inside vs. outside. At a high level, our pipelines take in data, perform actions on that data, and produce outputs in the form of data. For simplicity, we will limit our external providers and recipients to just a few specific examples.

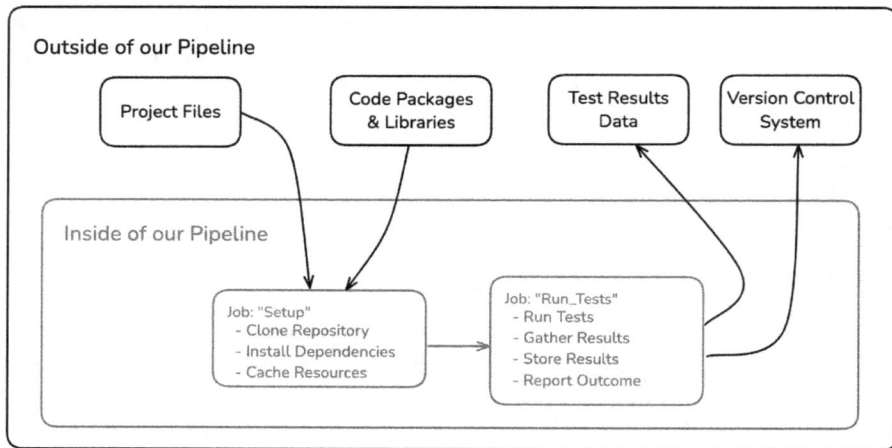

Figure 6.4: Distinction between the instructions in the pipeline and the assets that live outside of it

In *Figure 6.4*, we have a pipeline that begins with the action *clone repository*, which copies project files from an external source into our pipeline environment. Then, the *install dependencies* step performs the action of reading the project files we just copied, and finding an external code library is necessary. The step then copies the necessary libraries from an external source into our pipeline environment, caching the results for use in our subsequent job. As each step is completed without error, it informs our job that it has passed and that further steps should continue.

The *Run_tests* job is then executed by first running our tests based on the information we cached from the previous *Setup* job. The step to *Gather Results* is then performed, and the results are stored outside of the pipeline for use at some point in the future after our pipeline has been completed. We are at the end of our pipeline's tasks and perform one last step, which sends the pass/fail result to our version control system. This pass/fail result informs our version control system so that it can be conveniently displayed and, if configured, deny merging should the result be a failure.

Although we refer to a version control system as the recipient of our pass/fail response in this example, there can be a wide variety of recipients. A pipeline can inform one or many other systems that are useful for our purposes. These other systems could include a chatbot to inform developers when their pipeline completes or errors out, or a service that tracks pipeline pass/fail metrics. In fact, any system that can receive calls is an eligible target for our pipeline's response.

Our pipeline does not need to perform all its jobs and steps before it can communicate with integrations on the outside. In this example, our dependencies fail to install because an external resource is not found!

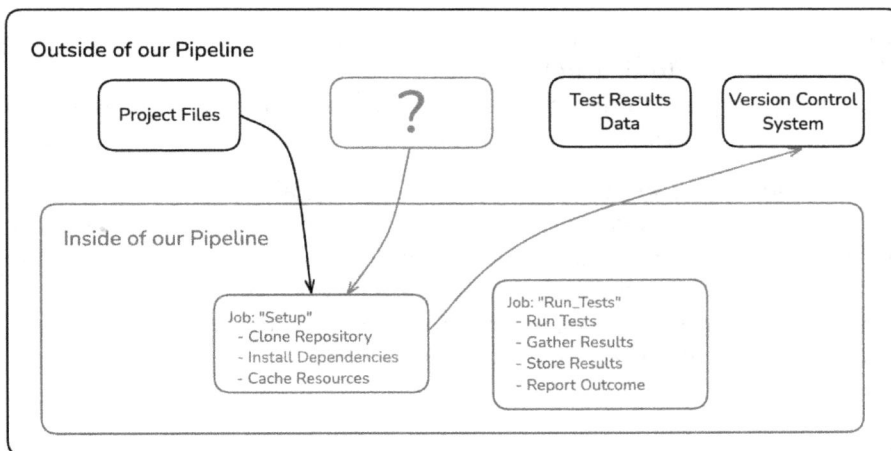

Figure 6.5: When our pipeline fails due to an external dependency

This failing step informs our job, which informs our pipeline that an error occurred. This, in turn, cuts the pipeline short of completing its duties, and the pipeline immediately reports a failure status to our external version control system.

Self-service as a design pattern

One of the major benefits of creating a pipeline is that if we have built the confidence required, we can open up our pipelines to additional developers outside of our team, role, etc. This allows us to empower teams by providing them with a simple interface to move software from one end to another without having to know how we get there.

We can reduce the permissions that our users need to have in a system if their interface for these sensitive actions is no longer directly through the system, and instead uses automation in our pipeline. Now, our pipeline serves as the agent to get a task done and requires only one set of permissions for itself. This is a great way to reduce the permission sets that developers and operators need in specific contexts.

For example, most developers and operators need to propose changes related to their SCM systems, both in content and configuration. Previously, we would have to create a ticket and wait for the service owner to get around to it. There is a better way. If our pipeline has access and automation to manage the same set of tasks, then we can shrink the developers' permissions down to content only, as we have changed the paradigm from performing changes directly to the system and instead are now collaboratively proposing changes, getting reviews, performing tests, and then applying changes with a bot. Notice how our pipeline concepts do not just apply to our applications or infrastructure; we can take any manual task, and automate it in a pipeline, which acts as a great form of change management, auditing, etc., in a more collaborative manner.

Reduce overhead

Automating manual tasks is a matter of quality control since it reduces the opportunity for mistakes. Pipelines afford a lightweight approach to automating small tasks like generating artifacts or publishing gem/module releases, which would otherwise require more workload on the developer, along with the risk of typing errors and silly mistakes.

We can think of our pipeline in this context as a guardrail that ushers our less-familiar teammates through complex tasks that only experts normally do. Self-service also reduces the communication overhead. which is often overlooked. Previously, when a developer needed to perform a niche activity, it required a conversation with the experts, pouring over documentation, and some wait time for detailed review. Pipelines remove this workload, replacing it with a collaborative experience where the owners simply need to review and approve the changes.

Security considerations

My favorite way of generally referring to CI and CD systems is **remote code execution (RCE)** as a service, as at the end of the day, we want our pipelines to support developers having the ability to set up all the necessary aspects of testing and deployments without requiring external assistance. As such, we need to be very careful about what kinds of access we give our CI/CD systems and how we should monitor these for compromise, which is something we will explore a bit more within *Chapter 9, Pipeline Mastery, Security concerns,* and *Chapter 5, Security.*

The more we use our automated systems to perform tasks, we must ensure that we protect these systems, and be aware of the sharp edges, especially as we ask others to use systems they are unfamiliar with.

Conclusion

Our software development pipelines were inspired by their physical counterparts. Defining flexible and scalable workflows empowers us to deploy frequently without sacrificing quality in our software development life cycle. Confidence is built through the implementation of *quality gates* that prevent defects (bugs, including business logic, reliability, availability, compliance, security, configuration, etc.) from progressing from one stage to the next in our pipeline. We discussed some core concepts of how we collaborate with humans and machines using pipelines. Remember that, due to the nature of the pipelines, they introduce a security risk that must be managed. Now that we have a foundation for pipelines, we will explore continuous integration and continuous delivery. Due to the highly interconnected nature of these three topics, we will follow up with another chapter diving deeper into extracting additional value from our pipelines. In the next chapter, we will focus on CI pipelines.

Join our Discord space

Join our Discord workspace for latest updates, offers, tech happenings around the world, new releases, and sessions with the authors:

https://discord.bpbonline.com

CHAPTER 7
Continuous Integration

Introduction

It is true that testing is critical at scale. Developer time is expensive, and we want to optimize the time it takes for us to get feedback from the system on whether our code behaves as intended. Setting up meaningful testing can be challenging and costly. Let us explore how we can introduce this concept of continuous integration against our codebase and proposed changes, and how we can apply it appropriately to increase developer confidence. We will explore the tool selection process, unlocking rapid feedback, scalability, pitfalls to avoid, and how a team can sustainably leverage the value of CI to improve their development and QA processes.

In short, CI means automatically running our tests with every change. Writing a test is only the beginning, in that our tests only bring value if we run them. These tests could be triggered via local updates to code when changes are pushed to a branch, on pull requests, or by integrating or merging changes into the target branch. We can have one or many tests run to give us feedback at various stages of development, informing the developer of the progress. Some testing takes longer than others, so we run only what we need based on the stage of development we are currently in.

Objectives

The objectives are to understand:

- What is CI?

- How is CI a powerful tool for rapid developer feedback?

- What environments should we consider when discussing CI, and how do we promote our changes safely?

- How did CI evolve over the years?

- Can we apply maturity levels to CI pipelines?

- How does quality assurance fit into CI?

- How should we think about selecting tools and frameworks for CI?

- What sort of ecosystem compatibility problems are we likely to encounter?

- How do we go about introducing new testing strategies into our organization?

- What do we do when we see failures in our pipelines?

Developer feedback

Armed with our new knowledge of testing, we can see the benefits of running our tests sooner in our development process rather than waiting till the end. Often, I have seen companies that have a heavy emphasis on testing right before production and almost nothing before that; that is not a good sign. We should push the developer feedback as soon as it makes sense.

In *Chapter 4, Importance of Automated Testing, X-driven development*, we talked about using tests in the context of a film scriptwriter to help us catch problems; what other common examples can you see everyday computer users running constant tests? How about our text editor? For Developers, this might mean running *linters* or other types of checks to improve our code. We have spelling, grammar, etc., and other types of checking for document writing. Rather than waiting until the completion of this book and then coming back and fixing all the mistakes, these programs are helping me *make fewer mistakes* every step of the way.

Ok, back into the developer context. Getting rapid updates directly to the producer at different stages of development lets us focus on optimizing our effectiveness, efficiency, and productivity. When we have good tests, we can spend more time focusing on our specific change and know that if we touched something in a way we did not understand, something should (nicely) yell at us and make us aware.

It is important that when we are setting up the feedback loop, the instructions are clear to the developers. What went wrong, and how can we fix it, if possible?

Environments

So, our local setup, including our editor, is now giving us feedback quickly. That is great, but we want to make it so that if we need someone else to test it easily, it is simple. Also, no one should have to take our word that we tested; we should want to see this directly within our pull request. To do this, we need some ability in our SCM solution to work with internal or external systems to perform the tests and report the results. This is typically performed on an external system and is referred to as a *continuous integration* server(s) or service. There are many frameworks and services, with new ones that come out with newer and shinier features. At the end of the day, we follow the processes we did earlier by mapping out our requirements and finding the best solution through elimination.

How many environments should we consider at a minimum?

Developers often make the mistake of oversimplifying the environments in which we work. These are typically thought of as development, test, and production. However, when we do a deep dive into building CI systems, it is important to distinguish our environments a bit further. Some of this depends on the nature of your chosen workflow, but as an example, let us refine our understanding of these environment groups with a bit more granularity.

Local

As development generally starts locally, it is easy to think of these two distinct aspects as one; however, they do not need to be.

- **Local development:** A developer's machine where code is written.
- **Local test:** A developer's machine where tests are run.

CI

CI test: An internal, external, or third-party server(s) or service(s) where a larger subset or a complete set of developers' tests are run. This on-demand and ephemeral environment frees a developer's machine for continued feature development in parallel while also affording collaboration with other individuals and groups that can optimize speed and help troubleshoot test issues.

Promotion

In *Chapter 8, Continuous Delivery, Implementing deployment strategies*, we will focus on using continuous deployments to promote our changes through the following environments. *Staging, Preproduction, Partners, etc.,* are environments designed to simulate production where developers, QA personnel, product owners, external partners, security researchers, etc., can collaboratively inspect new feature behavior before it is released to the customer and isolate the impact of the testing.

Each of these environments aims to build confidence, as the same code is being deployed multiple times and increasingly passes various verifications.

Evolution of CI

CI can be traced at least as far back as the 1980s, when change coordination and specifically ordered test executions were implemented as a method of managing large-scale software projects[1]. Later in the 1990s, *Kent Beck* took the concept to what was considered *extreme* for the time. In contrast, it was common for companies at the time to deploy only once or twice every year!

The notion of continuous deployment was extreme at the time, but it would never have been possible without the stability and confidence provided by continuous integration. To get a fresh understanding of CI's value, let us consider a very simple example of an application in its infancy. This might be a single developer sitting down at their computer and writing a few lines of code with a test.

Independent and local

For an individual developer, running a test suite is very practical (and fast) for small apps and teams; however, as an app grows in its feature set and complexity, so does the number of tests that ensure its correct behavior. Here is a simple representation of a developer working without a team:

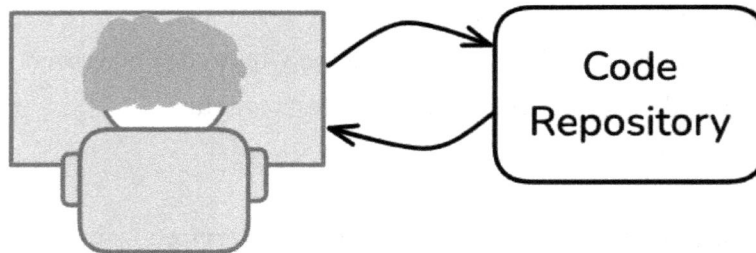

Figure 7.1: *The pulling and pushing interaction between a developer and a code repository*

At first, a developer will run tests during code authoring without breaking their stride, but over time, the duration of running the test suite grows until it reaches a tipping point. That point is when a developer realizes their tests take a long time to run, their eyes glaze over, thoughts wander, and the context of their work is mentally diminished or lost. This tendency worsens as the elapsed time of the suite slowly increases over time. To avoid adapting to slower test feedback and, by extension, slower progress, we need to optimize our tests to make them run faster. Little delays are expected at this point, such as time spent optimizing tests and waiting for the entire test suite to run locally. Progress is moving forward, but it is limited to a single contributor.

---

1 (Kaiser, Perry, & Schell, 1989)

As the team scales to support a growing app (as depicted in the following figure), the time cost also scales, affecting the workflow of each team member who attempts to run the entire suite locally. Differences in app state or local environments may also introduce test failures that surface on some but not all computers, causing further delays in resolution.

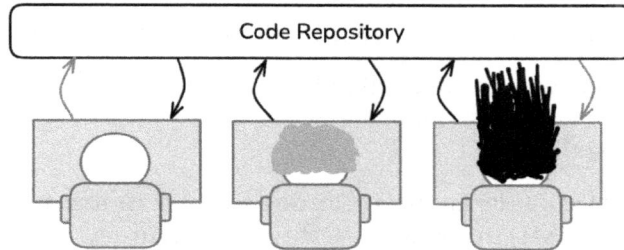

Figure 7.2: Multiple developers pulling and pushing from a code repository

Collaborative and remote

The developers then turned to running their test suite in an environment that is optimized and decoupled from the developer's local environment. Something that provides a consistent and fast experience for the whole team. This remote environment could be a dedicated server with more resources within the same building as the developers or a hosted service that manages the server for them. Now, there is a little bit of overhead when running the test suite remotely, like copying the app and spinning up a database, but the developers no longer wait for their test suite to finish running on their own machine, and issues with the suite are now contained within a consistent environment. To be clear, this remote environment augments a developer's testing capabilities and is not a replacement. You may want to run some subset of tests locally to speed up the feedback loop for syntax and style while deferring additional tests to the remote environment.

Storytime with Sean, the no tests company

Let us look at how deferring tests can play out at a small company where delays begin to mount and collaboration challenges start to bog down progress.

A while back, I worked with a team that consisted of a single senior developer who would build the basic structure of a feature, and everything else was built by a third party overseas. We will call them *Offshore Inc.*

I quickly discovered a troubling pattern in my company's software development cycle. When *Offshore Inc.* introduced new features, existing features would break, even though, on the surface, those broken features seemed unrelated.

I had a lot of manual testing to do to ensure the new features and the rest of the application continued to work. This involved checking every path through the app from multiple browsers on multiple devices.

I had arrived at a tipping point in the company, where its core application had become complex enough that no single person could comprehend how the entire feature set was implemented. The larger our application became, the slower and more error-prone our manual QA process also became. The time spent working with each author to correct the newly found bugs would burn a considerable amount of the day. As development progressed, we needed a way for the wider development team to merge confidently.

The challenge was to increase the maturity of our process.

Maturity levels

Let us define levels of confidence in our testing, similar to many **Software Assurance Maturity Models** (**SAMM**), introducing testing as a journey that requires iteratively building and measuring our progress:

- **Level 1:** Developer:

  The feature author manually tests behavior to ensure it is intentional and correct.

- **Level 2:** Developer:

  The behavior is tested on a staging environment that is more representative of production than their local machine.

- **Level 3:** QA:

  A product owner, stakeholder, or dedicated QA tester manually exercises the behavior in a staging environment that is representative of production.

- **Level 4:** Developer:

  The feature author writes automated tests for the behavior to ensure that it is intentional and correct.

- **Level 5:** QA:

  A dedicated QA tester will rely on manual and automated testing in an environment that mirrors production.

In a mature software development project that needs to scale and reduce customer impact, its deployment will rely on pipelines and quality gates to tie this all together.

Quality assurance

Quality assurance (**QA**) is an important responsibility of everyone involved in the design, development, deployment, and maintenance of the product or service provided. We often have dedicated roles for people to focus on, ensuring that we meet the quality without also having their own deliverables. We, as developers, can help these folks by writing great tests and integrating them into the development and deployment workflows. This frees up these specialists to spend more time building out better automated and manual QA processes or prioritizing exploratory testing beyond the most common paths used.

With extra QA capacity freed by our automated test suite, we increase our QA team's ability to perform app inspection faster, with more depth, or both. This, in turn, increases the quality of feedback needed to support developer confidence. Without rapid feedback from QA in addition to our test suite, the tendency to resist change begins to set in. We naturally want to limit the frequency of deployments as a form of risk management.

Manually reviewing test failures

Manual review in the context of a test failure also has its place. While on the one hand, tests for continued coverage should be reviewed as a part of regular code reviews, human eyes on a test failure help answer the question, *Is this a valuable-test-failure that caught unintended behavior, or is it a worthless-test-failure that now requires troubleshooting?* If discerning whether a test adds value is desirable, then yes, manual test review in this context applies.

Selecting tools and frameworks

Many CI/CD tools are available to help us better manage our pipelines. As the needs of our product and team change, so should the tools supporting them. The size of our team and organization will greatly impact our needs.

Features to look for:

- Documentation on structuring a config file, often in a YAML or vendor-specific format, to describe how to get from **A** to **B**, **B** to **C**, etc.
    - Groups of actions
        - steps (lines of instructions typically written in a shell script)
        - jobs (groups of steps)
        - job-streams (groups of jobs)
        - pipelines (the entirety of your project configuration)
- Options for selecting your execution environment (Docker, virtual machine, language-specific runtimes, etc.)
- Parallel test runs on multiple containers or workers
- Visualizing the order in which these pieces connect, like a flowchart
- Reusable jobs and configuration
- Productivity, performance, and debugging metrics (run frequency, speed, failure rate)

Some features are not offered on every tool/platform but are valuable enough to guide your choice.

Parallelism

A test suite should run jobs in parallel, splitting tests into groups so that each group can run at the same time. The execution of each test group is best kept isolated, along with its own resources, environmental variables, database, and supporting services. Running a test suite in parallel is a powerful tool that can cut down large suite run times by an order of magnitude.

Cost concerns

It all boils down to cost, but if your project is very sensitive to cost, then understandable pricing and tracking accuracy will carry a high priority. As such, you will want a way to access current and projected costs by everyone on our team, and as a bonus, we may even want a way to access this information with an API for the flexibility to slice our own key performance indicators or set up custom alerts.

Ecosystem compatibility challenges

Often, developers who have been in the cloud for many years tend to discount some of the common compatibility challenges that many of our practitioners who are running a hybrid or on-premises system face. This comes into play when building and testing our software.

For example, I have worked for many software development companies that ran their entire infrastructure on Linux but had one or more random *Mac Mini(s)* in a closet somewhere to build and test *iOS* apps. Another example of this was when Apple moved to their new **Advanced RISC (Reduced Instruction Set Computer) Machines (ARM)** chipset, and most companies' software broke despite Apple's compatibility promises. This required many companies to either invest heavily in adding support for ARM into their stack or move their development off of those architectures.

[Sean says] I have seen examples of this also in the way of Android and iOS testing, where a product manager kept a bank of mobile devices fastened to a sheet of plywood in their home office. The array of smartphones served as a shared staging environment to connect and upload recent features for testing.

Vendors should embrace interoperability so that we can achieve better outcomes.

Introducing testing, tactics, and strategies

Sean continues his story at *The No Tests Company:* We were caught in a cycle of developers breaking each other's work. I proposed that we insist that *Offshore Inc.* provide us with tests in tandem with their features. Several days later, a new feature arrived from *Offshore Inc.* in a pull request that also had tests! I ran the whole suite, and it passed! Then, I scanned through the tests. There were multiple files! The titles were descriptive and seemed relevant. Then to my disappointment, I noticed the body of these tests simply returned `true`, which is to say, they could only ever pass.

None of the tests added any value because they made no assertions to validate any application behavior. It was clear we still needed tests of real value. I ended up writing many tests myself as a way of modeling what was expected, but more generally, I had come across some of the many pitfalls we all stand to face when introducing (much less maintaining) a valuable test suite to an existing project. Remember how we discussed that *Volkswagen misrepresented their vehicle emissions in Chapter 4, Importance of Automated Testing, is our test valuable or harmful?* Without an understanding of a test's value, incentive misalignment can even find its way into a test suite.

Negotiable or Non-Negotiable

> *You've got to know when to hold them, know when to fold them,*
> *know when to walk away, and know when to run*
>
> *- Kenny Rodgers, The Gambler*

How to manage testing on a project depends on the situation at hand. *Believe it or not, this is a very controversial statement.* Some developers believe that 100% test coverage at all times is a hard rule for every project of every kind, with no exceptions. Anything less deserves a mass walkout and total project abandonment, some fasting and repentance for good measure. We will call this camp of developers Non-Negotiable. Each camp is right, depending on the situation.

The *Non-Negotiable* camp can be right in their 100% coverage stance for the following concerns:

- Real-time safety systems (think airbag deployments and things that keep people safe)

- Financial transactions (think money ledgers and things that combat fraud)

- Public health (think nuclear, aviation, and pharmaceutical safety mechanisms)

- Information security (think a person's identity, and privacy)

- There's more, but you get the idea

The *Negotiable* camp can be right in their *less than 100%* coverage stance for the following:

- Deferring supplemental feature coverage for the sake of prioritizing coverage on core business features, and our *Non-Negotiable* list above

Admittedly, that Negotiable bullet was long-winded, but we walk a tightrope discussing this topic, and it must be very specific. After all, software projects can vary widely in their commit history, scope, language, regulations, and internal cultures. Certainly, if you find yourself on a new project, then take the opportunity to set a quality precedent by demonstrating excellent coverage to your co-founders.

That said, we are not here to peacock about test coverage absolutism, but rather, give you practical ways to join a team's existing project, evaluate the test coverage as-found, and steer the team's culture of quality in the right direction. All, without driving the project into bankruptcy. If your management tells you to risk human life or break the law, it is time to take *Kenny Rogers'* advice and walk away. For situations that fall into the *Negotiable* camp, let us proceed with caution.

A strategy to consider

Let us look at a fictional example about a developer we will call Sam. It is Sam's first day on a fast-growing food recipe platform. He is excited to be solving the question of *What's for dinner?* He busily catches up on the history of decisions made by team members of the past and present. He quickly discovers a backlog of technical debt, such as a deficient test suite with numerous gaps in coverage on critical organizational features. To make matters worse, a discussion with the team reveals a fundamental misunderstanding of test suite value. Instead of *abandoning ship!* Sam assumes the best intent, gathers together some empathy, and decides to navigate these rocky shoals. Besides, he needs this job.

The following is a simple flowchart to help map Sam's course towards quality. Consider your own project, and any parallels you might see that overlap:

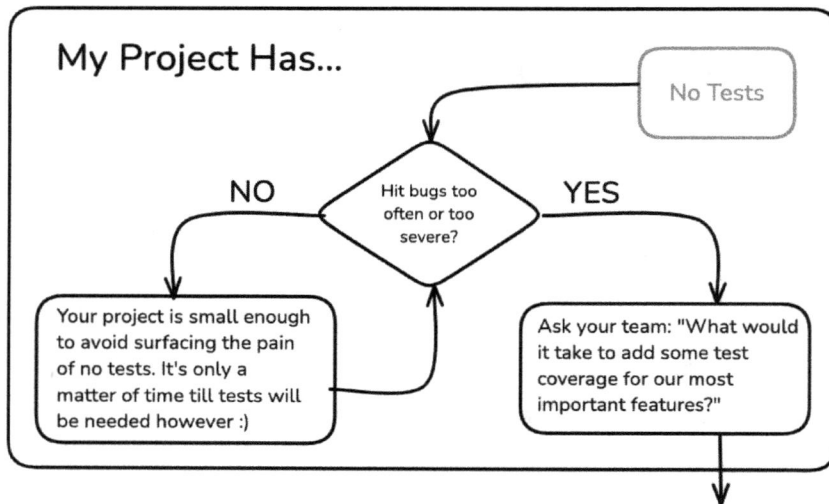

Figure 7.3: A flowchart depicting the rationale behind adding tests for the first time

Getting back to our story, Sam talks with his team about the lack of tests he found and asks about any regressions the team may be experiencing. The other members agree that broken features have not slowed them down, so Sam considers the small size of the team and the simplicity of the app as the underlying possibility. Sam offers help to anyone wanting to write tests and continues covering his new contributions. The next release does not go so well when the ability to tag recipes as a favorite breaks. After the team scrambles to fix the issue, Sam brings up the matter in their next meeting, asking *What would it take to add coverage for our most important features?* The pain was undeniable, so the team decided to identify core business features and boost their coverage. Let us take a look at the next stage in our flowchart:

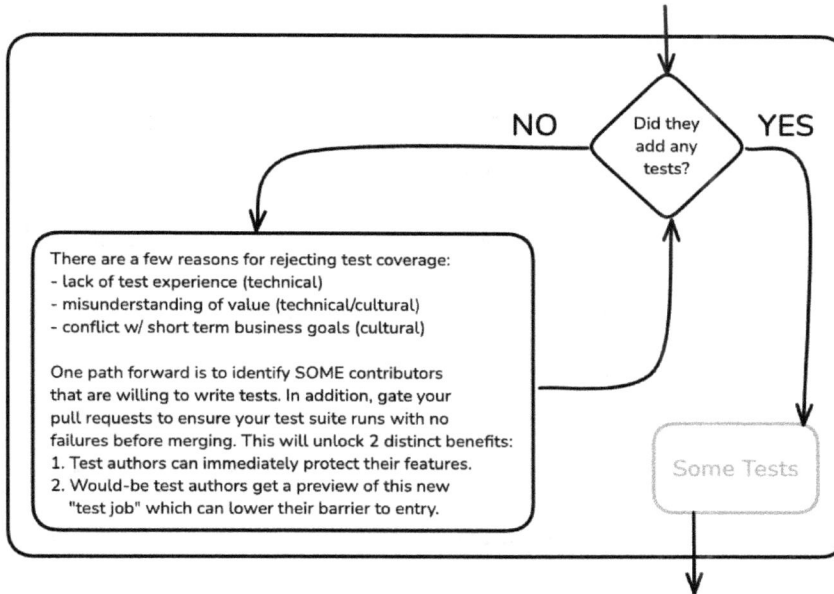

Figure 7.4: Flowchart depicting that once we have agreed that we need to add tests

Sam is happy to hear they are going to add tests but given the team's history of prioritizing short-term business goals, he wants to make running the tests an unavoidable part of the development workflow. Before the team concludes the meeting, Sam suggests a quality gate is added to require the test suite runs cleanly before a merge. The team recognizes Sam's willingness to work under the same constraints, and it encourages them in their decision.

As the next sprint draws near to the end of its cycle, Sam is pleased to see the test coverage go up, but also notices complaints from teammates about being blocked on account of someone else's broken tests. Now that we have buy-in, we keep writing tests as long as they keep running smoothly. Sam wonders how broken tests managed to get past the quality gate and into the codebase to begin with.

Hoping to make the testing transition as smooth as possible for the team, he runs the problem test a few times in succession on his own and discovers that it seems to be failing *randomly*. Removing all instances of random data, and replacing them with consistent and unique data, seems to solve the issue. Sam takes the next opportunity to chat with the team about how random data devalues the test suite by increasing maintenance costs. The team is encouraged by Sam's example and leans into more complex and involved test scenarios.

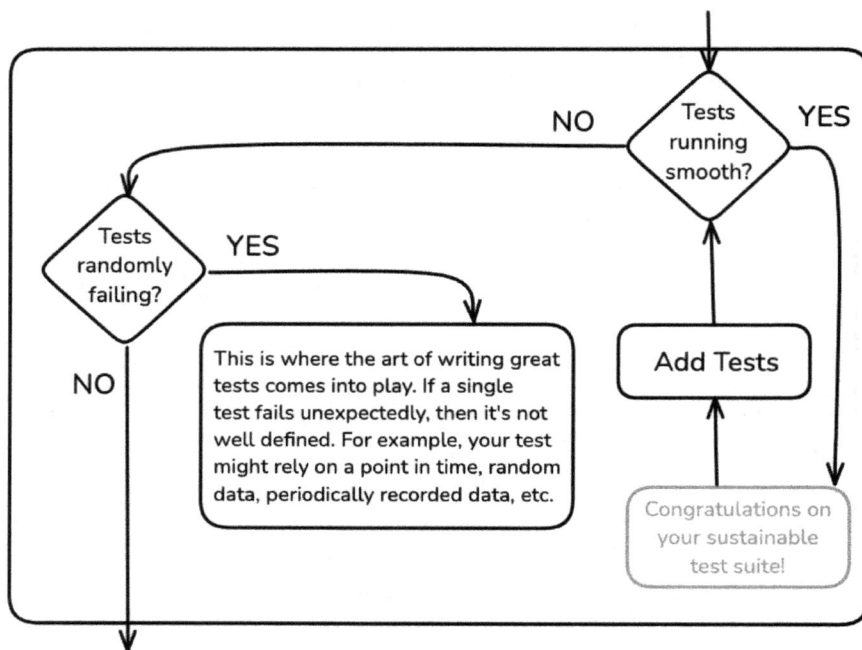

Figure 7.5: *Flowchart to evaluate what to do based on how smoothly our tests are running*

Let us pause our story for a moment to talk about large, long-running tests. The terms *large* and *long-running* are relative and will be defined differently across teams, their chosen tech stack, and mission requirements. It is common for developers to overlook tracking the performance of their suite since the issue generally has a slow onset. Here is where our empathy kicks in—It is easy to grow accustomed to a long-running test suite. It is important to have a performance target identified and agreed upon by all stakeholders so that when a test or test suite surpasses the target, there is no debate over prioritizing cleanups and optimizations. Such a target should aim for efficiency instead of a hard time limit for individual tests or full-suite runs. Over time, a healthy test suite must take longer to run to be commensurate with its growing coverage. Therefore, we recommend a target that scales, such as an average duration per test. It would also be beneficial to consider reasonable resource expenses on a per-test basis. This will ensure the servers running your test suite will also scale. Remember that hardware is a factor in the speed of your tests, so it is important to balance software efficiency with hardware capability. I have seen a situation first-hand where a talented team spent a good bit of time grooming the suite to squeeze as much performance as it could, only to look back and realize that for all of the time spent, it would have been a better value to direct some of that effort elsewhere and simply buy more server resources. Let us see what Sam is up to.

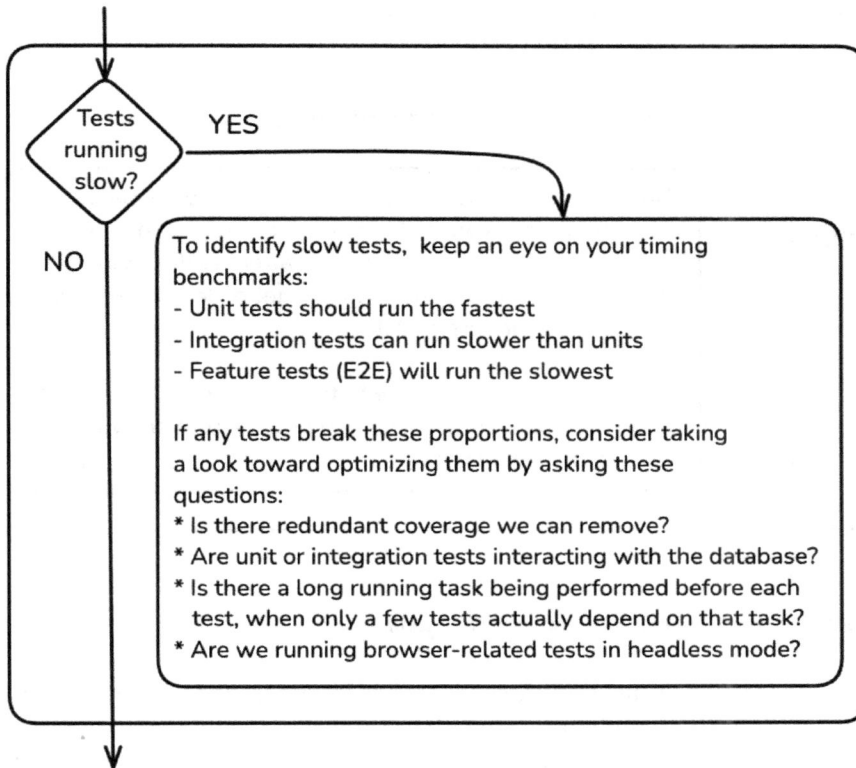

To identify slow tests, keep an eye on your timing benchmarks:
- Unit tests should run the fastest
- Integration tests can run slower than units
- Feature tests (E2E) will run the slowest

If any tests break these proportions, consider taking a look toward optimizing them by asking these questions:
* Is there redundant coverage we can remove?
* Are unit or integration tests interacting with the database?
* Is there a long running task being performed before each test, when only a few tests actually depend on that task?
* Are we running browser-related tests in headless mode?

Figure 7.6: Flowchart for when our tests are taking too long

Sam takes a look at the full test suite run duration and notices a significant spike since the team began writing E2E tests. That seems natural since they are focused on writing tests that thoroughly exercise the app, but one E2E test stands out. Once in a while, the test takes several times longer than its peers to run. On closer inspection, Sam discovers that the test is making calls to an external social site, which sometimes takes a long time to respond. Sam asks his team why their project's test suite is concerned with content outside of its control. Management says it is very important that content on *Tubular* is accurate so it must be tested. Sam decides to balance the needs of management and his team over this issue. Knowing the worst that could happen would have very little impact; he preserves the test by moving it onto a schedule that runs once per day in the afternoon, just after new postings. Now the check will run close to when it is actually needed, instead of on each commit, saving time and preserving confidence.

As time passes, the group grows significantly into many small teams working on different areas of the same application. Then one day, a not-so-straightforward issue arises when a developer tells Sam (who is now the official point of contact for test suite-related issues) that they are blocked by an unrelated test failure and need to push an urgent update.

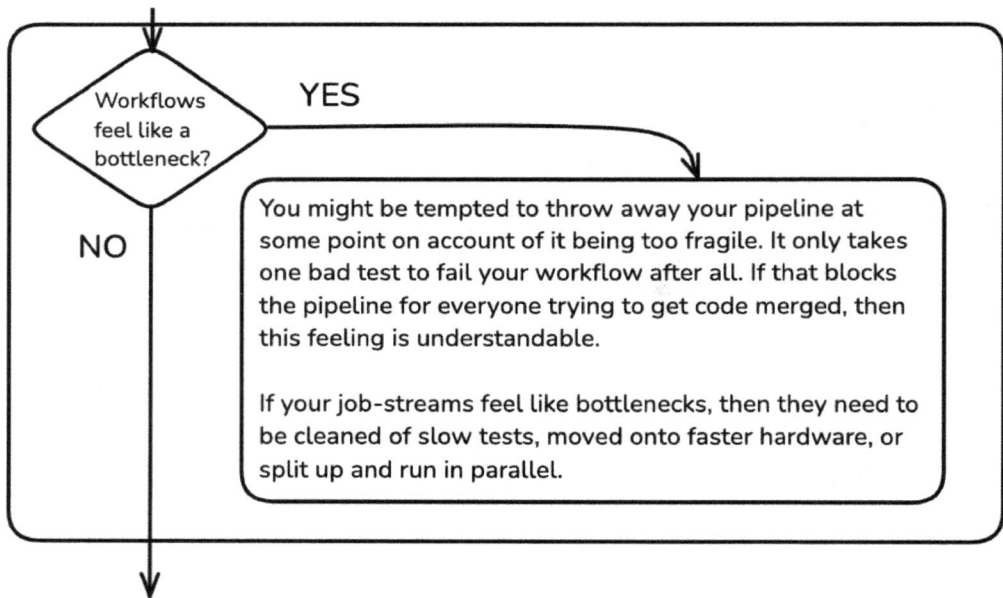

Figure 7.7: Flowchart to encourage continued investment when the workflow feels like a bottleneck

Sam does not want to risk an additional bug entering the code base due to bypassing the test suite, so he immediately looks into the issue. As he looks, management asks the affected group what is blocking the update, and they respond with *Some unrelated test failure*. Sam adds that the team cannot be sure it is unrelated and insists that bypassing the suite could introduce a bug and even affect the success of the update. Sam stands up for quality like a true Non-Negotiable. The team nods in agreement and starts investigating the failure's root cause. Then there is a plot twist—the test suite ran again without any changes, but the test did not fail this time!

The test is fragile because it is not well-defined. The team decides to go ahead with pushing the update since the test did eventually pass.

While Sam is looking into the issue, he notices the test suite failure rate for pull requests begins to rise, and it becomes clear that recent merges with the codebase have spread the same fragile test into the broader team's working branches. This fragile test is now slowing down *multiple* teams. They begin reaching out to Sam for an exception since he is the only one with permissions to overrule the quality gate. Sam starts to weigh the value of this fragile test and its true cost to the company.

Engineering hours and server time are not cheap at scale, but neither are bugs. Without more time to solve the issue, the broader team will have to re-run the whole test suite multiple times for every change to the codebase until all tests pass. Sam starts to evaluate each requested exception and realizes that if the problem test does not get fixed, responding to developers will become his new job!

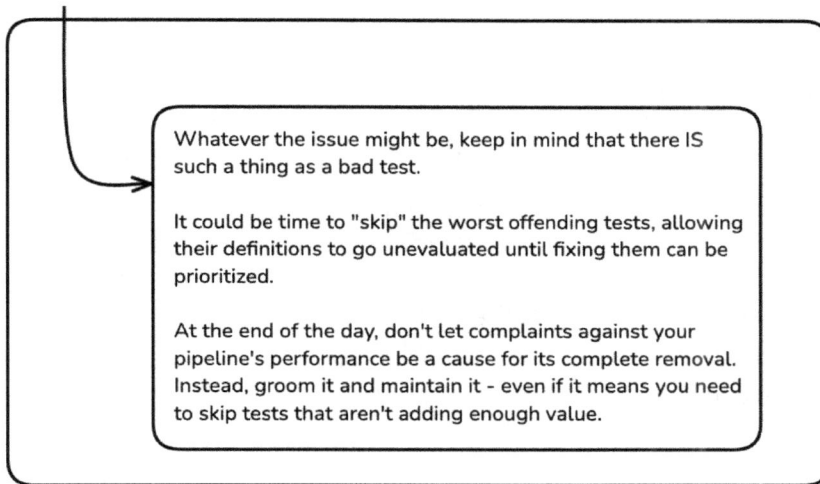

Whatever the issue might be, keep in mind that there IS such a thing as a bad test.

It could be time to "skip" the worst offending tests, allowing their definitions to go unevaluated until fixing them can be prioritized.

At the end of the day, don't let complaints against your pipeline's performance be a cause for its complete removal. Instead, groom it and maintain it - even if it means you need to skip tests that aren't adding enough value.

Figure 7.8: When something is not working optimally, it means we can improve it

Sam gets approval from his lead and project manager to pull the fragile test out of the suite for the time it takes to get fixed. This move would temporarily reduce overall code coverage, but the test's trustworthiness is in question, and the cost to the broader team is much more obvious. Sam steps over from camp *Non-Negotiable*, and into camp *Negotiable* by removing the problematic test, and notifies everyone to update their branch to avoid further issues. Now fixed, the test is reintroduced to the suite, coverage goes up, and the rest of the team barely notices the test is back in place as they are heads-down busy working on their features. Nice work, Sam! The app, test suite, team, revenue, and user base are all scaling! There was pain at times, but you came out the other side as both a champion of quality and an understanding teammate who is in for the win.

Overall, we can focus on the quality of our tests while looking for ways to optimize the components of our pipeline. We should look at each test to determine if any tests are useless, and we can simply delete them. Like Sam in our story, there are situations where if the tests are otherwise valuable, but flaky or unreliable, we can choose to skip them temporarily until we can address the root cause. While we can look at automating this, it should require an engineer to approve the temporary changes.

As we know, pipelines can bring significant value; if the *job-stream* is a bottleneck, it means it is fixable.

What to do when our pipeline breaks

Pipelines can quickly become an integral part of any team's workflow. When a pipeline fails for one developer, that could just be the test suite doing its job, but it can be a bad day when it breaks down for everyone. External dependencies can implement breaking changes; tests can suddenly fail for unknown reasons; global states like environmental variables can be tampered with, etc. What is important in these situations is to mitigate downtime and balance keeping bugs out. Those in charge of the broken pipeline might find themselves flooded with developer requests to manually *bypass* it. This makes it more difficult to troubleshoot. Try to separate the task of troubleshooting and that of triaging developers between our teams so that both tasks can be done effectively.

Keep in mind that a pipeline working in some capacity is better than no capacity, so having jobs defined as essential (our behavior validating tests) beforehand helps. Then, if an essential test is blocking the pipeline (for everyone), consider temporarily removing it from the suite while the issue is investigated.

There are many techniques to diagnose and fix issues that we will not get into here, but in general, remove the broken piece to unblock your pipeline, track its removal, fix it, and reinstate it.

Shared space

Consider the nature of your CI pipeline. It is like a break room that everyone shares. Everyone benefits, and everyone needs to clean up after themselves for it to continue adding value. For CI to serve a team's needs, it is the team's responsibility to promptly address CI issues.

Conclusion

We have covered many of the benefits our continuous integration pipeline provides, from rapid feedback and reduced troubleshooting costs to boosting development confidence and unlocking scalability for teams. A CI pipeline comes with some maintenance, but that cost buys us the key to sustainably adding change after change to our application without backsliding into broken features.

Now that we have our CI pipeline humming along, in the next chapter, we will dive into how it serves as a prerequisite for CD, allowing us to ensure quality while automating delivery to our users.

Join our Discord space

Join our Discord workspace for latest updates, offers, tech happenings around the world, new releases, and sessions with the authors:

https://discord.bpbonline.com

CHAPTER 8
Continuous Delivery

Introduction

This chapter explores the continuous deployment side of **continuous delivery (CD)** and its crucial role in consistently delivering value to production. We begin by exploring the fundamentals, and throughout, we will equip you with all the essential pieces and explain how they relate.

Objectives

The objectives are to understand:

- What is continuous deployment and continuous delivery?
- What are the common shapes of continuous delivery?
- When are we ready for fully automated deployments?
- Why is versioning crucial to automation and continuous delivery?
- Where do we store our artifacts for deployments?
- What are some common deployment patterns?
- How do we introduce or implement these deployment strategies?

Introduction to continuous deployment

Continuous delivery is the goal, while continuous deployment is the final stage that safely enables this. Only with proper testing will it be possible to deliver on the promise and value that *continuous delivery* will reduce risk and improve our efficiency. The following figure depicts the relationship between *continuous integration* and *continuous deployments* as *continuous delivery* components:

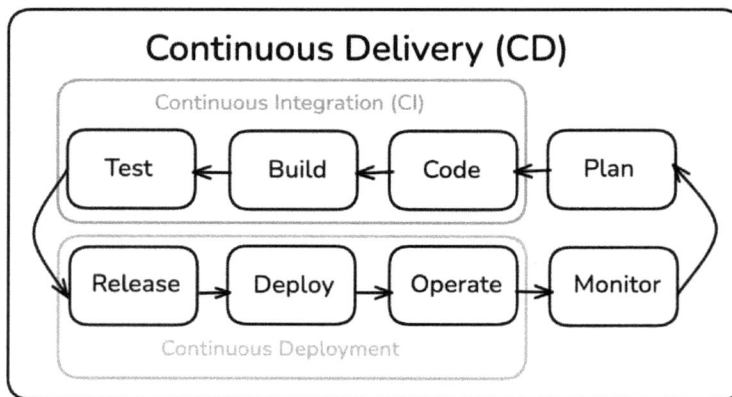

Figure 8.1: Continuous delivery requires implementing continuous integration and continuous deployment

The process of continuous deployment

Like runners handing off a baton in a relay race, our continuous integration pipeline hands off the baton to the continuous deployment pipeline. This transition marks the beginning of a phase commonly known as *release,* during which files are created and stored to support our next phase of *deployment*. This deployment phase involves provisioning our production compute capacity, which runs our application for end users.

Note: **For clarity, in this book, continuous delivery will often be referred to as CD, while continuous deployment will always be spelled out. They differ in that deployment is one piece of the delivery process.**

Shapes of continuous delivery

Our goal with setting up continuous delivery pipelines is to enable the organization to deploy as many changes as needed in a repeatable and quick manner. Some in the industry might say that *it is not continuous delivery if there are manual steps* or if it is below some frequency of deployment. Let us unpack those statements for a minute. While it is true that we strive to reduce the number of steps in our deployments, there are different ways to think about how to deliver. Our deployments may require several quality gates with automated and human reviews or approvals.

One common pattern for continuous delivery is to have the entire process orchestrated by our SCM, typically on the pull request, which we discussed in *Chapter 6, Understanding Pipelines, Collaboration techniques, Source Control Management, Pull Requests*. This includes code reviews with comments, which can act as soft gates, and test passes/failures, which can be either soft or hard gates. There are a lot of benefits to this. We get an audit trail of all the changes, the test results, the human code review, approvals or requests for change, etc., all in one place, and it is very natural for our developers.

We should consult with our developers to figure out what best suits them, as perhaps what we have in mind may not be the best shape for them. For example, an organization chatbot or communications platform could be the most appropriate option to consider when talking about systems that have been set up to pull the *latest* (which is generally unsafe for production) or a specific tag such as a version number, stability or environment indicator (such as *stable, testing, production*), etc., that are pulling on an interval to either update the existing system or bring up new resources to replace the current ones when we detect drift from the current state to the desired state can be a very simplified version of implementing continuous delivery and is not a bad place to start for our lower tier environments.

> Tip: **We need to be careful of caching when we contemplate retagging a new version of an asset with the same label; depending on the implementations, we might accidentally miss deployments we intended to receive. For example, pulling a container image tag from your artifact repository such as latest can yield different results on a fresh machine vs. one that has already queried and therefore cached, until busted or expired. Using version-specific tags rather than latest, production, or similar is safer and clearer to troubleshoot when multiple versions are deployed simultaneously. It avoids questions like, Which latest? Yours or mine?**

Should we never deploy manually?

After all that work to automate everything to this point, why would we stop here? We are so close to the promise of continuously delivering value to our customers; is there any reason we should pump the brakes?

One good reason has to do with the tradeoffs between confidence and speed. We recognize that not every team can transition from zero to fully automated overnight, so let us consider the use of manual steps as an instrument of that transition. Although it is likely we began our DevOps journey with many manual steps, it is our suggestion that these manual steps be replaced by automated ones incrementally until the limit of the team's comfort level is reached. This limit could take the form of retaining one or more manual steps that trigger a deployment. In any case, look to automate over time wherever possible.

While we should strive to provide robust pipelines, we must recognize that these are systems of software that run on hardware; they are susceptible to failure. When things go bump in the night, we need a way to manually kick off our automated deployments, even if it is inconvenient. Make sure we have documentation on how this is done. Why can continuous deployments only be done after successfully implementing CI?

While it is tempting to start here, I must warn against this. I have seen companies attempt to start with continuous deployment before proper testing and continuous integration are in place. The results, at best, lead to teams not wanting to deploy on Fridays, around demos, board meetings, etc. If we only automate our deployments without the appropriate testing and quality controls, we bring the deployments out quickly and often, regardless of the stability.

Storytime, versioning

Let us visit a scenario I have seen multiple times in my career, where real problems creep into production, having implemented continuous delivery on a portion of our infrastructure. We were using versioned artifacts, which we will discuss shortly. Even though we had implemented CI before our artifacts were published, there was a missing link. We had a mechanism that locked specific versions of artifacts in each environment. When we wanted to promote a new version, we would either open a pull request ourselves or rely on a chatbot to do the same. However, there was no validation that the versions inserted were valid. The first issue here is that we may insert a new version that does not exist (typically due to a typo), which results in our automation failing, but has little impact otherwise. The more dangerous scenario still often relies on a typo, but instead of it being an unknown artifact, it is an artifact version that was not intended (like accidentally pulling up **1.2** when we mean **12.0**). The problem is that the code had changed fundamentally in ways that, in one case, did considerable damage, which resulted in minor downtime. In some cases, some systems were able to be recovered by simply rolling back, and we needed to bring up new instances to restore the system entirely. This is an excellent opportunity to potentially insert a new input validation, automated test, or quality gate to ensure that this does not happen again.

Versioning

Does versioning have to be hard or complicated?

Opinion: A version number is nothing more than the communication of the program's evolution. I may be biased due to my long background in operations; however, I find that the only meaningful conventions focus on safely integrating modules.

What do we mean by that? We write code in distinct modules for portability, reusability, etc. Many times, there are dependency and compatibility concerns between modules. We will look at **Semantic Versioning (SemVer)** as the primary versioning scheme. We will focus on why having a good versioning scheme is important in the context of CD and what some things we should consider when looking for alternatives in the future.

SemVer

SemVer emphasizes communicating the impact of software changes from one version to another. This format uses several important concepts and strings them together. Before addressing it directly, let us consider the questions we would want to ask ourselves to understand the impact of the change.

Format

The format consists of several key components: a *major, minor,* and *patch* separated by a *dot (.)*, with optional *metadata*. Let us examine it more closely to understand why it is so powerful:

- **Major:** We use *major changes* any time the software has been changed in a way that makes it incompatible with previous versions. Many developers like to pretzel their way into saying something is not breaking. We probably all have heard the excuse after tracking down a bug with an upstream provider *that was not part of the publicly documented API,* as if that changes anything. Let us be clear, breaking is breaking; our customers do not care about how statistically unlucky they are when they happen to be part of the 100%, 10%, 1%, or 0.0001%, etc., of users impacted; *breaking is breaking!* In the context of continuous delivery, this is critical as we will be deploying our changes automatically; there is no human to evaluate if something else needs to change, regardless of how small it might be. It is only acceptable to break something intentionally without calling it a major change when a project has yet to reach a **1.0** milestone, which means we should not trust it for production usage. Prior to this, the project is considered unstable and should require rigorous testing for each version, as the API makes no compatibility promises. When using these dependencies, we should be pinned to specific versions until it reaches a certain level of maturity.

- **Minor:** We use *minor changes* any time we add new features, updates to existing features, and other miscellaneous updates to the project that are backward compatible and do not look to solve a known bug.

- **Patch:** We use *patch changes* any time a bug is fixed in a backward-compatible way. We must use a Major instead if we break something even while fixing a *bug.*

- **Optional labels:** We can use these *optional labels* for additional descriptions, commonly used in prerelease or release candidate stages.

- **Combined:** The format then looks something like this:

  `MAJOR.MINOR.PATCH-OPTIONAL_LABEL`

  What are some examples?

  `1.2.3`

  `1.2000.0`

```
1.2.3-rc1
1.2.3-$name
1.2.3-$buildnumber
1.2.3-$name-$buildnumber
```

Impact of versioning in continuous delivery

Why are these degrees of change important in the context of continuous delivery?

We need to keep our dependencies up to date. If we integrate with stable projects that clearly communicate when things are intentionally breaking, and we have good testing to catch any non-intentional changes, we should be able to pinpoint any new non-breaking change (major).

Pessimistic versioning

Many frameworks that have adopted *SemVer* have the concept of a *pessimistic version constraint*. We define an acceptable range rather than pinning to exact versions or accepting the latest.

Here are some examples:

```
1. # package name = acceptable versions
2. pkg1 = "~> 1.0" # at least 1.0 and less than 2.0
3. pkg2 = "~> 1.2" # at least 1.2 and less than 2.0
4. pkg3 = "~> 1.2.0" # at least 1.2.0 and less than 1.3
5. pkg4 = "~> 1.2.3" # at least 1.2.3 and less than 1.3
```

These allow operators to clearly outline their level of comfort and trust in a project regarding its upgrade strategy. For example, we probably never want to intentionally pull in a change when the developer tells us that they are aware of a breaking change.

Hint: **It is any time we cross a major version.**

Artifact management

This means different things depending on what our technology stack looks like. These would typically be the executables and configuration files in stacks where the code is compiled. Even in the context of interpreted languages, we have the code itself as an artifact; additionally, we can consider other types of assets that we could do dynamically but are more efficient statically, such as common *JavaScript* or *CSS*. As containers rose in popularity, many practitioners preferred to package their applications as a single artifact in the form of a container image (which is just a special **archive/zip/tar** file), representing the entire service with its necessary dependencies.

In other words, an artifact is nothing special; it is just something we store during our release phase and retrieve at deployment time. Good artifact management solutions allow

API support for specific format understandings (language/framework) and ad hoc HTTPS retrieval. If we are Python developers, please do not force us to learn Ruby to use your artifact storage product!

There is no one-size-fits-all; some companies like to have different artifact hosts for production and pre-production stages, while others prefer to use the same and rely on tagging mechanisms to denote whether the artifact is production-ready.

In addition to performance considerations, we should consider hosting external dependencies internally on our artifact management system to make ourselves more resilient to external failure or even support air-gapped (no internet) environments.

Understanding common deployment patterns

The rest of this chapter, until the summary, is geared towards the engineering audience. It is accessible to all but may not interest other personas as much [NOTE: **GOTO Chapter SUMMARY**].

As we explore automation further and start deploying more frequently, we need to ensure that our deployments do not disrupt our customers. To that end, let us explore different ways to roll out changes.

Immutable vs. mutable

In computer science, mutability is the ability of an object or resource to be changed or updated.

Mutable

When we can affect a resource without needing to create a new one, we refer to it as mutable. In the context of deploying systems, this refers to updating our existing resources (cloud, hosts, containers, configuration, processes, etc.). An example would be using an automation framework, such as Chef, Ansible, etc., to update the live-running system.

The pros are as follows:

- Easy to conceptualize.
- Efficient use of resources.
- Quick iterations during development.

The cons are as follows:

- It is harder to test changes.
- It is harder to roll back changes.
- Potentially slower deployments in specific use cases.

- Increasing risk of external dependencies causing issues. For example, an external API that needs to be hit.

- It requires a mechanism to detect and correct the configuration drift from the original defined state to whatever state it may be in.

Immutable

Well, if mutable means changeable without new resources, we can assume this means we need new ones for immutable deployments. The earliest examples of this were byte-level disk image deployments, which, with the rise of virtual machines and containers, became much easier to use in a practical manner. Please note that just because we have a container does not make it immutable. The deployment might be immutable; if we want to achieve real immutability, we must set the container's filesystem to be read-only.

The pros are as follows:

- Fast deployments
- Consistency
- Separation of build vs. deployment
- Rollback and recovery

The cons are as follows:

- Hard to conceptualize
- Increased cost (virtualization helps mitigate)
- Increased network traffic
- New deployments are inherently slower than applying an incremental update
- Data persistence is a greater challenge

Picking

Due to technological advances in virtualization, immutable deployment patterns have greatly advanced. Some people might say that immutable is always better. Is that always true, or is it only true for some organizations?

As an industry, much of our infrastructure has been shifted from mutable to immutable, especially given the rise of virtualization.

The notable exception is when the updates are so frequent that it becomes infeasible or undesirable to rebuild and deploy new resources every time a change is made.

Blue/green

In a blue/green deployment model, regardless of mutability, we have two groups of resources: blue and green. One group is currently serving customers' requests, and the other is for testing and validating our deployments. When customers are routed to the new deployments, the old resources remain available, even though they are not being used by customers anymore. If there are issues, we can reroute to the old group. We can completely remove the older group when we are confident there are no issues.

Rolling deploys

Rolling releases are a common deployment pattern. This involves slowly rolling out the new versions across our server fleet in groupings. For example, we could split our infrastructure into **n** groups and then deploy to each group serially until all are completed, halting if there is a problem.

This has many advantages. Through incremental updates, we can minimize disruption and impact while optimizing recovery by shrinking the *blast radius* to a smaller subset than if we had applied the update to all instances at once.

Canary deploys

This deployment pattern gets its name from the concept of using a canary in the coal mine to warn miners when they are approaching dangerous levels of toxic gases. We deploy our changes to a subset of the infrastructure and then monitor them. We will keep rolling them out only if we deem the change safe. Canary deployments rely on more observability data than rolling deployments to decide if they can move to the next one.

Reducing risk

These deployment strategies go hand in hand with our testing processes, reducing risk to our consumers. Below are a number of levers we have at our disposal.

Proactively communicating risk when making changes to a system

As we discussed in *Chapter 3, Automation, Communication,* we need to ensure that we notify all the relevant stakeholders in our planning phases. When we get closer to deploying our changes, we should again reach out and ensure that we communicate if we have learned anything new or if something has changed before we push it out. We should notify them again after we have deployed.

Failing forward or backward in the face of errors

We could probably debate this extensively and discuss a lot of nuance, but throughout my career, I have found that we must first answer the question, *Have we modified any state (such as data, schema, changed image names, etc.)?* This applies to all failure situations. To be clear, we are trading efficiency in some cases for safety in all cases, but the trade is ultimately more valuable in the long run when we are dealing with production problems.

Failing forward or backward has its benefits. If data has not been modified, it is typically safe to roll backward. However, the problem is compounded if the state has changed, as we may be doing more damage by rolling backward. The error needs to be addressed in the context of the current state. Otherwise, by returning to the original state, we risk a third state where the data has been modified, but the application does not know how to handle both formats.

When our new deployments fail, we should page an engineer to decide whether to proceed backward or forward.

Feature flags

What is the safest way to deploy changes? Deploy them in a way that does not affect system behavior until we signal otherwise. We do this by using *feature flags. T*hese allow us to change the code's behavior at runtime. This approach gives us faster recovery times, as we do not need to redeploy but instead simply flip a switch. There are many frameworks out there that allow us to define feature flags for a specific user, a percentage of users, the entire system, etc. We will explore this with the use of **pseudo code** to keep all audiences engaged:

```
1.  def feature_enabled(feature, user):
2.      # check for any number of enabled features
3.
4.      # lightsabers are tricky, only weapon masters
5.      # should use the new prototypes so that we can
6.      # sort out any of the design issues to ensure we
7.      # protect less skilled duelists
8.      if feature == 'prototype_lightsaber' && user.is_jedi_weapon_master
9.          return true
10.     else
11.         return false
12.
13. def prototype_lightsaber(user)
14.     if feature_enabled("prototype_lightsaber", user):
15.         # new feature
16.     else
17.         # feature is not available
```

In the *Star Wars* universe, lightsabers are incredibly difficult and dangerous (initially more to self) to wield and require extensive training, typically spanning multiple years in both *the force* and specific saber techniques before wielding them safely. In this case, we are working on an *experimental* new lightsaber; we only want it in the hands of a Jedi weapon master, and not just any Jedi. When we have worked out all the kinks in the lab and our quality assurance processes, the new prototype is safe to be used by any Jedi who wishes; we can remove the condition, making the feature available to everyone. Note that this is distinct from typical permissions in approaches such as **role-based access control (RBAC)**, even if we can use these as criteria. These feature flags can be enabled and disabled based on any criteria that make sense to a business or an operator.

Feature flags can be used for many different use cases; some of the most common are to assist us with rolling out features with limited impact, which are generally considered short-term, while others are meant to enable/hide a feature for maintenance, availability, and security needs. Feature flags allow us to define our logic and rely on an input, such as an environment variable, cookie, database record, request parameter, etc. When we write features behind short-term feature flags, it is critical when scoping the work that we include the cleanup of the flag once we have achieved our desired outcome.

- **Controlling feature rollout:** Often, product owners want to roll out a change while only impacting a small portion of our users. The simplest solution matches our pattern above with the lightsaber. It is only useful during its development and rollout and should be cleaned up when it no longer has value.

  o **Releases**: When we want to integrate incomplete and untested features into our target branch for production without impacting customers, these should be considered short-term and cleaned up shortly after completing the functionality and flipping the release to *on*.

- **Experimental:** When we develop new features and want to allow a subset of users access to a feature while preventing others from doing so, these are typically longer-lived feature flags. We may wish to collect information for several months before deciding whether to proceed.

  Our example with the lightsaber is a typical example of rolling out an experimental feature flag.

  An example of this is **A/B** testing. In short, this is when we want to ask our users whether **A** or **B** is better. However, they may not even know what they like until we present them. We do this by deploying functionality that presents users with either **A** or **B**. We capture data about the interactions and look to draw conclusions based on it. Once we have made our decision, we need to clean up. This can include removing the *dead code* and wherever the flags are being generated, such as environmental variables, database entries, configuration files, cookies, etc.

  Canary deployments are another common pattern that uses a feature flag to control the percentage of deployed resources.

  o **Kill switches**: Some feature flags are intended as *kill switches*[1] for products during outages or maintenance. Taking down a single feature to keep the rest of the application or system online is generally preferable. We should be careful about overusing this and keep this for critical features. As these are meant for long-term usage, cleanup is only needed once we no longer want to use the feature.

---

1 (Kill Switch)

     o   **Restricting access**: While our example feature flag with the lightsaber is technically more of an experimental feature flag, it also shares characteristics of permission feature flags. In short, we are specifying that the feature is only available to entities that have a particular role or permission assigned. These are considered long-term feature flags and are only removed once the feature is no longer needed.

Implementing deployment strategies

Typically, we deploy multiple environments prior to production to facilitate development and ensure quality. This should always be where we start with hooking up our CI and CD processes. Building our environments should follow the order in which our code advances: first development, then test, followed by staging, and lastly production, as outlined in *Chapter 7, Continuous Integration, Environments, Promotion*.

In the real world, before we take this to production, we pause to ensure that we have all the documentation, quality gates, observability, alerting, and processes ready to flip the switch. Near the end of our journey, we will dive into some burning questions to understand what happens once our applications are deployed in *Chapter 12, Observability, Taming monitoring, alerting, and on-call demons*.

Having met our criteria, we need to decide what human steps may still make sense in our process before deploying to production. While we can gain a lot of confidence in our automated testing run in our prior continuous integration pipeline prior to its deployment, we should consider which manual gate(s) will best facilitate our automated transition. Here, a gate could be represented as approval from someone responsible for QA or an action from SRE who has knowledge of our deployment availability.

Conclusion

We discussed the continuous deployment side of continuous delivery and why it is important that we work on this after continuous integration. As the frequency of our deployments rose, it became more important that we considered versioning schemas that communicated the impact of changes to ensure the safety of our automated processes. These packages are typically deployed to an artifact repository once all our quality gates have been cleared. We then looked at common deployment patterns to bring our strategy into reality, all while reducing the risk of errors. Finally, we delivered on the promise of continuously delivering value to our customers without sacrificing velocity or quality to get there. Our CD pipeline now provides a deployment that maintains high availability for our customers and users.

In the next chapter, we will be looking at how we can refine and master our pipelines to squeeze even more value out of them.

CHAPTER 9

Pipeline Mastery

Introduction

Now that we know how to create automated test workflows and deployments, let us consider how they come together. We will also examine how basic pipelines can be improved to maximize their value. All the distinct processes we have built up to this point serve an organization's overall goal or objective. Pipelines allow us to bring these concerns together. At the end of the day, customers are the indirect beneficiaries of pipelines and other engineering process enablers within an organization.

As we begin conceptualizing our pipeline scaling needs, we explore improvements that can be made. This includes optimizing the pipeline's configuration, addressing maintenance concerns, and optimizing the actual pipeline to squeeze out the last drops of efficiency. To avoid vendor-specific terminology, we will explore *job-streams* in the context of **continuous integration (CI)** and **continuous delivery (CD)** to help us improve.

Objectives

- Who benefits from pipelines?
- How do we improve our pipelines' efficiency, effectiveness, and scalability?
- How do we reduce the maintenance costs of our pipelines?

- What security concerns exist with pipelines, and how can we minimize risk as much as possible?

Everyone benefits from pipelines

As we discussed in *Chapter 1, Introduction to DevOps, Organizational silos, How busting silos makes life easier, Customer focus*, we often have multiple types of customers that we are supporting. It is important to determine who we serve and in what priority when we are unable to satisfy them all at once. Depending on the nature of our team, that can change. The following hierarchy is just one example (which is recommended):

Who (needs)	Priority (lowest value is most urgent)
External customers	0
Internal customers within our organization	1
Immediate team	2

Table 9.1: A priority matrix helps us know who to serve first when multiple problems arise

This customer hierarchy is important enough to be included in a team's mission statement or reason for existence.

Pipelines can be improved over time. Their scope and depth should increase as the need becomes apparent. On that note, do not worry about upending our current process to implement a large, sophisticated pipeline. It is most important to consider whether we have automated the task of running our tests, and then consider what other supporting tasks could also be automated.

Transparency

Earlier, we discussed the need for *job-stream* naming conventions, which we will discuss in more detail here. A naming convention helps anyone in the organization view a *job-stream* and get a general idea of what is going on.

Single responsibilities

We may have seen *job-streams* that perform multiple types of setup, testing, and artifact creation, all within a single job named **Main** or **Pipeline**. What does that job actually do? Should we conclude that such a job does everything? Would it not be nice to know without digging through the config details? Even if it is not all maintained within a single job, I have seen ambiguous names like **check_js**, while another job in the same *job-stream* was called **run_js_tests**. Not knowing with any certainty what a job does means we cannot trust our names and must inspect each job configuration for clarity. We suggest saving valuable time by defining job name prefixes as a lead to help others (and our future self) navigate the many *job-streams* we will likely review.

There is a lot of flexibility here, but consider placing boundaries on a job's activities with a naming scheme like this:

`<type>_<concern>_<utility>_<whatever_else_you_like>`

Please keep in mind that this specific scheme and the examples below are not prescriptive but rather should give us an idea of what names make sense to our team. The goal is to increase the readability of our *job-streams* at a high level, which is bolstered by a consistent and clear separation of activities.

General job activities	Suggested job names
Assemble resources for downstream	`build`, `setup`, `setup_js_assets`
Test functional behavior	`run_js_tests`, `test_js_unit`
Test non-functional behavior	`check_a11y`, `check_quality_sonar`
Create artifacts for use within the CI	`generate_report`, `generate_test_coverage`
Create artifacts for use outside of CI	`publish_image_dockerhub`, `publish_gem`

Table 9.2: Example job names based on function

Make sure our *job-streams* naming convention begins with high-level specifics. Do not waste characters, as the full name will likely be visually cut off in many situations.

Small job-streams

Each job usually involves some computational overhead, such as pulling down dependencies, hitting the cache, spinning up services, etc.

Accordingly, it does not always make sense to split a job if the duration of the overhead is greater than the work performed! In these situations, it is reasonable to make an exception by having a single job do everything and naming it **build**, **main**, or some other indicator that we are doing everything at a small scale. The assumption is that the configuration for such a job stream is also small and easily understandable. Configs have a way of growing in size and complexity.

How do we know when to split a single **build** job into multiple prefixed jobs? This is a judgment call, but a recommended rule of thumb is that an all-inclusive job with up to three responsibilities should be considered the maximum. Responsibilities like setup, test, and report should be considered the maximum, and adding another type of test should trigger the split of the job stream into jobs with single responsibilities.

Cultural balance and critical path(s)

It is reasonable that a CI pipeline's most important role is to integrate changes through tests. Following that logic helps us decide what is critical to pass within our pipeline and what should be considered optional quality gates. Pipelines can branch and split to form many paths of connected jobs throughout their *job-streams*. If tests are critical to our CI pipeline, then at a minimum, we can trace a path between our connected test jobs to form a critical path. This path represents a *hard gate* that must be passed before changes are merged. It ensures our *job-stream* outcomes are concise to a strict measure of pass or fail and clear-as-day to our developers if their changes have achieved the right level of quality. The following figure depicts a job-stream with a failure, but it can continue without stopping:

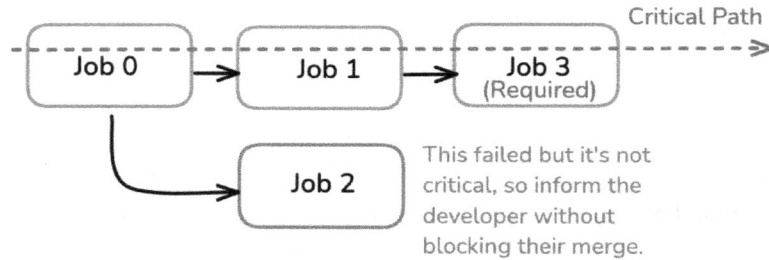

Figure 9.1: *A job-stream with a failure on an optional job that does not block the pipeline*

Notice how **Job0** and **Job1** are *implicitly* required because they are dependencies of the *explicitly* required **Job3**. The more jobs we tag as required, the more maintenance we will have to budget to keep everything running smoothly.

Scaling

Let us consider how this approach works in a large organization with many teams, apps, and pipelines. Some teams will likely see linting or style checks as *critical*, or a certain level of coverage, as *critical* to maintaining. This reality puts us at a junction where we must decide between team flexibility and *job-stream* standards. Hmm, tough spot! We do not want to let teams dictate what is required on the flexibility front since this compromises our quality standards with bias. On the other hand, we do not want to be the caretakers of fickle teams that continually shuffle around required jobs! With a simple technique, we can facilitate flexibility while minimizing the cost of shuffling required jobs.

Select or create a job that is farthest downstream in our *job-stream* and identify it as critical (i.e., required). Then, for whatever job is critical, specify that job as a dependency on the required job. Now, managing what is critical needs to be specified only in the structure of the *job stream's* configuration, free of edits to SCM rules, Terraform, or any other external governance.

External team maintaining CI (Omakase)

The CI/CD configuration must have clear ownership. That said, we would not recommend that multiple teams within an organization each manage their own CI/CD configuration, even though they contribute to it. This will result in every configuration having its own standard, which is synonymous with an organization having no standard. As teams and organizations reach a certain size, it becomes valuable for a single contributor or team to uphold pipeline standards to minimize collaborative overhead. This also ensures best practices propagate organization-wide. If a contributor claims that standards does not matter, be sure they are responsible for regular pipeline maintenance; otherwise, they can be safely ignored.

One structure of CI/CD management that has proven its value is a team dedicated to its development and maintenance. This can be seen as something of an *omakase* approach, where the experts promote and implement best practices for all things CI/CD. The developers then trust the CI/CD team's judgment, and the organization gains transparency, efficiency, and cost savings.

Another approach is to have a couple of engineers get together and determine best practices for our organization, and rely on embedded engineers, or a hybrid of both; either way, we want to reduce the cognitive overload on the product and infrastructure engineers when creating good CI and CD pipelines.

Quick wins and low-hanging fruit

Here are a series of *quick wins* and *low-hanging fruit* that we can generally apply to existing pipelines to improve their security, resiliency, performance, and our producer and consumer experiences.

Simplify test encryption

Our app should use strong hash algorithms to secure passwords, but only for some [1] tests in our ephemeral CI environments! The test data is and should be completely disposable, and also, the computational work required to hash a password should be purposefully set to the minimum.

Depending on how you secure passwords, check the library you are using for hash algorithms (such as **BCrypt** or **Argon2**) and make sure our test environment is set to the minimum cost, saving valuable computation time for disposable passwords.

Assets worthy of caching

There are many opportunities to cache information in a CI/CD context. To begin assessing these, we need to ask two questions:

What should we cache? While this depends on our organization and tech stack, here is a good place to start:

- First, we should examine dependencies, which typically change far less frequently than our app's behavior, while simultaneously requiring every *job stream* run.

---

1 Tests that specifically verify password hash related behavior should be preserved with careful consideration.

- Static asset images like `.jpg`, `.jpeg`, `.gif`, `.png`

- A very different type of image, like large container and virtual machine images, should be our next priority in the cache.

- Building artifacts is another great candidate, but be careful. It is easy to create unused artifacts, wasting resources. Consider invalidating the cache when a fresh-built artifact is desired.

- In general, look for files frequently required by the pipeline but changed infrequently. Dependencies like this are a happy hunting ground for caching opportunities.

Where should caching take place in the context of a pipeline? While this depends on our organization's needs and tech stack, we can start with any of these places:

- **Artifact management solution:** Caching our external dependencies on an asset host, which could be the artifact management solution we are using.

- **Web server:** Specifically for caching Ruby gems, Python packages, modules, or direct dependencies. The goal is to isolate failures and improve performance.

- **Localized cache:** Many CI/CD solutions can offer a cache to move temporary artifacts that are leveraged during the pipeline process to facilitate shared storage between multiple jobs, but are discarded once all the *job-streams* have been completed.

Tip: **To help conceptualize this, we can think of a minimum caching solution, such as storage and networking, to speed up our pipelines and reduce running costs. This can be as simple as cloud blob storage, a web server, etc.**

Sizing our runners appropriately

There are several factors to consider when selecting the resource profile of our runners, listed as follows:

- The speed of test suite growth. If our test suite grows relatively fast or unpredictably, we may want to size our runner for extra margin. If our runners' utilization is between 80% and 90% for a given job, bumping the resource size to a lower utilization (e.g., down to 60%) may add reaction time. It is amazing how strange the failures can be when a server reaches 100% utilization.

- The variability of current performance. Runners who share resources often have inconsistent performance between runs. This is due to the other tenants competing for those resources unpredictably. Consider the peak of our utilization as our reference point when allocating extra margin.

- The effect of parallelism. Sometimes, our runners are sized according to an expensive operation, such as pre-compiling assets. Ask if this operation must be performed in multiple jobs/containers or if it can be performed in a single job. There could be an opportunity to perform the expensive operation once, then cache it for consumption by multiple jobs downstream.

The resources available to our runners should fit like kid shoes, with room to grow.

Fail fast

The faster we realize a test will fail or a bug is in our application, infrastructure, or system, the cheaper it is to fix it. So, the name of the game is to *fail as fast as possible*. Almost. There are different schools of thought regarding leveraging a fail-fast approach, and teams can get into a pattern of waffling between them. The opposing view to failing fast usually involves the argument that all failures should be discovered in a single job-stream run, with the goal of fixing all failures at once. On the surface, this sounds efficient. However, the argument does not consider that fixing one bug can create or surface another entirely new one.

We recommend running as many tests in parallel as possible, but stop the build immediately when a blocking failure is discovered.

Stack the jobs

Favor short *job-streams* by running your jobs in parallel *stacks*. Maximizing parallelism in a *job-stream* structure requires understanding each job's dependencies. As soon as a job's dependencies are satisfied, it should be run. This means static analysis of our codebase can pull down our repository and run immediately. When a large, expensive operation is complete, everything that depends upon it should be run. You may have heard the phrase *A dollar waiting on a dime* before. We do not want any jobs in our job-stream waiting unnecessarily for jobs that are not truly a dependency! Squish job-streams into tall, pancake-looking structures wherever possible, such as in the following figure:

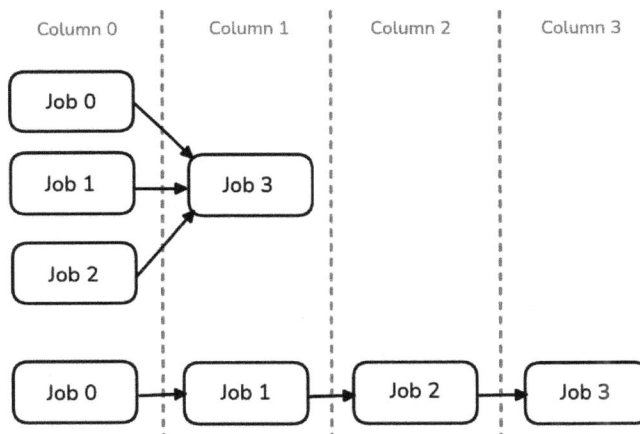

Figure 9.2: A squished job-stream with parallelization

The above diagram illustrates how we can cut our overall *job-stream* runtime in half. To realize a gain of this scale, the workload must be balanced across each parallel job. Even an imperfect balance can offer significant time savings. The blue numbered columns are just a point of reference to highlight the sequential nature of our pipeline.

Boost confidence

Running jobs in parallel can have utility beyond execution speed. In a scenario where a language upgrade is taking place, some tools offer convenient syntax to define *matrix builds*. This is where our test suite can be run against different language versions. Although this can dramatically increase the compute time, a *job-stream* that addresses this concern is very useful. It gives developers confidence that their changes are both forward and backward-compatible. Depending on your selected system and availability, consider implementing matrix builds for any critical upgrade, GitFlow, or versioned release planned.

Everything should finish at the same time

Running our tests is the common case we have in mind here. This is due to the nature of the work involved, which is typically a set of similar activities (the tests) with common dependencies. Just like a pipeline can only be completed once its jobs are finished, a job can only be completed once all its processes are finished. Whether virtual machines or containers facilitate these processes, the goal is the same: they all need to finish at the same time to maximize efficiency.

To illustrate how parallelism can play out in different ways, let us look at some perfectly balanced examples that happen to run their processes within containers:

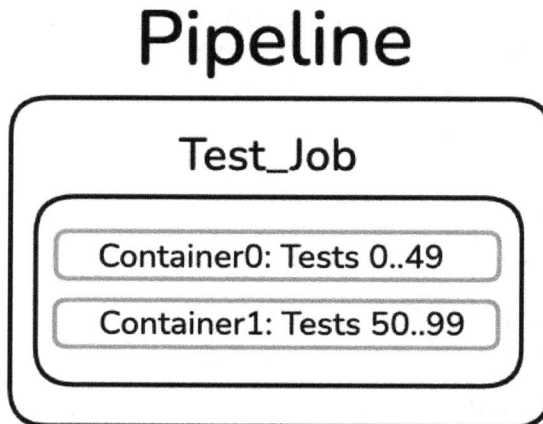

Figure 9.3: *Putting our test suite execution across two containers within the same job*

Above, our tests are evenly split between two containers in a single job and finish at the same time.

Pipeline

Test0_Job

Container0: Tests 0..49

Test1_Job

Container1: Tests 50..99

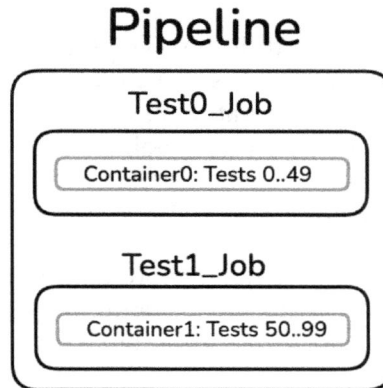

Figure 9.4: *Putting our tests in distinct jobs with their own containers*

In *Figure 9.4*, two jobs run in parallel using a single container. Within these simplified scenarios, the outcomes are the same: all the tests are completed around the same time.

Let us explore our container a little more. The runtime of our container depends on the total duration of the tests within. Some tests can take a long time, while others might run quickly. Knowing the duration of each test allows us to balance the tests between containers. This way, we can split them evenly between containers and further split containers between jobs if we choose.

Now, let us consider a situation where parallel jobs are *not* completed at the same time. Here, we represent the container runtimes within each job as a green bar, where the length indicates its duration. The work performed in *Job 0* is unbalanced between its two containers. This causes a domino effect of delaying job completion and subsequently delays the whole pipeline, illustrated as follows:

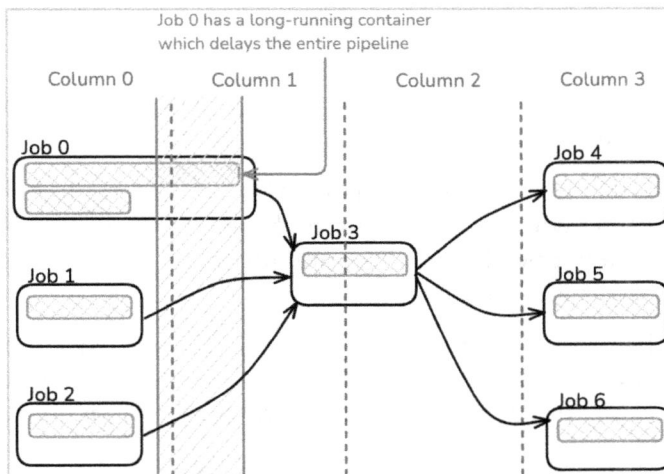

Figure 9.5: *A process in Job 0 is a bottleneck that affects our entire pipeline performance*

Depending on our tools, balancing the workload of tests between containers could be variable and may not always be worth it, but we will focus on the ones that merit the effort. There are many ways to balance tests, which we will not go into detail in the book, but in essence, we need to track the duration of each test and assign those tests to our containers in groups whose total duration is equal.

Optimizing project structure

This might seem silly to call out, but talking about a project's layout is essential. A well-planned layout can simplify collaboration. For example, rather than grouping all logic into a single or small set of files/directories, consider breaking them down to allow for better collaboration.

Many systems leverage some form of the *CODEOWNERS* concept. This allows us to define a set of rules that map sections of our repository to specific owners so that we can use them to ensure we get reviews; we get them from all the relevant parties. Instead of pinging everyone on the engineering teams all the time, we get the best review by asking the specific **subject matter expert** (**SME**) teams. This also will greatly help us when we talk about building pipelines to help meet security and compliance needs by tying these reviews to quality gates.

Good structure can also help with a wide range of useful improvements. For example, instructing our linters not to be as sensitive on our testing files as we would be with our production code.

Yet another benefit of well-defined project structures is that they promote easy targeting of test groups to optimize CI jobs. For example, if your test suite has unit, integration, and end-to-end tests organized in their respective directories, we can target those directories when running related jobs.

Consider automatic re-runs

Let us define a *re-run* as running a test twice without changing app logic, behavior, or configuration in between.

Sometimes, when a test fails, we are tempted to run it a second time, hoping it will pass. This is a *code-smell*. Something within the behavior of the app or the test itself is unpredictable, and either the app behavior needs to change, and the test is correct, or the test needs to be fixed to behave in a deterministic way.

We recognize that there are different schools of thought about re-running tests. Although there might be good business reasons for doing so in certain circumstances, *the need to continue* should generally be considered tech debt rather than long-term sustainable.

At worst, rerunning will hide poorly written tests from sight, which will only be discovered later. When the need to rerun our tests lengthens our *job stream* beyond what is practical, the pipeline becomes blocked. We will call this phenomenon *re-run overload*. At this point, there is no quick fix that also upholds quality. Fixing usually ends with fixing the most important tests and throwing away the rest, diminishing test coverage and deployment confidence.

Re-run overload

To the team that is facing this exact problem, we would suggest the following actions depending on the urgency of the situation:

- **Low urgency:** Mark the worst offending *test examples* as *skipped*, then create tickets to track their status and spread the workload of fixing them. Prioritize the workload for the next available work cycle.

- **High urgency:** We will want to consider this approach with our team's comfort level in mind. One method to unblock a pipeline immediately is to skip each *test file* where the failure occurs. This is to avoid situations where test examples within a file surface and fail one at a time. This requires multiple pull requests and multiple *job-stream* runs, which are likely undesirable in this situation. Once resolved, it is important to put forth the effort of restoring the test suite. This should involve reactivating (I.e., unskipping) the relevant test files and proceeding to process failures according to the Low Urgency guidance previously described.

Some CI tools and test frameworks advertise *automatically* rerunning tests as a feature. This feature, however, is more like a Band-Aid, where it can help in the short term but bite us in the long term. When automated, these Band-Aids can accrue outside of our view and block our pipelines with re-run overload at the least opportune moments.

Under the best circumstances, rerunning a test should be done with human intentionality, out of business necessity, with plans to fix it immediately.

Only run job-streams when necessary

To avoid wasting resources (such as time, money, and developer time), we should only run job-streams when it is valuable. Here are some opportunities to optimize this:

- **Auto-cancel:** See if the CI configuration options include *Auto-cancelling* redundant pipeline runs. Consider the situation where a developer makes rapid commits to a repository. If each commit kicks off a *job-stream*, you could run multiple overlapping *job-streams*, which is not usually of great value. As a bonus, ensuring only one *job-stream* runs at a time per developer per project makes it much easier to determine the pipeline's current pass/fail state.

- **Leveraging rules:** Let us focus on *job-streams* that should only run under special circumstances. Running a *job-stream* when we do not need to is like leaving the lights on after leaving a room. It is a waste. We should only run our CI *job-streams* when it makes sense. Regulating when the appropriate *job stream* is triggered goes by many names depending on our framework, some of which include *rules*, *filters*, and *schedules*. These simple conditions specified within our CI/CD configuration determine when a specific *job-stream* in our pipeline runs.

- **Alternative rules:** There are situations where it may be desirable to trigger a *job-stream* in ways outside of the configuration itself. This could take the shape of an approval that must be clicked within the *job-stream* UI itself. Also, marking a branch or commit with specific text (for example, **"[CI Ready]"**), a label, a tag, or any purposeful indicator that can be detected is useful here. In these latter cases, the agent that detects a marker and subsequently triggers a *job-stream* can be a chatbot or command line interface.

In larger applications, the opportunities can be abundant regarding small changes that translate to significant savings. For instance, if a developer commits changes to a Readme file, we do not want to run a lengthy *job-stream* of 20+ minutes to verify app behavior that should not have changed! For lengthy *job-streams*, consider adding a way to verify intentionality and throttle its use based on necessity.

Scaling our pipeline configuration

We now understand how to build pipelines, but how do we scale their configuration?

Our pipeline definitions should be in code

As we discussed in *Chapter 3, Automation, Automate all the things!, Everything as code*, we realize that manually defining our configuration is an exploratory action. This becomes apparent as we need to scale many various tasks. The goal is the same whether we define it centrally within the CI system or rely on the project to contain its own CI instructions. We want to ensure that we can clearly communicate what the *job-streams* are, collaborate on them, and meet the scale of our organization's pipeline needs.

Copy/Paste

Any pre-existing CI/CD configuration within an organization will be used by default as the basis for the next project's configuration. This is manageable for a small team with only a few projects since a broad update needs only to be copied to a few other places. As we might have guessed, this is not a scalable practice. If our organization is large and has hundreds of projects, then we will find ourselves in a difficult situation. For maintainers of CI/CD configuration, updates will likely get missed or implemented incorrectly due to the similar but different nature of these many projects. What is worse is that others within the organization will continue to copy and paste configurations from existing ones, even while we are in the process of rolling out updates. Now, we are hustling to clean up their changes, which, at best, is inefficient. We need a way to limit the number of places from which the implementation of our configuration can be copied. Moreover, we need a single source of truth that can be reused across the organization.

Pipelines making pipelines

When brainstorming this section, the factory scene in *Star Wars: Attack of the Clones*, where *C3-PO* says, *Machines making Machines. How perverse.* came to mind. Since pipeline definitions are little more than instruction sets, we should be able to templatize our configuration. Whether this is done with a vendor-specific mechanism (such as a plugin) or whether we directly templatize our configuration is irrelevant; what matters is that we have a mechanism to scale the needs to create similar pipelines with different inputs, such as project names, environments, etc.

Keep it composable at the project level

To manage our growing complexity, take stock of the tools available. Does your CI/CD framework offer a way of defining reusable configuration units? It might be called an *orb*, *shared action*, or *component*, for example. In general, these concepts provide a way to define a common section of configuration that can be reused across projects. This powerful feature opens up the ability to manage changes to a single concern in a single place for all relevant configurations! Consider an organization with *hundreds* of projects. If a better way to cache dependencies is implemented on one project's config, similar work will need to be done on all relevant projects to scale that benefit. With a composable configuration, the special tools, the scripts, and the manual labor involved in rolling out these changes disappear. Here is an example of what this could look like:

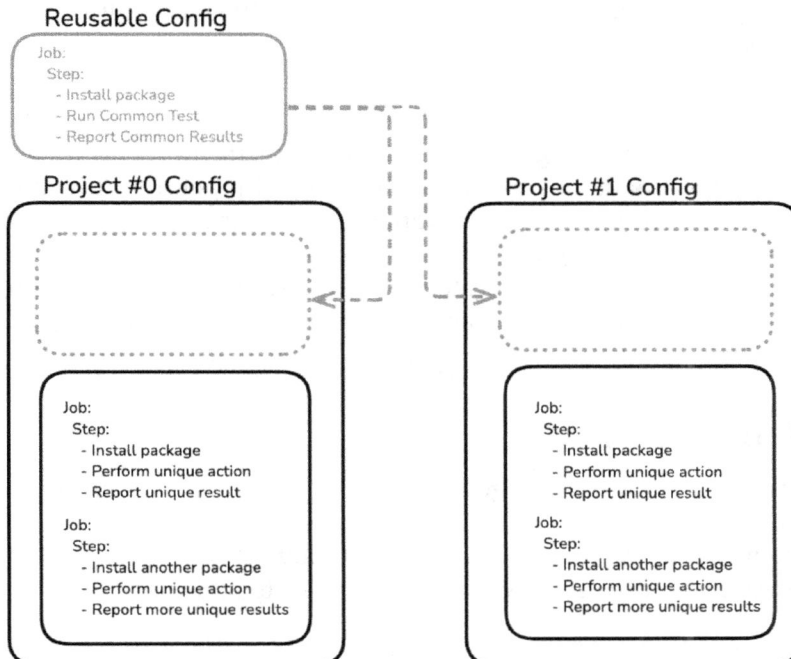

Figure 9.6: Reusable configuration can improve jobs with similar needs

Keep it composable at the file level

At a lower level, our CI/CD framework should be able to define reusable groups of steps within a single configuration file. This can significantly reduce the need to define the same concerns multiple times within a large configuration. Like rolling out changes across projects, reusable groups can update a piece of your configuration once and passively multiply its benefit everywhere that piece is referenced.

Dealing with large chunks of config

There are situations where even composable pieces of configuration can become lengthy and difficult to break up. If a configuration section is irreducibly complex, consider moving the instructions into a script and labeling the configuration piece and file with a descriptive name. An example might be waiting for a database to become available and then performing actions like loading or creating. This could all be performed under a script titled **prepare_database.sh**. We have seen configurations that are thousands of lines long, and when configurations are difficult to read, they become a barrier to contributors.

Go higher if we need to

Some tasks might be easier to develop and maintain with higher-level languages beyond our default operating system shell scripting language. For example, if our script needed to perform API calls, make a complex set of decisions based on that response, and post JSON data for tracking metrics, we could wrap all of this up in a configuration snippet called **gather_test_metrics**.

Dynamic configuration

Generating and managing configurations can be cumbersome in an organization, with hundreds or even thousands of repositories needing CI pipelines. A feature that allows for dynamic configuration, that is, generating configuration files automatically based on project contents, can add significant value, especially when there are many ways of performing the same task. In a large-scale setting such as this, dynamic configuration can provide standards and reduce maintenance costs for our CI pipelines organization-wide.

These concepts apply whether we use an externally hosted CI solution or self-hosting.

Isolate dependencies

We discussed broad artifact management earlier, but more specifically, we want to highlight the benefits of copying those dependencies into our project and checking them into version control. This follows the principle of moving issue discovery *as close to your development environment as possible*, where it is cheapest to address.

Sean says: *At a previous company, I used to get pushback from some folks about packaging/ installing dependencies bundled with the application code. This was to isolate pipelines from external calls failing. Managing dependencies this way can be slightly more labor intensive, and I could see* *their point when version conflicts inevitably surfaced. What some folks did not fully appreciate, including myself at the time, was the durability this approach brought in times of crisis. A long time after defending and maintaining dependency isolation, another team responsible for managing artifacts mentioned how our isolated/cached dependencies saved their hides during service outages. Being so well isolated, I was unaware they'd been having issues!*

Valid reasons not to put our dependencies in SCM

In deploying our applications, we see the value of isolating our dependencies by ensuring smooth deployments even when there is upstream disruption. We must decide which dependencies are appropriate to isolate rather than consume externally.

We will assume that a package manager of some form is used on our project, with version selection and dependency locking to ensure compatibility between developers and environments:

- **License Compliance and Terms of Service (TOS):** Ensure compliance with any restrictions or attributions among our dependencies. For example, a proprietary package may require us only to download it from a specific distribution infrastructure and may not redistribute it with our own mechanisms.

- **Security status:** Verify any vulnerabilities that pose a risk to our project.

- **Types of dependencies:** Not all dependencies are appropriate for all source control methods, since some platforms are only optimized to handle text.

- **Size of dependencies:** If a dependency is quite large, it might not be worth the tradeoffs involved with including it in the project.

- **Documentation:** Make sure our project has clear instructions on setting up a development environment, including installing dependencies.

Operational maintenance

Here, we will look at some suggestions to improve operational maintenance on our pipelines.

Rotating our focused attention

The aspects surrounding pipeline management are very different from those of building a pipeline. The task's duration is key, since building a pipeline takes a relatively short time, whereas managing a pipeline can continue indefinitely. Each aspect we discuss should be the focus of an individual or team and prioritized such that each is actioned on a regular rotation, as illustrated in the following figure:

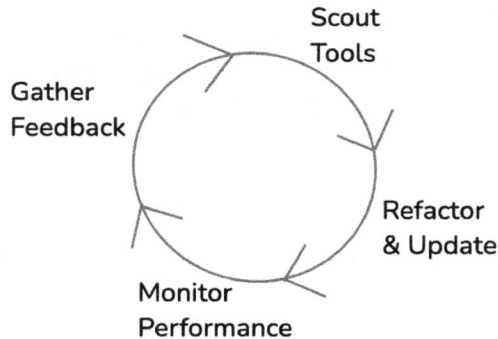

Figure 9.7: *Cycle attention to various aspects in improving the operational maintenance of our pipelines*

Monitor performance

We suggest monitoring performance as a first maintenance step after the pipeline is built. We need to monitor benchmarks for speed, failure rate, and cost at a minimum to avoid major issues that could be avoided with just a small amount of observability. I have seen improvements added to pipelines that accidentally disabled their ability to fail, nullifying the pipeline's value! How would we notice that every run was passing without monitoring? Fortunately, in this case, the issue only lasted several days before it was caught, and only had a handful of minor failures to fix. Issues that surface from monitoring should be worked into regular work cycles, while urgent issues should be dealt with immediately. We will take a deeper look when we discuss observability.

Gather feedback

Feedback from our developers can be gathered simply by asking questions about the pipeline's readability, speed, and usefulness in catching bugs. Any face-to-face gathering is perfect for this, while video meetings can be a good second option. When interviewing users, we should prefer open-ended questions to allow the users to tell us what they want, avoid our own biases, and prepare for an unpopular opinion; some examples include *How is CI/CD treating you?*, *What can we do to improve?*, and *What do you dislike the most about the current system?* This is a happy hunting ground for improvements, and confirming CI/CD benefits are being received as intended. Gather feedback at every opportunity.

Scout for tools

There are tools, features, and improvements popping up every day. Imagine the loss felt when realizing we have been doing something the hard way for years! Reading tech news regularly is not good enough; it can be a springboard that piques our interest and leads to further investigation. As painful as it might seem, we need to get to know our rival tools and refresh our knowledge regularly. We recommend setting aside time either as an individual habit or formal team process to find, play with, and understand tools that are new (or new to us) on a regular basis. Familiar with *GitHub + GitHub Actions*? Try *GitLab + GitLab*. Think we know all about *CircleCI* or *Jenkins*? Try *BuildKite, Spinnaker, Azure Pipelines*, etc. This is a great candidate for prioritization using *Friday Tasks* or similar.

Refactor and update

Although the previous activities require study, research, and dialogue, it is now time to update your code and configs to make a real impact on your project. Refactor and update your configurations with all the insights we have gathered in the previous steps regularly. Be aware that your regular goals have a variety of maintenance activities, or our CI/CD system will get stuck in a rut.

Optimizing pipelines

Here are some additional optimizations that we can use to improve our pipelines.

Review from various teams

As we briefly mentioned, the separation of responsibilities and *CODEOWNERS*, there are good reasons why we might need to have multiple teams review a change set to ensure that it brings good outcomes to the customers. The more we automate without testing, the more we free up our reviewers to focus on their domain of expertise and not get distracted by checking out other potential blockers. The same is true about having checklists of baseline requirements, which will be very useful for security and compliance teams to ensure that the needs are met while making it easier and faster for our teams to bring out products. You might be wondering how this is possible. We will explore this in *Chapter 5, Security, Where does Security fit into DevOps?, Building blocks for reusability and encapsulation*.

Quality gates

There is a difference between rules and quality gates that should be noted. Rules determine which *job-streams* run and when, but the spirit behind them is to orchestrate *job-streams* for the sake of efficiency. In contrast, a quality gate requires a certain outcome before advancing the software life cycle. Rules can easily be subverted, but quality gates on the other hand should be difficult.

Ideally, if a quality gate is worth implementing, it should be done as a hard gate. Soft gates are a concession to the fact that there is no practical way of enforcing them. A soft gate should only be implemented to tie these ideas together when there is a strong justification, despite it being impossible to enforce fully. An example of using a soft gate could be the point where only human eyes can determine if software should proceed to the next lifecycle step. These situations sometimes arise when an extensive amount of automation has been applied, and software cannot easily determine the intention behind a change.

Tip: **As both soft and hard gates are conditions that determine whether we can proceed, permissions may very well come into play. Consider that a hard gate on an admin in a system is more of a soft gate, as they can circumvent the protections we have put in place.**

Security considerations

Pipelines run on platforms with internal and public interfaces; just like applications, they are vulnerable to bad actors. Environment variables (variables specific to our deployment), credentials (access keys, username + password, etc.), our **intellectual property** (**IP**), and the automated systems that leverage them to get work done are all subject to being exposed or misused without careful attention. Attackers are looking for systems with high levels of permissions and the ability to move laterally, making CI and CD systems a juicy target. With these considerations in mind, we need to tightly control access to these systems. The more granular capabilities a service offers, the more likely that security teams will approve additional debug capabilities. Some pipeline services provide **Secure Shells** (**SSH**), **Remote Desktop Protocol** (**RDP**), **Virtual Network Computing** (**VNC**), etc., access to our CI servers (available + usable), while others intentionally do not choose to offer such access. As these pose risks to our organizations, we need to ensure that we review these options and decide whether we should allow these features even if they are available.

Ultimately, we must make an informed choice to balance these considerations based on the nature of our project, the culture and resources of our organization, and the availability of services that can be procured externally or in some cases, built internally.

Security and compliance stages

We previously discussed how, during our CI process, we will create security and compliance testing. Depending on our customer's needs, these will be integrated into our overall pipeline, and our organization failing to meet these requirements should result in the pipeline failing the build and preventing it from reaching production until it is addressed. For example, we may want to prevent a build from making it into production if it introduces a security vulnerability higher than a desired threshold. Typically, these security and compliance steps are behind a quality gate. While we always start with using a soft gate, our goal is to get into a state where we can move it to a hard gate. We do need to be careful and take a scalpel rather than a sledgehammer; we certainly do not want to block a production push because of a low-impact security finding.

Tests vary in value

Remember our conversation about how tests are all about value? When we make a change, the first tests we should run are written specifically to cover *that* change. This is because they specifically protect the changed file's behavior. We still need to run the entire suite to ensure we did not break anything else, right? Let us pause for a moment to look at what makes a test worth running.

If a feature's most valuable tests directly cover its behavior, then it stands to reason that tests become less valuable as they become less related to that feature. Their value decreases as their degree of separation increases. The degrees of separation are more evident with a dependency graph, such as the following one:

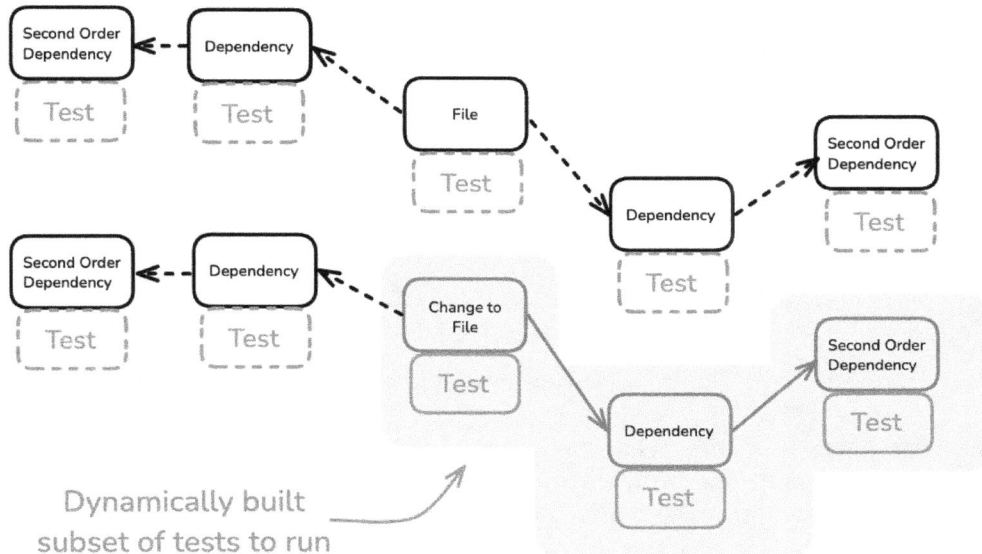

Figure 9.8: *Graph showing the relationship of a file change to its downstream impacts on dependencies*

Shopify engineers pioneered a new approach[2] to determine which tests should be run rather than simply running them all. At its core, they dynamically build a dependency graph to track the relationships between the tests and the code. A roster of tests is then determined based on the graph, which is a subset of the full test suite. They found that they could cut down on 25% of their *job-stream* runtime by running only tests related to changes, and with only a 0.06% rate of failed tests that should have run. They decided that the speed and cost improvements were worth the risk of a few failures going temporarily undetected. In other words, the risk-to-reward ratios made sense; it was a good value.

We are not advocating that we should not run our entire test suite. Still, knowing that a test's value depends on multiple factors, including its quality and relevance to our change, is important. If a team is willing to allow a fraction of failures to pass, then their risk tolerance might be compatible with Shopify's approach.

Benchmarking today's issues

Other industries put time towards assessing their risk tolerance, and likewise, we recommend teams consider their comfort threshold in the context of their own product. The following example is a way to visualize risks to our software project:

---

2 (Xie, 2020)

Risk Assessment Chart

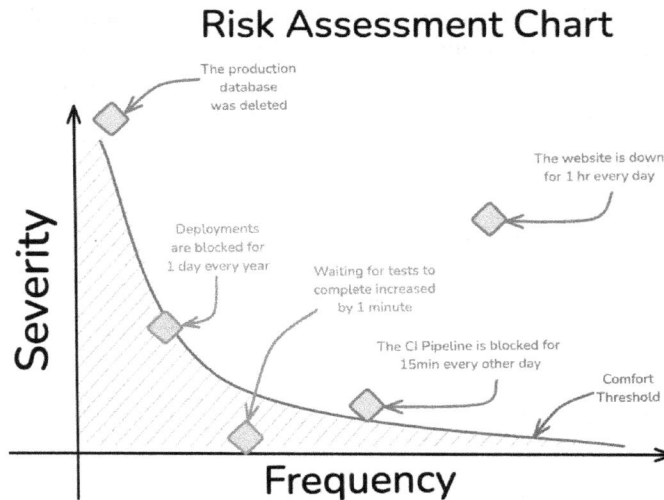

Figure 9.9: A graph illustrating the severity and frequency of an event for risk assessment

This exercise helps us define what matters to our team in the context of our product. Assuming there is only one product in question, we list the issues that potentially (or currently) affect it and place them on the chart.

Inspecting our axis, *Severity* is just a relative level of how bad the issue might be, and *Frequency* refers to how often it occurs. The scales are relative and do not need to be precise. Next, notice the curve that separates what is considered acceptable and unacceptable. This curve represents our *comfort threshold*. As our software and pipelines mature, the severity and frequency of undesirable events should diminish. For example, we can reduce the severity of losing a production database by adding redundant backups to our infrastructure.

A chart like this quickly sketches out and costs very little to produce. It is a great first step to get our team thinking about what matters enough to justify tracking and measuring.

Conclusion

We have finally come full circle on what is necessary to ensure that we can empower the business to rapidly deliver our shiny features to customers at the needed scale without sacrificing quality. In this chapter, we explored advanced pipeline topics focused on optimization, scalability, maintainability, security, and compliance considerations. If this were an Agile book, we would stop here; however, as we are a DevOps culture book, we are focused on the entire **software development life cycle** (**SDLC**) rather than only the creation and delivery phases.

In the next chapter, we will continue discussing how and what to measure. We will look at various aspects of value within our organizations with an eye for improving efficiency and effectiveness at a variety of different levels.

CHAPTER 10

Trusting Our Metrics

Introduction

You may be familiar with the phrase *Lies, damned lies, and statistics,* popularized by *Mark Twain*, which I find hit home with many standard industry metrics. It is important to be data-driven; however, for the analysis to be sound, we must ensure the entire process's integrity. Everything falls apart if there are issues with measuring the initial data and its integrity in storage or presentation. We will examine what makes a good metric, why and how we create meaningful metrics, spot useless ones, and how to game the system when necessary.

Objectives

- What is a metric?
- How are metrics used to improve processes and outcomes?
- Why should we be a metric skeptic by default?
- What makes a quality metric?
- What are some bad or smelly metrics?
- How do we establish a baseline and targets?
- How can we use metrics to get what we want?
- Why do we need to revisit our metrics regularly?

Finding valuable metrics and KPIs

The acronym soup can be confusing; let us take some time to understand what metrics, KPIs, and OKRs are.

Definition of a metric

While I have seen many definitions, the best is *a standard measurement of something*. This definition is both generic and specific enough that we do not have to keep redefining it to fit our needs. We should think of metrics as the nuggets of data necessary to answer a specific question. While there are some nuanced differences between a statistic and a metric, we will use them interchangeably for this book.

A **key performance indicator (KPI)** is a metric that we have determined is an important performance indicator. We will track it to understand better how our people and systems within our organization interact to achieve a specific objective.

An **objective and key result (OKR)** is a set of short-to midterm objectives that we establish. These objectives include a set of KPIs to ensure we can measure our results.

To illustrate the difference between an OKR and a KPI, we will define a KPI that we will use within an OKR. Let us say that we work for a software company selling video games. We can use the number of sales as a long-term KPI that we will track till the game is no longer sold. An OKR would be to become the #1 game company in a particular genre in for a given year or quarter as measured by a specific dimension, such as the total sales, downloads, highest rated, etc. Our OKRs must be time-scoped to ensure that they are meaningful for the life of the measurement.

Metrics could represent the measurement of distance, time, resource consumption, allocation, cost, sales, etc.

How metrics are used

Data points, or the output of a metric function, are often recorded and analyzed using time as the lens, as they are crucial measurements of other metrics.

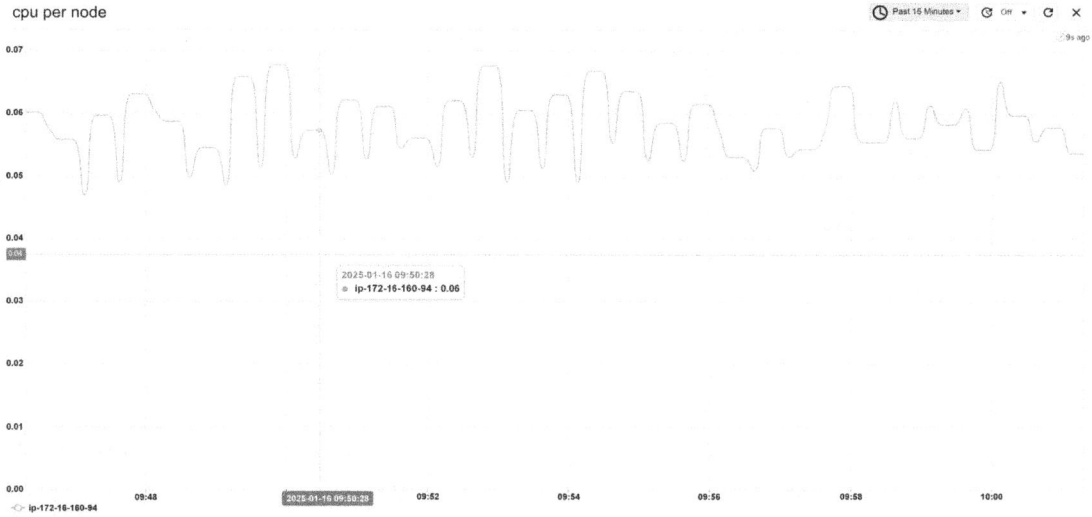

Figure 10.1: *A time series graph of CPU usage*

One common manifestation of this is when we store these data points in a **time series database** (**TSDB**) or other data structure to represent each of our captured data points as representing the points on a line on a graph or function. If this process of defining a collection, performing a series of steps to put it in our desired format, and then saving the newly mutated data externally sounds familiar, our metrics collection process is just a pipeline! In a data engineering context, this could be considered an **extract, translate, load** (**ETL**) *pipeline,* which we will discuss later in *Chapter 12, Observability, Taming monitoring, alerting, and on-call demons, Observability pipelines.*

Metrics, lies, and statistics!

We are constantly bombarded with metrics or statistics throughout our lives. While many of these metrics are critical to understanding what is happening, others are low quality and erode our overall trust in analytics, which is closely associated with statistics. Our experiences dictate the integrity or trustworthiness of a metric with it. When we see that our metrics accurately represent what we are looking to measure, we can use them to better understand a specific aspect of a system, problem set, etc., as well as the relationships between data points.

When we encounter a metric for which the data does not seem to match our understanding, we need to take a step back and ask ourselves why this is the case. Before jumping to conclusions, we should ask ourselves whether we are measuring the proper dimension and fully understand what it represents. This leads us to the sentiment that *97% of all statistics are BS; the remaining 3% are made up on the spot.*

What makes a high-quality metric

Metrics that do not lie or attempt to misrepresent themselves; good metrics are clearly understandable, why we want to measure them; we ensure that they are properly collected and represent what we hope to capture.

No, we will not give you a list of good metrics

Instead, I will give you a bunch of bad metrics that could be used, but they typically do not paint a complete enough picture to be acted on alone. They can be more misleading than they are worth. Buyer beware!

Metrics that smell

As we discussed *code smell* in *Chapter 3, Automation, Automate all the things!, Code for 3 AM, Bens ten commandments of clean coding, In seriousness*, we have the same concept for metrics. Here are some examples:

- **Lines of code (LOC):** Thankfully, this metric has fallen out of favor with the industry. At one point, many companies started using it to indicate how productive an engineer was. However, this fails to acknowledge that the quantity of code is not a good indicator of the code's progress, quality, or overall value. This scenario is a typical case of incentive misalignment, where developers are incentivized to write lengthy programs for non-technical reasons purely to game their performance metrics.

- **Number of commits:** This suffers from the same problems as LOC and has waned significantly due to how versioning control systems work. It is possible to write over history when we finish a feature, a common pattern in many developers' workflows. They are doing this to help our reviewers optimize their time by providing them with a clean changeset without necessarily having to inspect every step of the development journey to get there. Yet, we are punishing these engineers for excellent communication skills, which is not ideal.

- **Number of pull requests:** This one is not entirely terrible, as a pull request generally represents the entirety of a change set, which has some bearing on how much someone contributes. However, be careful of how automated pull request generation can skew these metrics. A single change across many repositories vs. a single change in one repository may seem more valuable than the other, which is not necessarily the case.

- **Story points:** Time to throw a grenade! I expect some fun review comments on this one. In theory, story points used in our project management are an excellent way to help us plan our capacity, help us with sequencing, etc. However, management or other portions of the business often start distorting this metric, which has the effect of losing its meaning. One example of this I have seen in my career was an executive insisting that we change and adopt a new point system, even though the team was happy with the current system. There was a lot of confusion for quite a while until I got them to explain that they wanted to use the story points for reporting on something for taxation purposes. This was a *black swan*; it made sense to them and them alone until we established a shared understanding of the matter. When we no longer feel a metric has any meaning, its meaning inherently changes to be a waste of the team's time. Suppose your organization has managed to do this correctly; *kudos to you, as you are part of the 3%!* I do not trust any story point system that is forced on it by another team, project manager, leadership, etc., as they are not focused on using it as it is intended, which is to give us some idea of our overall capacity and capabilities to meet the organization's needs.

- **Tickets, stories, epics, etc. completed:** We can represent a body of work as many small tasks or one larger task. If we are measured based on this rather than the value we bring with our changes, we will see folks game the system.

- **Feature or bug count:** Focusing on the number of features delivered and bugs addressed is an example of how incentive misalignment may lead teams, engineers, product managers, etc., to prioritize work without considering the value that it brings.

- **Code test coverage:** This metric only reveals which lines of code our tests exercised, but nothing of the validations that ensure expected app/system behavior. While we do advocate tracking this metric, we must emphasize that we must be conscious of people who fall into gaming this metric unintentionally or otherwise. When contributors abuse our trust with *defeat devices*, we should discuss it with them. We need to emphasize how tests exist to build confidence. At the end of the day, however, we want to assess the confidence gained by our overall testing process and suite rather than some singular dimension that only tells us part of the story. Use this as a guide to help us monitor overall test suite health.

- **Total vulnerabilities:** While it is essential to understand all our vulnerabilities, what is crucial is that we know the impact or risk these bring to our organization. We should look to refine this to ask more nuanced questions, such as *How many publicly facing systems have at least one or more high or critical vulnerability?* and a follow-up question might be counting them based on *of these systems, which single vulnerability patched addresses the most assets in terms of risk reduction?*, we should ask specific questions that focus on value rather than relying on broad strokes. From a long-term perspective, one of the better metrics to track is the time from reporting (to a CVE database, organization, etc.); we want to ensure that we are quickly patching known vulnerabilities. This is especially true when engineering groups do not have enough time for maintenance work to address their risk. Start with our *critical* and *high* severities, then move to *mediums*, eventually ensuring that *lows* are patched in a reasonable time frame.

Establishing baselines and targets

When capturing data for metrics, we often try to understand changes to typical system behavior. Typically, we must capture and analyze the metric data for some time to establish whether the system is doing what we expected and understand what the data shows us. We need to refine our metrics over time before they become trustworthy. This is the sign of a healthy metric. Once we know that our metric is trustworthy, we can deploy it to help us understand. When we do, we typically need to see how the system works over time to know if our desired changes make sense. This is especially true when we are looking to optimize our processes and systems with our typical Venn diagram problem of *cost*, *performance*, and *velocity*, and we only get to pick two.

Continuous improvement powered by metrics

Before introducing a new process or changes to an existing process, we should consider our associated KPIs, OKRs, and other metrics to gauge whether our resulting efforts bring a positive or negative impact. Once we define our metrics and establish the baselines, we need to regularly look at the data without having knee-jerk reactions or biases. When we see a smelly metric, such as our Engineering Hours, we should attempt to understand how the data is collected and what it tells us before we discount it. Is the data flawed? Did we ask the wrong questions? Did we think that affecting X would bring a positive result, only to have the opposite? When in doubt, we should leverage user feedback and surveys to check the sentiment against what we believe the data tells us.

When we have a great metric, establish baselines, and identify target(s), we realize that this can be seen again through the lens of a maturity model. When working on large-scale changes, we should adopt an incremental progress mindset. We do not need to go from 0 to 100 instantly; we need to define milestones and quality metrics that we can track to help us understand as we move the needle.

Let us take a common example: we want to reduce the latency, or the time that one process is waiting for another process to finish and respond. We currently average 20 milliseconds of latency and would like to get it down to 10. Your engineering team immediately says *it cannot be done!* Let us break this down into two goals to reduce it by five each. We can break down one story into a *low-hanging fruit* category and use it to make an initial pass to see how much we can improve with limited investment. We could decide if more optimizations are worth pursuing depending on the results. By taking this mindset, we acknowledge that there may be no more easy wins, and it may be too expensive in terms of time and resources to get the desired results. In this way, we can iteratively address our tasks in smaller pieces to the point where they have diminishing returns on value.

To support our planning needs, we will likely need to capture a number of metrics, such as cost and time estimates on projects, our status as we move towards that goal, and time blocked by external teams, etc. This will help us understand how efficient and effective our processes are. On the other hand, the folks responsible for project management will typically focus on metrics that highlight inefficiencies, such as duplicative efforts and time spent waiting, and identify opportunities to improve our efficiency, to name a few.

A common manifestation of reviewing these types of metrics in an agile world is a sprint retrospective, which we covered in *Chapter 2, Planning and Reacting to a Changing Organization's Needs, What agile fits you best?, Tour of the big bands, Scrum, Sprint review, and retrospectives*.

Using metrics to get what we want!

There are two ways I look at this. The first is about identifying what we want, who can get it for us, and what they want to see in return. Suppose we can quantify this using a trustworthy metric. In that case, it will make it much easier to track progress, build confidence, etc., and ensure that our investments make sense and that we should continue to do so rather than cut losses.

Sometimes, we are given bad metrics and told to use them; ideally, we should try to understand the needs first before we judge. There may be an interesting reason that makes sense from their perspective. Most poor-quality metrics are the manifestation of a *black swan*. Sometimes, they are flat-out wrong, which is OK, as all humans are error-prone, and we acknowledge our humanity. When they are wrong, we should simply look to game whatever terrible metric they want as long as there is no moral or ethical concern. The danger here lies in that it comes down to integrity and intent. If the intent is good and we have integrity, there should be no problem. The problem arises when we have misaligned incentives that force someone to compromise their moral or ethical standpoints, such as the case in Boeing and VW scandals we have already discussed in the book and will likely revisit one last time in *Chapter 11, Valuation, Bridging Management and Engineering, Decisions and events that affect value*.

Revisiting our metrics for relevance and impact

Over time, the meaning of a metric can change, and what previously made sense to monitor, observe, or alert needs to be reevaluated. What would be an example of this?

A stand monitoring metric is CPU usage, which is good if used correctly. With the rise of virtualization, cloud, autoscaling, clustering, etc., the context of how we use it changes depending on our deployment topology.

When we deploy an application to our infrastructure on-premise, we have a finite number of resources, and our processes risk waiting for resources to become available. The finite resources often translate to system delays, which impact the customer. When we discover resource exhaustion, we need to investigate the root cause even after an alarm has cleared without human intervention. Maybe the only outcome is an update to our scaling policies and alerting.

When we deploy the same application in a public cloud, we suddenly (should) have *infinite* (in concept/theory) scale potential. So, how does this change how we think of resource exhaustion? Due to this capability, we can leverage auto-scaling groups and load balancing rather than paging an engineer. We can also alert our teams when the threshold of our auto-scaling group's cost exceeds our expectations, which correlates to the number and size of the instances. This is a prime example of how the context of our metrics can change, highlighting the need to think about what our metrics truly mean and what we are looking to achieve.

We kind of cheated here by introducing the concept of combatting alert fatigue early and rerouting our alerting data, which we will cover in further depth in *Chapter 12, Observability, Taming monitoring, alerting, and on-call demons, What should we alert on?*

Conclusion

Metrics are the distillation of data to answer a specific question. Data affords many awesome possibilities; we need to be conscious of our limitations in understanding, measurement, and collection processes, etc., to ensure we follow high-quality and understood metrics. We explored what makes a good vs. a flawed metric, how we establish targets and baselines, achieve continuous improvement through continuous feedback and measurement, revisit our metrics to ensure we understand their relevance as context shifts over time, and use metrics to get what we want out of people even when they do not want to give us what we seek.

In the next chapter, we will define *value* (a commonly misunderstood concept), how we measure it, and how we can use it to make better organizational decisions.

Join our Discord space

Join our Discord workspace for latest updates, offers, tech happenings around the world, new releases, and sessions with the authors:

https://discord.bpbonline.com

CHAPTER 11

Valuation, Bridging Management and Engineering

Introduction

The first topic we cover is the inherent conflict between engineering and management, which arises naturally from the nature of the work in which each type engages and the differences in personality types.

We then cover valuation as a type of time travel, forecasting future values from amounts invested in the present or the reverse, discounting future forecast cash flows to value in the present, known as present value. Valuation requires thinking through time, which is not a skill natural to most people, but one that can be learned. My original first draft of this chapter contained much more how to, much more mathematics; however, I learned that was inconsistent with the general theme of this book, and therefor this chapter focuses much more on the what and the why of *value*. Why value a business? What good would it do for you?

Of the original 20 or so equations, there still remains four that I felt essential: equations [1] and [2] are the future value equation and the present value equation. Each of these converts a single value in the present to a value in the future or the reverse, a single forecast cash flow in the future to present value. Equation [3] is the **Annuity Discount Factor** (**ADF**), which converts a finite series of cash flows with constant growth to present value. It is the most complex of the formulas, but the good news for you is that we will not use it. Its main use is as a stepping stone to equation [4], which is the **Gordon Model Multiple** (**GMM**), also known as the valuation multiple, which is the present value of an infinite series of cash flows with constant growth.

This is very light exposure to valuation concepts, which are very important in business. When you really need valuation help, it will be time to call in a professional, but if you have no concept of valuation, you will not recognize that you need the help.

We also speak about actual rates of return in the stock market, which form the basis for calculating discount rates, which are the rates of return that we use to discount forecast cash flows to present value. Later, we will use that to value Boeing, the aircraft manufacturer.

Next, we have a large section on decisions and high-impact events that major effects on an organization's value. In this section, we measure the loss in value sustained by famous companies that made big mistakes by measuring the loss in value of their stocks in response to their mistakes becoming public knowledge. Without knowing this, it is impossible to make intelligent, rational mission-critical decisions.

The purpose of our *Strategic Blunders* analysis is to derive the measures that will enable to use of valuation techniques to help companies make strategic decisions, such as how much they should invest in **Quality Assurance and Cyber Security (QACS)**. This is the ultimate purpose of this chapter and the reason why valuation is important to Engineering and Management, as it is the only common measure and only language that should be common to both disciplines, and it is the criterion by which companies should be deciding their budgets.

During this process, we also measure stock market reactions to other giant events, the 9/11 terrorist attack and COVID-19, to provide us with benchmarks to compare the effects on value of company-generated mistakes with these international phenomena that affected value, sometimes dramatically so. We also provide a table to present and analyze various characteristics of the companies involved in the train wrecks, the competence of the business, its morality and ethics, whether the mistake involved loss of life, how many competitors the company had, and whether it was too big to fail to begin to provide a theory and the ability to measure the effects of the different characteristics on value. This is a new discipline in its infancy.

Finally, we use a valuation analysis as an example of the optimal method to demonstrate how to decide how much to spend on QACS rather than engineers hyper-focusing on risk and management doing the same on sales.

Objectives

- To bridge the natural gap between engineering and management.
- That *value* should be the common language throughout an organization, as it simultaneously aligns people with maximizing company value while seeking to optimize the necessary tradeoffs between the desire for higher sales and profits and the risk that goes along with them.

- That valuation is about thinking through time. This is not a natural way for most people to think. This is the stock-and-trade of MBAs, valuation analysts, and economists.

- To develop a working elementary understanding of future value and present value.

- That large firms and high-growth early-stage companies typically have much higher valuation multiples than most small and medium firms.

- How *Three Multi-Billion Dollar Businesses*, The *Strategic Blunders*, Lost 35% to 100% of their value in their moral, ethical, and technical failures.

- How valuation should help management determine how much to invest in QA and cybersecurity.

Why value matters to engineers and leadership

Why would a book on DevOps engineering culture have a chapter on business valuation? On the surface, it seems totally unrelated and out of place, yet we believe it is essential for both engineers and leadership to understand. Why? Let us answer this question with a tragic real-life story.[1]

Tragedy of the Challenger

Six months before the Challenger exploded upon launch, a booster rocket engineer at a company contracted by the **National Aeronautics and Space Administration (NASA)** predicted *a catastrophe of the highest order* involving *the loss of human life* in a memo to his managers.

The problem, he wrote in the memo, was that the elastic seals at the joints of the multistage booster rockets tended to stiffen and unseal in cold weather, and NASA's launch schedule included winter lift-offs with risky temperatures.

On January 27, 1986, the forecast for the next morning at *Kennedy Space Center* included a launch-time temperature of 30 degrees Fahrenheit (–0.5° C) NASA had never launched in temperatures that cold, and he and his four colleagues at their headquarters concluded it would be too dangerous to launch.

He fought for hours to stop the launch. At first, his managers agreed with them and formally recommended a launch delay. One of the NASA officials challenged that recommendation, stating, *I am appalled! I am appalled at your recommendation!* Another shuttle program

1 The following story is almost verbatim, with some very light editing, from the NPR article at https:// www.npr.org/sections/thetwo-way/2012/02/06/146490064/remembering-roger-boisjoly-he-tried-to-stop-shuttle-challenger-launch

manager showed his disdain with biting sarcasm, ... *When do you want me to launch—next April?* In other words, NASA management shamed and chastised him rather than address his technical arguments about why he feared a life-threatening disaster.

He and his colleague told **National Public Radio** (**NPR**) that the NASA pressure caused his managers to *put their management hats on,* as one source told us. They overruled him and the other engineers and told NASA to go ahead and launch. It is critical to note that in *putting on their management hats,* they first must have taken off their engineering hats, with disastrous consequences.

The explosion of Challenger and the deaths of its crew, including Teacher-in-Space *Christa McAuliffe,* traumatized the nation and left this heroic engineer disabled by severe headaches, steeped in depression, and unable to sleep. When NPR correspondent *Howard Berkes* visited him at his home in April 1987, he was thin, formerly tall and stocky, tearful and tense. He huddled in the corner of a couch, his arms tightly folded on his chest but ready to speak publicly. *I am very angry that nobody listened, he told me.* He asked himself if he could have done anything differently, but then a flash of certainty returned.

We were talking to the right people. We were talking to the people who had the power to stop that launch. He testified before the Challenger Commission and filed unsuccessful lawsuits against his own firm and NASA. He continued to suffer and was ostracized by some of his colleagues. One said *he would drop his kids on his doorstep if they all lost their jobs,* according to his wife.

He took it very hard; she recalls. *He had always been held in such high esteem, and it hurt so bad when they would not listen to him.*

What can we learn from this tragic story? Unfortunately, it is highly likely that the Challenger story is not unique. It is quite common. Why?

As engineers are closest to the problems, they are the ones who build it and have professional pride in it. If there are any issues in the program, whether it is a space launch or launching the next version of company software, the ones most likely to know about it are the engineers, as they are closest to the details, and they often care about the risks.

Businesspeople, especially entrepreneurs, are a different breed. They tend to be risk takers, some even daredevils. The world needs both types, and they need to learn to respect and communicate with each other. There is the rub. These are different breeds of people who do not naturally respect each other and communicate well, and that lack reared its ugly head with NASA and the contracted company.

The engineers may respect and more likely fear the boss, but they may not respect the boss' flippant disregard for risk and danger. The boss, on the other hand, tends to think in terms of prioritizing product features to increase sales and net income, and, of course, delivery needs to be now! This builds pressure to put out new features before they are ready and to overly economize on testing, operations, and security, which, after all, are *just cost centers that bleed the bottom line for no great purpose other than to enable marketing to emphasize how stable and secure the product is, right?* In the bosses' eyes, the engineers are a bunch of fearful wimps.

This leaves the operations and security engineering staff feeling disempowered and undervalued and can dangerously alienate them from the engineering and other executives while potentially inflating the egos of executives, as they are rewarded for ever-increasing levels of net income, which they naively imagine also optimizes *value*. However, *value* is an often misunderstood term and topic. This creates and widens the communications divide until it appears unbridgeable. What can we do to bridge this gap?

The answer is to think in terms of *value* and to learn how to measure, create, and retain it. *Value* should be the common language to tie together all departments and leadership with engineering. By that, we mean that engineering and management can speak about the probable effects of each major decision on the value of the company.

Two pillars of value

The two pillars of value are *love* and *fear*, which translate as *risk* and *reward*. These two pillars act like an accelerator and brakes on a car. Reward, i.e., higher forecast cash flows, increases value, while higher risk holds value down. It is the net effect of these two opposing forces that determines value.

Why future and present value

Some reasons to invest your time and concentrated attention in this area are:

- **Company business:** It will greatly help to make your company more successful. Why? Since value is the ultimate measure of a business's success.[2]

  o As we discussed earlier, the two pillars of value are reward and risk. Top management tends to focus on rewards. C-level management often own stock options in the company, so their compensation is directly tied to the value they help to create, but because most of them do not understand how one values a business, they will instead mentally substitute sales and net income for value, ignoring the pillar of risk and frustrating the engineers.

  o Engineers create the product and often identify with the pillar of risk, while the pillar of reward remains more distant. How good is the product? What are its vulnerabilities? *How can you ask us to put out these new features in this ridiculously short period of time? The product will be garbage!*, *Shut up and do what you are told!*

  o The sad truth is that management and engineering in many companies are like a married couple who each grew up in dysfunctional homes, never

---

2 I am not meaning to minimize the importance of ethics and morality. I am presupposing that is the only way one should do business.

read *Men are from Mars, Women are from Venus* and have never done couples therapy or a Marriage Encounter seminar. There is just no common language to break out of frustration and coercive behavior. The best solution for this is that everyone in the organization should understand enough of the basics of value, including future value and present value, to provide that common language. Then management can understand how rushing inadequately tested products to market, while it may increase sales and net income in the short run, may reduce value right away and in the long run, while engineering may come to understand why it pays to take some intelligent, calculated risks in order to bring the product to market perhaps earlier than its comfort level would dictate.

o   Thus, understanding value is the single most important tool to facilitate intelligent and relevant communication across all levels of a company.

- **Your finances:**

o   Understanding present and future value is critical to becoming a more successful investor. For example, you may be interested in investing in a company whose **price-earnings** (**PE**) Multiple is, let us say, 20. Is that a good thing, a bad thing, or just a thing? What makes a good PE multiple? Most investors have no clue. If you work to master the basics of future and present value, you will develop the basic skills necessary to become a more successful investor, even if you remain an employee for the rest of your life and never start your own business.

Valuation approaches

So, how should one go about trying to measure the *value* of a business? In *business valuation*, we have three different valuation approaches. A valuation approach is a way of looking at *value*. It is not a specific valuation technique, which we call *valuation methods*. Each valuation approach has two or more valuation methods. The relevant approach for you to understand is the *Income Approach*, which is the main approach business appraisers use in valuing businesses. The Asset and Market Approaches are outside the scope of our discussion.

The *Income Approach* looks at the company's income and, more accurately, cash flow generating capacity to measure value. **The Discounted Cash Flow (DCF)** method is the most widely used valuation tool in the business appraiser's toolkit. It is the go-to method that applies in almost all valuations.

A *DCF* method involves the following steps:

1.   Forecast the company's cash flows.

   a.   For an existing firm, this first involves analyzing the past. Obviously, this is impossible for valuing a startup company, which has no past. There are entire books written on this topic, and it is beyond the scope of this chapter to delve into this topic. To simplify, we will assume we have a forecast of next year's cash flow and a constant growth rate of forecast cash flows. This is accurate only for a mature firm.

b. For an early stage, high-growth firm, typically, forecast growth is very high in the early years and comes down over time until it levels out to a modest, long-term growth rate. However, it does not matter. Even if your firm is in high growth, the insights we will gain from this simplification are completely valid, even if the fact pattern is not literally true.

2. Discount the cash flows to present value. A dollar that we forecast to receive in the future is worth less than a dollar that we are receiving right now. The present value is higher the closer the cash flow is to the present and the lower its risk. We will cover this topic in a fair amount of detail.

After those two steps, there are other adjustments a professional business appraiser must make that are beyond the scope of this chapter.

Value as time travel

In teaching the basics of valuation, I find it helpful to think of valuation as time travel and the investor and appraiser as time travelers. Valuation requires the ability to think through time. In the simplest sense, that means being able to translate a known value or investment today into value at some time in the future or the reverse, translating known or forecast cash flows or value in the future to value today. We will begin with the skills of calculating future values.

This begins the most difficult section in this chapter, which is the mathematics of **Future Value and Present Value** (**FV and PV**). We will begin with an introduction to the types of skills you will develop in this chapter.

Skill progression in this chapter

This chapter will help you develop your financial skills in the following:

- **Single cash flows:** We will begin with learning how to convert a single cash flow to future or present values.

- **Annual cash flows:** We will present the mathematical formulas to convert a series of annual cash flows to present value:

  o An **Annuity Discount Factor** (**ADF**). An ADF is the present value of a *finite* series of cash flows with a constant growth rate.

  o A **Gordon Model Multiple** (**GMM**). A *GMM* is the PV of an *infinite* series of cash flows with a constant growth rate. It is the major mathematical formula that we use in valuing businesses and intangible assets with a presumed potential infinite life. However, the majority of the value of businesses derive from their first 10 years of forecasts.

The GMM is the formula we use for valuing businesses, and it is far more important that you understand it than the ADF.

The sale of Manhattan Island

To add some flavor and a bit of fun to what some people may consider a dry topic, let us learn about future value in the context of posing a question of interesting historical significance in the USA—The Sale of Manhattan Island. The settlers of Manhattan Island paid the Native Americans $24 in the year 1624. The question is, what would it be worth 400 years later at the end of 2024? This is a Future Value question.

The Mathematics

NOTE: **This section gets math-heavy compared to the rest of the book. Please feel free to skim or skip ahead, please [GOTO: The Mathematics—Value of $24 in 2024] section.**

A few comments on the mathematics. *FV* and *PV* mathematics are not simple. To maintain as much readability as possible, we use certain simplifications. For example, we assume the annual returns are the same every year. While that is not realistic, it simplifies the math, and the insights that we can gain from the simplified math are every bit as valid as the more complex math with varying returns every year.

Another simplification we use is that we assume **End-of-Year (EOY)** *cash flows*, i.e., that the *cash flow* comes on the last day of every year, December 31. Business cash flows typically come much more frequently and evenly than that, but the mathematics are more complex and do not add to the insights that engineers and management need to understand in valuation. The bottom line is, *Do not try this at home!* When there is a lot of value involved in an analysis, get professional help. However, the simpler math is more than adequate to begin to understand the language of *value*.

Finally, we removed most of the mathematics from the chapter to make it as readable as possible and refer the reader to one of my books for the details. Hopefully, we will present the mathematics in a follow-up book.

Definitions

Let us define the following terms:

- **CF= Cash flow:** An expected amount of money to come in at some time in the future or an actual amount of cash invested at the present, determined by the context of each analysis. We generally use $1.00 of cash flow in year 1, which enables us to scale the future or present value for each $1 of year 1 cash flow, which we explain further on.

- **FV= Future value:** The value of some asset, money, or otherwise, in the future. For simplicity, we will speak in terms of cash flow.

- **PV= Present value:** The value in today's dollars of some asset, usually money but not necessarily so, that you expect to receive at some time in the future. PV is the reverse process of FV.

- **n=** The number of years out in the future that one expects to receive the cash flow.

- **r=** The constant investment rate of return.

Future value equation

Equation 11.1 states that the future value equals the present value invested times one plus the rate of return to the nth power:

$$FV = PV\ (1 + r)^n$$

Equation 11.1: *Future value equation*

Future values with various rates of return

Here, we will look at how future value changes with a 5, 10, and 20% growth over 20 years:

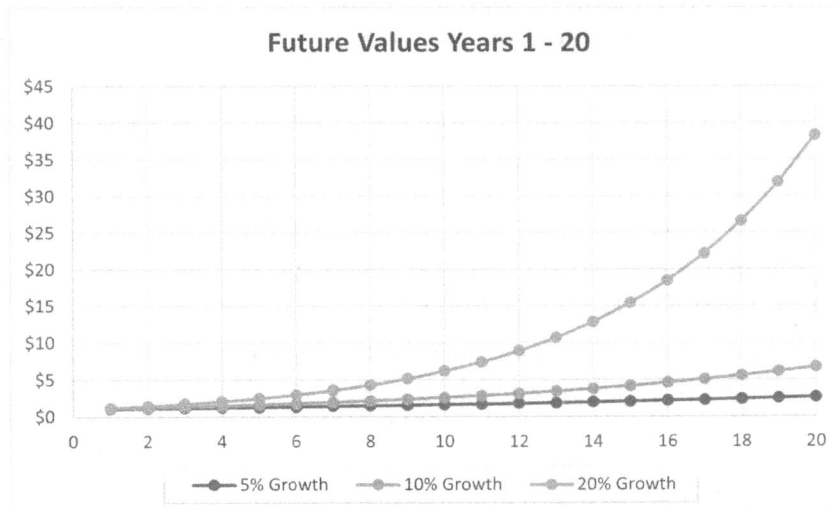

Figure 11.1: *Value at various rates of return*

Future values experience *Compound Growth = Exponential Growth*. The higher the growth rate and, the larger the time invested, the greater the curvature.

To answer our question of what the $24 sale would be worth in 2024, let us fill in what we know in *Equation 11.1* as *Equation 11.1.1*. We know that 400 years have passed since that transaction. Thus, our equation now is:

$$\text{Value in 2024} = \$24 \ (1 + r)^{400}$$

Equation 11.1.1: *Value of the original sale invested 400 years*

The only thing we are missing is the appropriate rate of return. Once we have that, we can answer our question. Thus, we need to delve a bit into historical rates of return.

There are two most commonly used types of average returns: *geometric* and *arithmetic* average returns. *Geometric* averages are the most appropriate to use for forecasting future values, while *arithmetic* averages are most appropriate to use for developing discount rates to discount to present value. *Arithmetic* average returns are higher than *geometric*.

The Size Effect

There is a phenomenon in finance known as the Size Effect, first documented by *Rolf Banz* in a 1981 academic article, which is that small firms outperform large firms in the stock markets. It is a topic about which there is much controversy. It is important to understand the Size Effect in order to understand rates of return on investment.

To speak about the Size Effect, we need some terminology. Academic researchers have split the public markets into 10 groups, called deciles, ordered by size, as measured by market capitalization, market cap for short. A stock's market cap is its value, as measured by number of shares outstanding times the price per share. For example, a firm with 10 million shares outstanding and a current market price of $100 per share has a market cap of $1 billion.

Decile 1 is the group of the largest 10% of publicly traded stocks. Decile 2 is the next largest 10%, …, and Decile 10 is the smallest 10%. There is a further breakdown of Decile 10 into four sub-quartiles (i.e., groups of four), which each represent 2.5% of public stocks. The smallest of these is known as Decile 10z, which is the smallest 2.5% of public stocks.

In my 1994 article,[3] the author demonstrated the following results based on data published in the Ibbotson and Associates SBBI[4] Yearbooks:

- The largest firms had the most stable returns, while the smallest firms had the most volatile returns. When all things are equal, investors prefer stability over volatility; they will only invest in more volatile assets if they are compensated for the additional *risk* with higher expected returns on investment. The data bore out this fundamental principle in finance theory.

- The largest firms produced the smallest long-run **return on investment** (**ROI**), while the smallest firms produced the largest long-run ROI.[5] However, there are significant time spans in which the above results are not true. It is a complex topic, beyond the scope of this chapter. This relationship works well enough over the long run for our purposes.

3 "A Breakthrough In Calculating Reliable Discount Rates," *Valuation*, August 1994
4 *Stocks, Bonds, Bills, and Inflation*. Roger Ibbotson, a finance professor at Yale University, was the founder. The raw data came from the University of Chicago's **Center for Research in Security Prices** (**CRSP**).
5 We sometimes use **Rate of Return** (**RoR**) synonymously with ROI in this chapter.

For 1926 to 2022 US stock market results, the *geometric average* returns rose from roughly 9.5% for Decile 1 returns, to 12.9% for Decile 10 firms. Decile 10z had a *geometric average* return of roughly 15.7%.

Value of $24 in 2024

Investing the $24 the Native Americans received for Manhattan Island in 1624, we have the following valuations of the $24 in the year 2024 for the various assumed rates of ROI:

Description/Decile #	1	10	10z	Inflation
Geometric Avg r	9.5%	12.9%	15.7%	3.0%
FV $1 400 Yrs = $(1+r)^{400}$	$5.8 $\times 10^{15}$	$1.2 $\times 10^{21}$	$2.2 $\times 10^{25}$	$136,424
$\times$ $24 = FV in 2024	$1.4 $\times 10^{17}$	$2.9 $\times 10^{22}$	$5.2 $\times 10^{26}$	$3,274,169
FV 2024 in Words	$140 Quadrillion	$29 Sextillion	$520 Octillion	$3.3 Million

Table 11.1: Future Value Varies Enormously Over Long Periods of Time

At the 9.5% Decile #1 Geometric Average ROI, the 2024 value is $140 Quadrillion,[6] and this rises to an eye-popping $520 Octillion at the Decile 10z geometric average return of 15.7%. However, at a 3% inflationary rate of return, the $24 in 1624 would have grown only to $3.3 million, enough to buy a condo in Manhattan!

As you can see, over a very long period of time, and 400 years qualifies for that, at least for the human race, small differences in rates of return make enormous differences in value.

Present value

This section is math-heavy compared to the rest of the book; please feel free to skim or skip ahead, [GOTO Decisions and events that affect value].

Now that we have learned how to go forward in time, which is usually from the present to the future, we need to reverse that process and go from the future to the present. We do that by dividing both sides of the *Equation 11.1* by $(1 + r)^n$, which results in *Equation 11.2*. However, we also switch both sides of the equation to keep the dependent variable on the **left-hand-side (LHS)** of the equation:

$$PV = \frac{FV}{(1+r)^n} = FV \times \left(\frac{1}{(1+r)^n} \right)$$

Equation 11.2: The present value equation

The last term on the **right-hand-side (RHS)** of the equation, , is known in finance as the **present value factor (PVF)**. It gives us the formula for the *PV* of $1 to be received *n* years from now when the investor requires an investment rate of return of *r*. While, in theory,

---

6 One quadrillion is one-thousand times one trillion. One trillion is 10^{12} and one quadrillion is 10^{15}.

it seems that this should be the same rate of return as in *Equation 11.1*, it is not, as for purposes of discounting to *PV*, we must use the larger arithmetic average rates of return, not geometric, as it is demonstrable that using the arithmetic average discounts forecast expected cash flows to their proper present value, while using the geometric average discount over-values the cash flows.

Present Value of $1 to be received in Year *n*

Figure 11.2 is a graph of the PVs according to *Equation 11.2*. The highest values are in the blue curve, which has a 10% discount rate. The lowest values are in the purple curve, which has a required rate of return of 25%, and the middle curve is the orange one, with a 20% required rate of return:

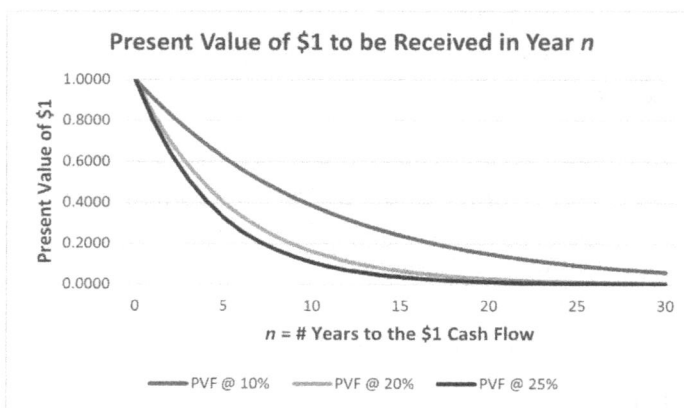

Figure 11.2: *present value of a future dollar*

Present value declines exponentially over time, which is why the graph is a curve and not a straight line, and the discount rate is the rate of decay. PV decays the fastest for $r = 25\%$, the purple curve.

These PVs are exponential decay curves that show how value *decays* exponentially over time, i.e., PV decays over time in much the same fashion that radioactive Uranium 238 decays into lead over time. The discount rate in the *PVF* has the same function as the decay rate in U-238. You can also see that the *PVFs* at 20% and 25% discount rates are not very different after a few years. The further out on time is the expected cash flow, and the higher the required rate of return on investment, the lower is the PV. A quick glance shows there is not much difference in the PVs of the orange and purple curves, especially after year 15. By year 18 or so, the PVs are indistinguishable.

Present value of a series of cash flows

For almost all businesses, appraisers forecast the company's cash flows annually and discount them to present value. That is very detailed and requires accounting and finance skills beyond the scope of much of the readership of this chapter.

We simplify and assume our forecast cash flows grow at the same percentage growth rate, *g*, every year. The resulting ADF is in *Equation 11.3*. The *ADF* by itself is not very useful in the context of this chapter. While it looks complex and daunting, you do not need to understand it:[7]

$$ADF = \left(\frac{1}{(r-g)}\right) \times \left[1 - \left(\frac{(1+g)}{(1+r)}\right)^n\right]$$

Equation 11.3: Annuity discount factor

However, when $r > g$[8] and n approaches infinity, then , and any number less than one raised to an infinite power equals zero. Then, the square brackets become $1 - 0 = 1$, and *Equation 11.3* simplifies to the **Gordon Model Multiple** (**GMM**) in *Equation 11.4*:

$$GMM = \frac{1}{(r-g)}$$

Equation 11.4: Gordon Model Multiple

Equation 11.4 is the GMM, which is the multiple that we use for valuing mature businesses. The *GMM × Next Year's Forecast Cash Flow = Value*.[9]

The Gordon Model Multiple

Figure 11.3 is a graph of the GMM as a function of *r* and *g*:

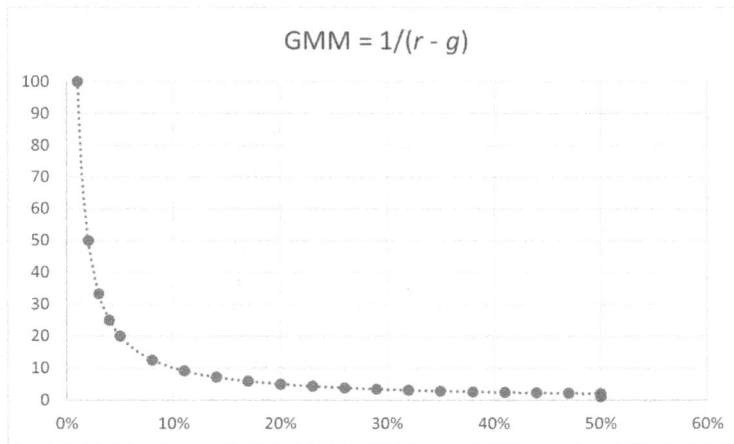

Figure 11.3: GMM approaches infinity as g approaches r

---

7 For those interested to see the mathematical derivation of the ADF, see my book, Quantitative Business Valuation, 2nd Edition, Jay B. Abrams, Wiley & Sons, ©2010, Chapter 4.
8 The ADF can work for finite series of cash flows when $r < g$, but not for infinite series, which is the practical application in this chapter. See the Mathematical Appendix for those details.
9 Again, there are likely to be adjustments for degree of control and marketability, which is outside the scope of this chapter.

The y-axis is the GMM, and the x-axis is $r - g$. The graph at the bottom shows the *GMM* rising asymptotically towards infinity as g approaches r. The GMM is the positive quadrant of a hyperbola and grows infinitely large as $r - g$ approaches zero, which happens on the left side of the graph.

This is an extremely important observation to understand. Very large firms tend to have high *GMMs* (aka valuation multiples), because their discount rates are low, due to the low volatility of returns, and their forecast growth rates are high. I call the very upper ranges of GMM the *valuation edge*. It is the zone in which *GMMs* are very high, and small changes in r or g produce large changes in the *GMM*. It is much easier to *move the needle* of value significantly in this zone than with small firms, which are the opposite and usually have high discount rates and low expected growth rates. Typical valuation multiples for them are 2 to 4 times after-tax cash flow, although there are exceptions. It takes much larger changes in r or g to produce a material change in value in a small firm.

Discount rates from publicly traded stocks

For 1926 to 2022 USA stock market results, the *arithmetic average* returns rose from roughly 11.2% for Decile 1 returns to 19.6% for Decile 10 firms. Decile 10z, the smallest 2.5% publicly traded firms, had an arithmetic *average* return of 25.0%, which is considerably higher than its 15.7% geometric average return for 10z.

Arithmetic average returns are considerably higher than geometric, especially for the smaller firms. The simple, intuitive reason for this is that geometric returns *smooth out* the ride from the starting point in 1926 to the end point in 2022. It excludes the bumpiness of the ride that the arithmetic returns capture. We would not want to forecast the future with arithmetic average returns, and we should not use geometric average returns to discount forecast future cash flows to present value, as that would result in a material over-valuation.

There is a more precise but much more technical reason why arithmetic means are the right ones to use for discounting to present value, which is that the arithmetic mean correctly discounts expected cash flows to present value, but demonstrating that is beyond the scope of this chapter.

Note that the Decile 10z arithmetic average return of 25% is the number we used for valuing small businesses above. Some small businesses may need an even higher discount rate than 25%, and venture capital and angel capital require even higher returns than that.

This concludes the theoretical/mathematical sections on valuation. We now move to the application of what we have learned to actual businesses.

Decisions and events that affect value

We examine a few business decisions and events out of their control that lose value for the following purposes:

- To learn from their stories. Specific stories have a more emotional impact than a dry succession of mathematics and statistics, from which you are likely suffering. Hopefully, stories of corporate hubris in which management failed to understand the hidden risks in the dust *swept under the carpet* will help those in top management do a better job of listening to the grassroots engineers who know the risks better than they do.

- To come to understand just how much value big risks can destroy.

- Hopefully, this will lead to more informed and intelligent investment in managing risk and value in making corporate decisions on how much to invest in quality control and cybersecurity.

Arthur Andersen and Co.

Arthur Andersen (**AA**) was my first professional job out of college. I worked in the commercial audit and small business divisions at different times from 1974 – 1976.

Fast forward to 2001 – 2002. *Arthur Andersen*, with 85,000 professionals, was involved as auditors of *Enron* and *World Com*, both of which were guilty of accounting fraud. The *Enron* scandal gave AA a serious wound, and *World Com* was fatal and put it out of business.

On Oct. 12, 2001, *Arthur Andersen* legal counsel told auditors to destroy all *Enron* files, except *Enron's* most basic documents, and on June 15, 2002, it was convicted of obstructing justice. Shortly thereafter it went out of business, a 100% loss in value.

Boeing

Boeing is so much in the news now that there is no need to explain much background.

I am writing the majority of this chapter as of March and April 2024, with a few edits as late as February 2025. The **Federal Aviation Authority** (**FAA**) audit found many quality control problems at *Boeing* and its supplier, *Spirit AeroSystems*.

Boeing stock prices

Our data consists of almost 62 ½ years of Boeing's daily stock prices from 1/2/1962 to 6/24/2024. As the table is more than 15,800 rows long, it would print on more than 320 pages if we show every row. Instead, we only show snippets of the table to ensure we focus on the most relevant material.[10]

Summary statistics

When analyzing large quantities of data, it is always important to begin with presenting summary statistics, minimum, maximum, etc., to get an initial *feel* for the data:

---

10 Even though the next several tables are from the same Excel table, the table numbering convention requires giving them separate table numbers.

	Summary statistics (A)	Amount (B)
15731	Min	-23.85%
15732	Max	24.32%
15733	Mean	0.06%
15734	Median	0.00%
15735	Std Deviation = Sigma (σ)	2.14%
15736	Std Deviation Pre COVID	2.02%
15737	Std Deviation During COVID	8.75%
15738	Count	15,724

Table 11.2: Summary statistics

We show summary statistics in rows 15731 – 15738. Thus, we are beginning our explanation from the bottom of the table. Column B shows statistics for all 62 ½ years of data, except for (B15736), which excludes all daily returns from the onset of COVID, and (B15737), which is the standard deviation during COVID. Let us dive into the details:

- There are 15,724 (B15738) trading days of stock returns.

- The largest loss (i.e., the minimum gain) is –23.85% (B14731), losing almost ¼ of its value, which occurred on 3/16/2020, right in the heart of COVID. The **Dow-Jones Industrial Average (DJIA)** dropped 12.94% that day, so Boeing's drop is consistent with the market, though more extreme, as one would expect, as air traffic drastically reduced during COVID. We will show excerpts from the table below.

- The maximum price gain was 24.3% (B14662) on 3/25/2020, which was part of the up-and-down paroxysms of the stock market during COVID, which we will cover shortly. In other words, in a single day, the company value increased by almost ¼.

- Average (mean) daily return over the entire 62 ½ years was 0.06% (B15733). If we multiply by 250 trading days per year, average annual returns are 15%. While not shown in the table, the average mean return was also the same if we measure only through 2/13/2020, the approximate onset of COVID, so COVID appears to have had no effect on average daily returns.

- The standard deviation of returns, which is a measure of dispersion around the mean and is known in statistics by the Greek letter σ (sigma), was 2.14% (B15735).[11] Recalculating σ to stop just before the onset of COVID, through 2/13/2020 (row 14634) lowers σ to 2.02%, which is lower, but not by much. We see that COVID had only a modest effect on standard deviation, undoubtedly because the COVID

---

11 Technically, this is a sample standard deviation, not a population standard deviation, but with so many observations, there is no difference.

period was such a small percentage of the entire 62 ½ years, as the early COVID period returns were very volatile. The standard deviation of returns during the first three months of COVID was 8.75% (B15737), which is more than four times the pre-COVID standard deviation.

Various times of interest

The following events are in chronological order, and we will discuss them thematically rather than the order of events:

- 09/11/2001   Terrorists destroyed the world trade center
- 10/29/2018   Lion Air MAX 8 Flight 610 goes down
- 03/10/2019   Ethiopian Airlines MAX 8 goes down
- 03/13/19–11/18/20   FAA grounded all MAX 8's
- 02/24/2020-12/6/2021 COVID Pandemic
- 01/05/2024   Alaska Air MAX 9 door plug blew out. ↓ 19.5% fair market value 1/5 to 1/16

Boeing stock prices around 9/11

Here we show an excerpt of our table for dates relevant to 9/11:

	Date (A)	Closing price (B)	Delta Δ^{12}(C)	Price change (D)	Notes / Comments
10000	09/17/2001	23.5615	-17.6%		6 Day drop after 9/11, no trading between.
10001	09/18/2001	21.8109	-7.4%	-23.7%	1 week drop 9/11
10002	09/19/2001	21.4621	-1.6%		
10003	09/20/2001	19.5863	-8.7%	-31.5%	Max drop 9/11
10017	10/10/2001	23.5363	-0.7%	-17.7%	1 month drop 9/11

Table 11.3: Boeing's maximum drop in stock price was 31.5% 10 days after 9/11

On 9/10/2001, Boeing stock traded at $28.6029 (B9999) per share. After the 9/11 attacks, there was no daily trading in the **New York Stock Exchange** (**NYSE**) until 9/17/2001 (row 10000),[13] at which time *Boeing* stock dropped 17.6% (C10000). It continued to drop

---

12 The Greek letter **Δ (Delta)** means *change*. In the context of this chapter, we will typically use it as the percentage change in stock price between two dates.
13 However, Airbus Industrie stock, being on several European stock exchanges, did trade during that week.

through 9/20, at which time it reached its maximum decline of 31.5% (D10003) before it began rebounding. On a daily basis, people were trying to understand whether this event represented the beginning of a new world war, was a unique, one-time event, or represented something in-between those two extremes. The market was reflecting investors' ongoing research, expert opinions, etc., and impounding that information and understanding into the stock price.

By 10/10/2001, one-month after 9/11, *Boeing* stock had partially recovered and was only down by 17.7% (D10017) compared to 9/10/11.

In 2017, a year in which *Boeing* fired 1,800 mechanics and engineers, the stock price increased 93.2% (D14101, not shown). So, apparently, the market liked what it was seeing, which was increased sales and profits. At least one[14] or two[15] of the articles that came out about *Boeing* and its many troubles in 2024 attributed at least part of its problems to moving production from Seattle, which had a long-standing, highly trained workforce, to South Carolina, which did not, but did offer a lower cost workforce.

A lot of analysis and research goes into investors betting their money, and more often than not, investors are pretty savvy and do get it right. However, this may be an example of investors being unable to see the hidden risks in *Boeing's* long-term decline from its focus on quality and safety.

This excerpt of our table shows Boeing's stock prices around its two fatal crashes of the Max 8, *Lion Air* and *Ethiopian Air*:

	Date (A)	Closing price (B)	Delta Δ (C)	Price change (D)	Notes / Comments
14309	10/26/2018	347.5210	-1.2%		
14310	10/29/2018	324.6154	-6.6%		*Lion Air* crash
14332	11/29/2018	332.8857	2.7%	-4.2%	1 month ↓ in FMV after 1st crash
14352	12/31/2018	313.3922	1.9%	10.8%	Stock price ↑ in 2018
14398	03/08/2019	412.6895	0.0%		
14399	03/11/2019	390.6847	-5.3%		*Ethiopian Airlines crash on 03/10/2019*
14400	03/12/2019	366.6582	-6.1%		*Ethiopian Airlines crash on 03/10/2019*

---

14   https://www.afr.com/companies/manufacturing/boeing-heard-all-the-warnings-it-just-wasn-t-listening-20240402-p5fgqt
15   https://www.library.hbs.edu/working-knowledge/why-boeings-problems-with-737-max-began-more-than-25-years-ago

| 14421 | 04/10/2019 | 356.4323 | -1.1% | -13.6% | 1 month ↓ in FMV after 2nd crash |
| 14422 | 04/11/2019 | 361.5306 | 1.4% | 3.2 | Ratio of the 2nd-to-1st crash after 1 month ↓ FMV |

Table 11.4: Lion and Ethiopian Air Crashes ↓ Boeing Stock 6.6% and 13.6%

Boeing's first disaster was the *Lion Air* crash on 10/29/2018, and its stock price declined by 6.6% (C14310). However, the next day, its stock increased 4.3% (not shown) and continued to increase for another three days. Thirty days after the event, the one-month decline in stock price was 4.2% (D14332).

Nevertheless, during 2018, which was *Boeing's* peak year of sales and net income, the stock price increased 10.8% (D14352).

The next major disaster is the *Ethiopian Airlines* crash on Sunday, 3/10/2019. In the first two trading days after, *Boeing* stock declined 5.3% and 6.1% (C14399, C14400), which is almost 11.5%—a huge decline in value.

Boeing's stock price one month after the event was down by 13.6% (D14421). If we compare the one-month declines of the two events, the second event caused *Boeing's* stock to decline 3.2 times (D14422 = D14421/D14332) more than the first crash. That is logical, as the market becomes increasingly worried the problem is with *Boeing's* planes and not with the pilots and airlines who were flying or maintaining them, which Boeing had initially insisted was the case.

Change in corporate values, whether real or apparent

It is very instructive to see *Boeing's* change in its Mission Statement in its Annual Reports. Look at the difference in Mission Statements from the 2018 versus the 2019 Annual Reports:

2018 Annual Report

Our purpose and mission is to connect, protect, explore and inspire the world through aerospace innovation. We aspire to be the best in aerospace and an enduring global industrial champion.[16]

To the Shareholders and Employees of the Boeing Company: Innovation is at the heart of everything we do—a fact that's truer now than ever before at Boeing...[17]

2019 Annual Report

Everyone affected by the Lion Air Flight 610 and Ethiopian Airlines Flight 302 accidents — including the loved ones of those on board and our airline customers and their people — has experienced unimaginable loss and sorrow. All of us at Boeing mourn with them and share their heartbreak.

16 Boeing 2018 Annual Report, p. 3. All page numbers cited are those of Boeings PDF documents, not the number that appears at the bottom of the page. The first two or three pages of the PDF document are the cover page, etc.

17 Boeing 2018 Annual Report, p. 4, stated by Dennis A. Mullenburg, CEO & President.

We will never forget the 346 lives lost in the 737 MAX tragedies. They have changed us and our industry forever. We are humbly learning from the accidents and are committed to using what we learn to improve safety and quality, because all who rely on our products and services deserve our best.

That includes our ongoing commitment to our values, with an emphasis on the highest standards of safety, quality and integrity. You can see this dedication throughout the company as our people work to strengthen our culture for the better and focus on our priorities. Foremost among these priorities is the safe return to service of the 737 MAX.[18]

Nothing is more important to us than safety. We are determined to restore the trust we lost in 2019. We will do it one airplane, one flight, one customer at a time.

This is what we stand for.[19]

Our values

The more than 160,000 people of Boeing are driven by our company's core values, including safety, quality and integrity. Their commitment to building safe and reliable products remains strong.[20]

The report goes on and on about safety, quality, integrity, etc. Shakespeare may have said, *The lady doth protest too much, Methinks.*

Comparing the two annual reports

The 2018 report, which Boeing would have issued after both crashes, emphasized innovation as its core value. The 2019 report emphasized safety. The Company *ate a lot of crow* in acknowledging its commitment to earn back the trust that it lost. The question is whether it was sincere or was it just optics to make a possibly cheap *mea culpa* to hopefully go back to business as usual.

Reports of rampant quality problems surfaced, including those that led to the *Alaska Air* door plug blowing off the plane in January 2024. That is more than five years after the *Lion Air* crash. This suggests that either they were not as committed to fixing their problems as they portrayed themselves to be in their 2019 annual report, or it was so steeped in mediocrity that their problems would take a huge amount of time to fix, which is the picture that appears to emerge as events continue to unfold.

It is troubling that Boeing referred to the *crashes* as *accidents* rather than *inevitable outcomes*, given the decisions made at the highest levels of the organization.

We would have thought that *Boeing* should have had its 2019 Mission Statement as its 2018 Mission Statement. After all, hundreds of people have already died from their faulty product. That it took until 2020, the year in which it would have issued its 2019 annual report, to make safety its core value suggests that, at best, Management was slow on the

18 Boeing 2019 Annual Report, p. 2.
19 Boeing 2019 Annual Report, p. 3.
20 Boeing 2019 Annual Report, p. 2.

uptake. Safety should have been Boeing's #1 core value from its inception. Every other value, engineering excellence, exciting features, etc., are fine add-ons, but they do not help when your planes go down and kill people.

Even more suggestive are the unethical and greedy decisions they made to intentionally mislead the *FAA* and their customers about the existence and therefore the dangers of the faulty *MCAS* system. This is especially true when you consider that they were selling the third sensor (which is needed to determine which sensor is faulty when one is giving inaccurate data), which would have led them to discover an additional issue with data corruption in the MCAS. The additional sensor would have added $80,000 to the cost of a nearly $100 million plane in 2024 dollars. If we assume the 2016 *737 MAX* price was $80 million, this would have been a 0.1% increase in the price of the plane, which its airline customers certainly would have paid. However, to make it an option without disclosing the danger in the plane without the third sensor?

COVID: While COVID has nothing to do with *Boeing's* design and quality control problems, it was a once-in-a-100-year pandemic that had a major impact on all businesses in general and airlines and airplane manufacturers in particular. It is instructive to see its effects on Boeing and compare that to the effect of the plane crashes on *Boeing's* stock price:

	Date (A)	Closing price (B)	Delta Δ (C)	Misc (D)	Notes / Comments
14634	02/13/2020	$342.82	-0.7%		Rough start date for COVID based on stock market pricing.
14650	03/09/2020	$227.17	-13.4%		DJIA ↓ 7.79% COVID.
14651	03/10/2020	$231.01	1.7%		
14652	03/11/2020	$189.08	-18.2%		WHO declared COVID a pandemic. Trump places travel ban on 26 nations.
14653	03/12/2020	$154.84	-18.1%	-55.2%	1 Month loss in value.
14654	03/13/2020	$170.20	9.9%	-4.6	Std errors.
14655	03/16/2020	$129.61	-23.8%	-11.1	Std errors. DJIA ↓ 12.94%
14656	03/17/2020	$124.14	-4.2%		
14657	03/18/2020	$101.89	-17.9%	-8.4	Std errors. Boeing applied for a $60B bailout.
14660	03/23/2020	$105.62	11.2%	5.2	Std errors. Suspends dividends, CEO will not take pay. News broke Friday night 03/20/2020.
14661	03/24/2020	$127.68	20.9%	9.8	Std errors.

	Date (A)	Closing price (B)	Delta Δ (C)	Misc (D)	Notes / Comments
14662	03/25/2020	$158.73	24.3%	11.4	Std errors. Stimulus package signed into law.
14663	03/26/2020	$180.55	13.7%	6.4	Std errors. DJIA ↑ 6%.
14664	03/27/2020	$162	-10.3%	-4.8	Std errors.
14667	04/01/2020	$130.70	-12.4%	-5.8	Std errors.
14670	04/06/2020	$148.77	19.5%	9.1	Std errors.
14673	04/09/2020	$151.84	3.4%	-56.0%	2 Month loss.
14695	05/12/2020	$125.22	-2.9%	-63.7%	3 Month loss.
14716	06/11/2020	$170	-16.4%		DJIA ↓ 6.9% due to increase in COVID cases.
14717	06/12/2020	$189.51	11.5%	-45.1%	4 Month loss.
14760	08/13/2020	$174.73	-0.4%	-49.4%	6 Month loss.
14886	02/12/2021	$210.98	0.2%	-38.9%	1 Year COVID loss.

Table 11.5: Enormous stock price drops and a few huge price increases

Using a starting date of 2/13/2020 for the pandemic, we see a long string of large price declines in February and March 2020. Look at the whopping price declines of 13.4%, 18.2%, 18.1%, 23.8%, and 17.9% on *3/9/20, 3/11, 3/12, 3/16,* and *3/18* (C14650 and rows below). The 1-month loss in share price is 55.2% (D14653).

The 23.8% decline on 3/16/20 appears to be in response to President Donald Trump's announcement of a travel ban on 26 nations. This was an 11.0 standard deviation event. An eight standard deviation event only happens once in 803 trillion times, so this is way beyond extraordinary. *Boeing's* stock declined 77% (not shown) from 2/21 to 3/20/2020.[21] This is a loss of more than ¾ of its value! One year after the start of COVID, *Boeing's* price had recovered to be down only 38.9% (D14886), still severe, but about ½ of its 77% loss.

June 11, 2020, is also an interesting date, as *Boeing's* stock declined 16.4% (C14716), but additionally, it is the maximum trading volume day,[22] with 103.2 million shares traded that day, while the average daily trading volumes were 8.2 million over the entire 10 years and 4.2 million before the first crash. An internet search revealed that on that day, the newspapers published that the USA reached 2 million COVID cases.[23] This is a real-life example of the **efficient markets hypothesis (EMH)** in action.

---

21 Boeing price on 3/20/20 was $95.01, and it was $407.8541 on 2/21/20.
22 Excluded trading volume from the printed table to conserve space and font size, as it is not the focus of our analysis.
23 https://theweek.com/10things/919412/10-things-need-know-today-june-11-2020, item 2.

EMH is a controversial hypothesis that states that *share prices reflect all available information, and consistent alpha generation (a fancy phrase meaning return without risk) is impossible. According to the EMH, stocks always trade at their fair value on exchanges, making it impossible for investors to purchase undervalued stocks or sell stocks for inflated prices. Therefore, it should be impossible to outperform the overall market through expert stock selection or market timing, and the only way an investor can obtain higher returns is by purchasing riskier investments.*[24]

While *COVID* brought larger losses than gains, there also are days of extreme gains as well, e.g., 3/24/20 and 3/25/20, with gains of 20.9% and 24.3% (C14461, C14462). The latter is 11.2 standard deviations.

In other words, big crises bring with them extreme stock market volatility, as people are trying to obtain and absorb information rapidly on often poorly understood phenomena. As information changes daily or even within a day, stock prices of publicly traded firms are adjusting to the new information. This information often causes investors to change their forecasts of future cash flows, their discount rates (i.e., their risk measures), or both, which causes market valuation to change.

Privately held firms do not benefit from the instant market feedback on their news. It does not mean their news has no or less impact on their value. It just means that it is more difficult to interpret how changing business operations and news impact a company's value.

The next section of our table shows Boeing Prices around the time of the Alaska Air MAX 9 door plug blowing off:

	Date (A)	Closing price (B)	Delta Δ (C)	Misc (D)	Notes / Comments
15614	01/05/2024	$249.00	1.7%		Alaska Air Max door plug blew off Friday 1/5/24, 5:14 PST (after mkt close).
15615	01/08/2024	$229.00	-8.0%		1st Trading day after event.
15616	01/09/2024	$225.76	-1.4%		
15617	01/10/2024	$227.84	0.9%		
15618	01/11/2024	$222.66	-2.3%		
15619	01/12/2024	$217.70	-2.2%		
15620	01/16/2024	$200.52	-7.9%	-19.5%	10 day ↓. (Market closed MLK day).
15634	02/05/2024	$206.63	-1.3%	-17.0%	1 Month ↓ FMV
15654	03/05/2024	$201.14	0.3%	-19.2%	2 Month ↓ FMV

Table 11.6: *Alaska Air Door Plug Blow-Off ↓ 19.5% in Stock Price*

24 https://www.investopedia.com/terms/e/efficientmarkethypothesis.asp, very lightly edited for brevity and clarity.

The last incident of interest is 1/5/2024, *Alaska Airlines'* MAX 9 door plug blew off the plane at 5:14 PM Pacific time, after trading hours. The next trading day, *Boeing* stock declined 8% (C15615). By 1/16/24, 10 days later, *Boeing's* stock declined 19.5% (D15620). On 2/5/24, one month after that event, *Boeing's* stock price was down 17.0% (D15634). On 3/4/24, two months after the event, its stock was down 19.2% (D15634).

As prices fluctuate on every trading day, it is difficult to state a definitive loss from all three incidents combined, as there is much *water under the bridge* (i.e., the passage of time, with all kinds of news), causing a lot of *white noise* in the trading prices. It often takes time for investors to figure out whether bad news is a unique, one-time event or whether it is a symptom of a systematic problem that means more problems in the future. One day after the event is usually not enough time. We could choose any time period—one week, two weeks, etc. We selected the one-month prices after each event to make a reasonable measurement of the magnitude of *Boeing's* losses from these events without polluting the measurement with other significant, unrelated events.

In D15758 (not shown), which equals the sum of D14332, D14421, and D15634, we calculate losses of 35.3%, which is the 4.7% one-month loss in share price after the *Lion Air* crash, the 13.6% one-month loss in share price after the *Ethiopian Air* crash, and the 17.0% one-month loss in share price after the door plug fell.

Notice that each subsequent event caused a larger magnitude of loss in value than the previous one, which makes sense, as the collective opinion of investors is that this is no longer a case of user error by the pilots on the first two crashes with no problems in Boeing's planes, but a systemic problem in the *737 MAX* that required a sensor for which *Boeing wanted to* charge an extra $80,000 to correct for its design flaw, and that sensor never should have been optional. Finally, the door plug problem eventually led to the *FAA* audit, with the conclusion that Boeing has substantial problems in its quality control.

Airbus Industrie Stock Prices[25]

The purpose of including *Airbus* stock prices is to provide some additional context on stock prices, as it is *Boeing's* only competitor of significance in global manufacturing of commercial aircraft on a similar scale. We were able to find stock prices for *Airbus* since 9/3/2001,[26] but let us begin with 9/10/2001, the day before the 9/11 attacks.

On that day of infamy, 9/11/2001, *Airbus'* stock price declined 11.6%, and it declined significantly through 9/21/2001, at which point its stock was down 43.7% (E19), after which its stock increased. The one-month stock price on 10/11/2001 was 26.4% (E34) lower than 9/10/2001—a significant decline, but less than that of 9/21. Again, it takes the market time to understand and price a new type and level of risk that was unheard of before.

---

25 Not shown due to space limitations. We nevertheless provide cell references.
26 Yahoo Finance, downloaded 3/18/24, AIR.PA

We note that 10/29/18 (row 4413, not shown) is the date of the *Lion Air* crash of the Boeing MAX 8, and it appears to have no effect on *Airbus'* value, with a –0.3% (D4413) drop in price, which is insignificant in amount and totally lost in *Airbus'* own white noise.

Airbus' stock price increased 1.3% (D4505) on 3/11/2019, the first trading day after the Ethiopian Air crash. This also appears statistically insignificant. I thought that perhaps Boeing's bad news would be *Airbus'* good news, but so far, there is no evidence of that.

Contrast that with the effect of COVID. One month after the onset of COVID, *Airbus'* stock is down 46.3% (E4763, not shown), and two months after the onset, it is down 54.1% (E4783). So, the market absorbed the horrible news of COVID substantially in the first month.

The first trading day after *Boeing's* door plug blow-out on *Alaska Airlines*, 1/8/24, *Airbus* was up 2.5% (D4792, not shown), which is significant, but not very large. However, *Airbus'* stock was up 6.7% (E5764) at the one-month interval after the door plug, and two months after, Airbus was up 10.0% (E5785), while *Boeing's* stock declined 19.2% (D2522). So it seems that eventually, Boeing's news did become Airbus's good news. Eventually, safety becomes a reputation. With apologies to Ecclesiastes, a good name is better than sales.

Summary of analysis of Boeing/Airbus stock prices

At this point, it is useful to summarize what we have learned by this detailed analysis of stock prices:

- Huge, catastrophic events cause valuations to decline significantly.

- The market responds differently to one-time events that have no future implications than it does to events that the market expects to continue. Each of the three Boeing incidents caused a successively larger decline in *Boeing's* value.

  o The *Lion Air* crash, which the market probably judged as likely to be pilot error but would have assigned at least a small probability to the problem lying with Boeing itself, caused a 6.6% (C14310) one-day drop in value; the *Ethiopian Air* crash caused a similar one-day drop (5.3% vs. 6.6%), but the two-day cumulative effects were very different—roughly –2.3% (C14310 + C14311, the latter not shown) for Lion Air versus –11.4% (C14399 + C14400) for Ethiopian.

  o The first two incidents were fatal crashes that killed everyone on both planes, but the third incident, which involved no fatalities, had the largest effect on a stock price of all, a 19.5% decline by the 6th trading day since the crash.

- It takes time for the market to accumulate and sort through the evidence as to how likely it is that any catastrophe may be a one-off vs. systematic in its cause, and it adjusts the value of the firm as each new piece of information affects investors' collective estimation of the future of the firm, or the industry, for that much.

Obviously, *9/11-style terrorism* affects plane travel more than taxicabs or Uber. At one point, COVID caused a 71% decline in *Boeing's* value and a 55.0% decline in *Airbus*.

- Adding the *Arthur Andersen* story, we can also add that trust, once lost, becomes hard or impossible to win back. After a bad incident, investors have to assess how deep the problem is and how long it will last. Every subsequent *Boeing* incident hit its valuation more than the previous one, as investors become more informed that, *No Toto, we are not in Kansas anymore.* Think about the effect of a cybersecurity incident, e.g., the Change Healthcare cyberattack cost UnitedHealth $872 million.[27]

Boeing financial highlights and valuation

The following is a series of excerpts from the Boeing financial highlights and valuation table. We begin with revenues and net income.

Revenues and net income

This table contains a lot of financial data[28] and prints on too many pages to present comfortably for non-financial analyst readers, so we will focus on only a relatively small subset of it. We begin with Boeing's revenues and net income (in millions of dollars) from its 2018 Annual Report:

	Description	2009 (B)	2014 (G)	2015 (H)	2016 (I)	2017 (J)	2018 (K)
5	Revenues (Billions USD)	68,281	90,762	96,114	93,496	94,005	101,127
10	Net Earnings (Annual Report Note 3)	1,312	5,446	5,176	5,034	8,458	10,460

Table 11.7: Boeing revenue and net income from its 2018 Annual Report

Revenues mostly rose from $68.3 billion in 2009 to a peak of $101.1 billion (K5) in 2018, after which they fell rapidly to $58.2 billion (M5, not shown) in 2020. The story of revenues is that *Boeing* was flying high until the end of October 2018 with the *Lion Air* crash. Even then, this was the first incident, and the market noticed but did not seem to ascribe great financial importance to it. Net earnings in row 12, not shown, also follow a similar upward pattern, rising from $1.3 billion in 2009 to a high of $10.5 billion in 2018. The company had much harder times in 2019 and after. The *Ethiopian Airlines* crash occurred on 3/10/19, and the *FAA* grounded all *737 MAX 8s* from 3/13/19 to 11/18/20. In one sense, *Boeing* was lucky, having almost half of its grounding period coincide with COVID.

Since 2018 was *Boeing's* peak year, I chose 12/31/2018 as the valuation date. All valuations <u>are only effective</u> as of a particular date and for a particular purpose. Think of what the

27 https://www.cbsnews.com/news/unitedhealth-cyberattack-change-healthcare-hack-ransomware/
28 Sources: 2018 Annual Report, p. 48; 2015 Annual Report p. 49; 2013 Annual Report p. 25; 2009 Annual Report, p. 17.

value of the **World Trade Center (WTC)** on 9/10/2001 vs. 9/11/2001. 2018 Net Earnings of $8.458 billion in J10 forms much of the basis for our valuation.

As a side point, the valuation purpose can change the valuation result. Two valuations on the same date for different purposes may or may not result in the same value. For example, if we are valuing the stock of a company president who has guaranteed a company loan with his personal assets, the value of his or her stock may be different than the same block of stock without the personal guarantee.

Growth

Let us look at the annual growth in revenues and net income. We show two types of growth, annual growth and **Compound Average Growth Rates (CAGR)**. A *CAGR* is a *geometric average* constant growth rate that takes us from a beginning number to an ending number, assuming constant percentage growth at the *CAGR* every year. The following are our calculations of Boeing's annual and compound average growth rates in revenues and net earnings based on the numbers in *Table 11.7*:

	Description	2009	2010	2011	2012	2013	2014	2015	2016	2017	2018
	(A)	(B)	(C)	(D)	(E)	(F)	(G)	(H)	(I)	(J)	(K)
32	**Growth**										
33	Revenue- Annual		-5.82%	6.89%	18.86%	6.03%	4.78%	5.90%	-2.72%	0.54%	7.58%
34	Revenue- CAGR to 2018	4.46%	5.82%	5.67%	3.62%	3.15%	2.74%	1.71%	4.00%	7.58%	
43	Net Earnings = Δ		152.06%	21.23%	-2.92%	17.63%	18.83%	-4.93%	-2.73%	68.00%	23.68%
44	Net Earnings- CAGR to 2018	25.94%	15.47%	14.67%	17.90%	17.95%	17.74%	26.43%	44.14%	23.68%	

Table 11.8: Annual and compound growth rates for revenue and net earnings

Annual revenue growth is in row 33, which is the annual growth of revenues in row 5. Revenues declined 5.822% (C33) in 2010 but then grew nicely from 2011 to 2015, highest in 2012 at 18.6%, declined in 2016, remained fairly flat in 2017, and increased at 7.6% in 2018.

The *CAGR* for the year 2018 is fairly stable. It is 4.46% (B34) from 2009 to 2018, increases to 5.8% and 5.7% for 2010 to 2018 and 2011 to 2018, and then declines as we move into the lower growth years. All in all, Boeing's revenue growth is fairly modest.

Net earnings growth is a very different story. It is much more volatile. Row 43 shows the annual growth in net earnings (row 12). Earnings grew 152% (C43 = C12/B12 − 1) in 2010, 21.2% (D43) in 2011, declined in 2012, grew in the 17% to 18% range in 2013 − 2014, declined in 2015 − 2016, and then grew 68% (J43) in 2017 and 23.7% (K43) in 2018.

The *CAGR* of net earnings appears in row 44. It is 25.9% (C44) from 2009 to 2018, 15.5% from 2010 to 2018, and increases over the next two years, holds steady in 2014, increases again in 2015 and 2016, and drops in 2017, but that drop is to a very healthy 23.7%. Note that the one-year *CAGR* equals the annual increase in the next year. For example, J44 = K43. Similarly, J34 = K33.

So, which rate or rates should we use to forecast growth in cash flows? First, we are actually using growth in net income as a proxy for growth in cash flows. But still, which rates should we use? It is a complex question that does not have any simple, easy answer.

My first thought is that growth in net income is closer to what we need than growth in sales. However, the sales growth rate is ultimately a limiting factor in the growth of net income. While the 152% (C43) *CAGR* from 2010 to 2018 is the most long-term *CAGR*, it also leads to a meaningless valuation, as growth will be greater than the required return on capital, i.e., $g > r$, which does not work. As we will see, it appears that *Boeing's* discount rate on capital should be 11% or 12%, which we will describe further in our explanation, so a meaningful growth rate must be under 11% or 12%.

Our next candidate is the 7-year *CAGR* in D43, 21.228%. However, that suffers from the same problem. Another reason why the high growth rates of net income do not make sense to use as our forecast of growth in the *Gordon Model* is that sales growth of around 5% to 6% with continued growth in net income that is much higher than that implies that eventually expenses eventually must trend towards zero, which also makes no sense. *Boeing* clearly went through a historical period where sales grew modestly while expenses grew at a much lower rate, but eventually, that is unsustainable.

Thus, long-term growth in net income and cash flow must be at least the sales growth rate and less than *Boeing's* historical growth rate in net income, i.e., somewhere between 5% and 12%. We will narrow that down shortly in the valuation section.

Valuation

Table 11.9 is a series of valuations of Boeing as of Dec 31^(st) 2018:

	Description (A)	Valuation 1 (G)	Valuation 2 (H)	Valuation 3 (I)	Valuation 0 (K)	Formula (L)
64	Discount Rate	r = 10%, g = 7.5%	r = 10%	r = 11%	r = 12%	
65	Adjusted Stock Price/Share 12/31/18	$313.3922	$313.3922	$313.3922	$313.3922	='11.5'!B14352
66	Millions of shares 12/31/18	570	570	570	570	=K27
67	FMV-Market Cap	$178,634	$178,634	$178,634	$178,634	=K65*K66
68						

	Description (A)	Valuation 1 (G)	Valuation 2 (H)	Valuation 3 (I)	Valuation 0 (K)	Formula (L)
69	Net Income 2018	$10,460	$10,460	$10,460	$10,460	=$K10
70	Payout Ratio	40.3%	40.3%	40.3%	40.3%	=$K26
71	Dividends 2018	$4,213.30	$4,213.30	$4,213.30	$4,213.30	=K69*K70
72	Discount Rate	10%	10%	11%	12%	='11.6.1'!B11
73	Growth Rate = Min(2012-18 CAGR, 7.5%)	7.5%	8.6%	8.6%	8.6%	=AVERAGE (B34,C34,C44)
74	Dividends 2019 (Forecast as of 12/31/2018)	$4,529.30	$4,575.00	$4,575	$4,575.00	=K71*(1+K73)
75	GMM-EOY	40.0	70.7	41.4	29.3	=1/(K72-K73)
76	FMV-Calculated with GMM	$181,172	$323,282	$189,427	$133,961	=K74*K75
77	Over <Under> Valuation	1.4%	81.0%	6.0%	-25%	=(K76/K67)-1

Table 11.9: Valuation—Mkt Cap vs. GMM in millions of USD

The valuation section is fairly small and consists of four columns and 13 rows. There are two dimensions of analysis that correspond to the rows and columns of the table.

The first dimension is the type of valuation, of which there are two. There are two vertical blocks of valuation calculations, *Boeing's* market capitalization (*market cap*) in rows 65 through 67, Boeing's price per share times the number of shares outstanding, and our own valuation calculations in rows 69 through 76 using the Gordon Model, with row 77 measuring how well our GMM valuation in row 76 approximates the market cap in row 67.

The second dimension in our valuation analysis is which key assumptions we use, primarily using discount rates of 10% in columns G and H, 11% in column I, and 12% in column K. In columns H, I, and K, we use an 8.6% (row 73) growth rate, and in G73, we use a 7.5% growth rate.

We start by calculating market cap, which is simply *Boeing's* stock price on 12/31/18 of $313.3922 per share (K65, which comes from *Table 11.4*, B14352) × 570 million shares (row 66, from K27, not shown in the table) = $178.6 billion (row 67). The market cap is the market's valuation of Boeing. Now, let us see what we get using our value fundamentals with the Gordon Model.

Using the *Gordon Model* to calculate the value, we begin with the 2018 Net Income After Tax of $10.46 billion in row 69. We multiply that by the **Dividends Payout Ratio (POR)** of 40.3% (K70) = 2018 dividends of $4.2133 billion in K71.

We use a discount rate of 12% (K72, transferred from Table 11.6.1, B11[29]) in our valuation in column K and a discount rate of 11% in column I. The 12% is from an actual calculation of the discount rate. However, our results with a 12% discount rate are OK, not great, so we try it a second time with an 11% discount rate to see what we get by lowering the discount rate by an absolute 1%. Additionally, we use a 10% discount rate (G72, transferred from Table 11.6.1, B17) in column G. We will describe this one last.

As mentioned above, the growth rate is the most difficult parameter in the *Gordon Model* that we must forecast. I chose to use an average of the 9- and 8-year sales *CAGRs* and the 9-year *CAGR* in net income (B34, C34, and C44), which average 8.6% (K73). I must emphasize that this is just reasonable guesswork.

We forecast 2019 Dividends as of 12/31/18, i.e., only using the information we have available as of the end of 2018, of $4.575 billion (row 74). The *End-of-Year Gordon Model* multiple is $1 / (r - g) = 1 / (12\% - 8.6\%) = 29.3$ (K74). Multiplying the latter by the former gives us our estimate of value using the *Gordon Model* multiple of $133,961 (K76) million, or $133.961 billion, which is a 25.0% (K77) undervaluation compared to the market cap. Had we used a midyear *GMM*, the undervaluation would have been roughly 21% (not shown).

Two questions naturally arise in this analysis:

1. If we already have a market cap, which is the market's valuation of *Boeing*, why bother using a *Gordon Model* multiple to perform a second valuation?

2. Which is the more accurate measure?

Those are fair questions.

- **The answers to question #1 are:**

    o In one sense, there is no need for a *Discounted Cash Flow* valuation using the *Gordon Model*. The market cap is the market's valuation of *Boeing*, so the *GMM* appears superfluous. However:

    o The market participants need to know how many shares of *Boeing* they want to buy or sell on any given day, and if one is stuck with using only the market cap, then there is no correcting mechanism if the market is wrong. Market participants—and remember that many of them are very sophisticated, professionally managed institutional investors—hedge funds, mutual funds, pension funds, etc.—are constantly looking for what they believe to be under- or over-valued stocks to buy or sell, and a *DCF* is the primary independent method to value stocks.

---

29 We do not show Table 11.6.1 in this chapter, as it is very technical and largely beyond the scope of the chapter. However, we do note that the discount rates that we use in the valuation section are consistent with Decile 1 discount rates.

- **Answer to question #2:** The author does not know which one is likely more accurate. There is too much information about *Boeing* that must be known to make an informed, professional judgment as to whether *Boeing's* stock was under- or overvalued on 12/31/18.

  o Keep in mind that most stock analysts are valuation people specialized in valuing publicly traded firms, while I am largely specialized in valuing privately held firms. There is a wide body of knowledge that deals with the difference in valuing public versus private firms that business appraisers like me must know that stock analysts typically would not know. However, stock analysts typically spend their every waking hour becoming experts in one or, at most, a few companies, while I have valued well over 2,000 companies and do not have time to develop the depth of knowledge over the decades that a *Boeing* analyst would.

  o If we had tens or hundreds of billions of dollars of trades depending on my stock recommendations, you had better believe that we would participate in every conference possible with *Boeing* executives, asking all kinds of questions. But writing this chapter for a book on *DevOps* engineering, we have not spoken to *Boeing* executives, as the company is under a continuing crisis, and we doubt it would want to allocate time for interviews for this chapter.

The lack of precision and certainty in forecasting the growth rate prompted me to explore a different possible discount rate—11% in column I. All calculations in I65 to I77 are identical to their analogs in column K, with the only difference between the discount rate of 12% in I72 versus 11% in K72. The result is a valuation of $189.4 billion in I76, which is 6.0% (I77) over the Market Cap of $183.8 billion in row 67.

I do not know which set of calculations is correct. Most likely, neither is correct, but they are both somewhere in the ballpark of *Fair Market Value*. Also, the most accurate discount rate may be higher than 12%, as *Boeing* is primarily debt-financed, with little capital. That may raise the discount rate above 12%, which would increase the *sell signal* at 12/31/2018.

However, *Boeing* is one participant in a duopoly and is a *too-big-to-fail* firm, which lowers its cost of capital. I can assure you that if any small, midsize, or even most large companies were underwater, nobody would be running with $60 billion to rescue them. Even Arthur Andersen, the largest of the Big 5 accounting firms in its day,[30] was allowed a fairly swift demise. Being *too big to fail* lowers *Boeing's* risk to investors, who can run to Washington, D.C. with *hat in hand*. Very few businesses have that safety net, which lowers investor risk.

At the end of the day, I know too little about *Boeing* to make a definitive valuation of it, and one must have a healthy dash of humility in attempting to value a firm about which I know so little.

---

30 When I interviewed for a position as an auditor there in 1974, it was then the *Big 8 accounting firms*. By the time of *Enron*, it was down to the *Big 5*. The loss of three came from mergers, *Ernst & Ernst* with *Arthur Young* to become *Ernst & Young*; *Price Waterhouse* with *Coopers & Lybrand* to become *PricewaterhouseCoopers*; and *Deloitte* with *Haskins & Sells*, then with *Touche Ross* to become *Deloitte & Touch*.

In *Table 11.6.1*, Calculation #2 results in a 10% discount rate. Using that directly in G72 while keeping all other assumptions the same resulted in a valuation of $323.3 billion in G76, resulting in an 81% over-valuation. However, combining a more optimistic discount rate with a somewhat optimistic growth rate results in a very optimistic valuation, i.e., a probable overvaluation. Thus, I lowered the forecast growth rate in G73 to a more conservative 7.5%, which resulted in a valuation of $181.2 billion (G76), which is 1.4% (– G77) above the *Boeing* market cap, a much more reasonable result and the closest one to the market cap.

What does this analysis show—that I fudge the numbers whenever convenient? No, my point is that a valuation is composed of a number of measurements and assumptions. We try to be *on the money* on each assumption, but sometimes we have a reason to select what others might consider a slightly more optimistic or more conservative assumption for one of our valuation calculations.

However, we must be very careful not to string together a series of assumptions that each tilt in one direction. That is how significant over-or-under-valuations can occur, even with an unbiased valuation analyst. This is especially all the more true when valuing a company near *the valuation edge,* i.e., low discount rate and high forecast growth rate. Small errors in our reasoning and/or inferences can cause fairly large errors in the valuation—a potential problem that largely does not exist in valuing small firms, where the same size small errors would have little impact on the final valuation outcome. We all make errors. Nobody is perfect, and certainly not all the time. I was perfect once last Thursday afternoon, and nobody even noticed.[31]

The author's assumption is that *Boeing* was more likely over-valued on 12/31/2018 than under-valued, and it is possible that it was correctly valued by the market, with one big caveat, which is all these calculations are assuming there was no hidden risk in *Boeing*—no dust swept under the carpet—no skeletons in the closet.

However, now, in retrospect, we know that Boeing was sweeping its dust under the carpet. We now know that *Boeing* had *design flaws* in its *MCAS* system for the *MAX 8 and 9,* and it has most recently come out that *Boeing's* manufacturing system has many flaws in it that resulted in missing bolts from its doors in addition to other likely problems.

In summary, we see that the *Gordon Model* multiple does a fairly good job of valuing *Boeing,* the task being made more difficult by our lack of knowledge of the company and lack of access to insiders. Usually, in my valuation assignments, we have ample access to the President, **Chief Financial Officer (CFO)**, Controller, and other C-level executives.

Volkswagen

According to the Guardian, The *Volkswagen* emissions scandal, sometimes known as *Dieselgate* or *Emissionsgate,* began in September 2015, when the USA **Environmental**

---

31 A bit of nerdy humor, with attribution to my dear friend, Christopher Hunt, who is anything but a nerd.

Protection Agency (EPA) issued a notice of violation of the *Clean Air Act* to German automaker **Volkswagen Group (VW)**. The agency had found that *VW* had intentionally programmed turbocharged direct injection diesel engines to activate their emissions controls only during laboratory emissions testing, which caused the vehicles' NOx output to meet USA standards during regulatory testing.

However, the vehicles emitted up to 40 times more NOx in real-world driving. *Volkswagen* deployed this software in about 11 million cars worldwide, including 500,000 in the United States, in model years 2009 through 2015.[32]

Thus, *VW* also plead guilty to committing fraud[33]. Unlike *Boeing*, there was no immediate safety issue from its fraud. No one was hurt or died. The only direct negative consequence to consumers is that the diesel cars polluted more than *VW* falsely claimed.

In valuation terms, *VW* decreased its probable future cash flows and increased its discount rate in committing the fraud.

Table 11.10 shows Volkswagen stock prices on key dates:

	Date (A)	Closing price (B)	Adjusted closing price (C)	Delta Δ (D)	Calcs (E)	Comments / Notes
437	09/17/2015	167.8000	111.7806	-1.1%		
438	**09/18/2015**	162.4000	**108.1834**	-3.2%		Notice of violation: Clean Air Act
439	09/21/2015	132.2000	88.0655	-18.6%		
440	**09/22/2015**	106.0000	**70.6123**	-19.8%	-34.7%	3 Day ↓ in FMV
441	09/23/2015	111.5000	74.2761	5.2%		
459	10/19/2015	99.1900	**66.0758**	-1.4%	**-38.9%**	1 Month ↓ in FMV
481	11/18/2015	101.4000	**67.5480**	2.8%	**-37.6%**	2 Month ↓ in FMV
503	12/18/2015	130.0000	**86.6000**	-0.6%	**-20.0%**	3 Month ↓ in FMV
510	12/30/2015	133.7500	89.0980	-1.2%		

Table 11.10: VW Stock ↓ 35% in 3 days

The *EPA* gave *VW* its *Notice of Violation* on 9/18/2015. On that and the two following days, its stock price dropped 34.7% (E440), or roughly 35%, about the same as *Boeing*. The 1-month drop in stock price was 38.9% (E459). The 2- and 3-month drops in *FMV* are 37.6%

32 https://www.theguardian.com/business/2015/dec/10/volkswagen-emissions-scandal-timeline-events
33 https://www.justice.gov/usao-edmi/us-v-volkswagen-16-cr-20394#:~:text=Volkswagen:%20On%20January%2011%2C%202017,The%20vehicles%20at%20issue%20include

(E481) and 20% (E503). Apparently, the market may have decided that new information trickling in between 1 and 3 months after the Notice mitigated some of the fears investors had. It takes time for people to find out just how big and bad the scope of the problem is, and investors are usually operating on partial information.

Table of strategic blunders failure attribute analysis

The following table shows various key attributes of our three *Strategic Blunders*:

Attribute	Arthur Andersen	VW	Boeing
↓ FMV	100%	35%	35%
Competence	↓	↑	↓
Morality	↓	↓↓	↓↓↓
Loss of Life?	No	No	Yes
# Competitors	4	14	1
Too Big to Fail?	No	Probably No	Yes

Table 11.11: Analysis of the effect of 5 attributes on loss in value

Here are a few comments about some of the rankings in this table:

- In terms of competence, VW actually demonstrated great technical competence to fool so many experts for so long.

- In terms of morality, I estimated Arthur Andersen's failings less harshly, as it committed its moral lapses under great pressure from the fallout of its lapses in competence. In contrast, VW and Boeing were under no unusual pressure that drove their moral lapses. Boeing's was the worst, because its callous business decision would inevitably lead to a loss in life. It would have been much different had Boeing informed everyone in advance of the intricacies of MCAS, made the additional sensor mandatory, and trained the pilots properly.

Lessons learned

What can we learn from these spectacular business failures:

- It is easier to maintain a good reputation than it is to restore it once lost. Once customers, investors, and other stakeholders lose trust, either in a company's competence, its ethics, or both, the company loses value, and it is hard to retrieve that loss.

    o In *Arthur Andersen's* case, it was a permanent, total loss.

- In the case of *Boeing*, many people died. If *Boeing* were not an American icon duopoly, with French-based Airbus being the only other alternative source of commercial jets, it would not surprise me if *Boeing* would have gone the way of *Arthur Andersen*. Of course, there is no way to know that, but Boeing had a better fact pattern in its favor, not better skills.

- It seems that these major corporate train wrecks tend to cost the firm 35% to 40% of its value. That is a heavy price to pay for arrogance and/or laziness, and callous indifference to other people's lives.

- Investing in quality is essential to reduce risk for building and retaining value within the organization.

Optimal spending for QACS

Table 11.12 is the culmination and ultimate purpose of this chapter. We show four different choices of how much to invest in QA and cybersecurity in columns B through E and run a valuation on the company under each assumption. The highest valuation points to the optimal spending choice:

	Scenario (A)	Current invest (B)	Invest $2M (C)	Invest $5M (D)	Invest $10M (E)
5	Forecast Sales Year 1	100,000,000	100,000,000	100,000,000	100,000,000
6	Net Income at Current Level of QA & CS	20,000,000	20,000,000	20,000,000	20,000,000
7	Enhanced QA & CS	0	2,000,000	5,000,000	10,000,000
8	Net Income Before Tax	20,000,000	18,000,000	15,000,000	10,000,000
9	Income Tax	(5,000,000)	(4,500,000)	(3,750,000)	(2,500,000)
10	Net Income After Tax	15,000,000	13,500,000	11,250,000	7,500,000
11	Dividends	6,000,000	5,400,000	4,500,000	3,000,000
12	Gordan Model Multiple	12.5	14.285714	16.66667	20
13	Fair Market Value[34]	75,000,000	77,142,857	75,000,000	60,000,000
14	Cost of Disaster as 35% of Base Case FMV	26,250,000			
15	Assumed Discount Rates	15%	14%	13%	12%

Table 11.12: The highest valuation reveals the optimal decision on QACS

---

34 For simplicity, we Ignore adjustments for control and marketability, as that is beyond the scope of this chapter, but in reality those are adjustments we must consider making.

In *Table 11.12* above, we make the following assumptions: Sales in year 1 is $100,000,000, Pre-Tax Margin is 20%, Corporate Tax rate is 25%, Payout ratio is 40%, discount rate starts at 15% and lowers by 1% for each additional level of investment, Long Term growth rate of 7%, and Cost of Disaster is 35% of FMV from their previous valuation[35].

Suppose a software firm with $100 million (B17, transferred to row 5) in forecast sales next year and a 20% (B18) profit margin has been spending 1% of sales = $1 million on QACS, and it wants to know whether this is the right amount. How might we analyze this?

Forecast Net Income before Enhanced *QACS* is $100 million × 20% = $20 million (row 6 = B17 × B18). In the Current Scenario (aka Base Case Scenario, column B), we assume no further Enhanced *QACS*. Thus, B7 = $0, and **Net Income Before Tax (NIBT)** is still $20 million (B8 = B6 – B7).

Assuming combined federal and state corporate taxes of 25% (B19) = $5 million (B9), which leaves forecast NIAT of $15 million.

We multiply this by our assumed Payout Ratio, which is forecast Dividends / *NIAT* of 40% (B20) to forecast dividends of $6 million (B11).

Let us assume the company has a discount rate of 15% (B15) and a long-term *Present Value Weighted Average Growth Rate* of 7% (B22),[36] so the GMM of the company is:

$$GMM = \frac{1}{(0.15 - 0.07)} = \frac{1}{0.08} = 12.5 \text{ (B12)}.$$

Equation 11.5: Gordon Model Multiple

The **fair market value (FMV)** of the Company, ignoring adjustments for control and marketability[37], is $6 million × 12.5 = $75 million (B13). While Arthur Anderson lost 100% of its value, we can estimate the Cost of Disaster at 35% (B23), which comes from our analysis of the *Strategic Blunders* and other *high impact events*—Boeing and Volkswagen. This implies a Base Case Cost of Disaster of $26.25 million (B14).

Now, the $64 million question: how much should the company invest in enhancing *QACS*? It is already spending $1 million, which is part of the 20% pre-tax margin in the Current Scenario. How much additional *QACS* spending is optimal? This is a valuation question, as opposed to an engineering one or the gut feelings of a business leader.

Our analysis in column C is identical to that in column B, except for the following:

- The Company invests an additional $2 million (C7) in *QACS*, which lowers *NIBT* from $20 million to $18 million (C8 versus B8).

---

35 Per our analysis of Strategic Blunders and high-impact events that affected the value of organizations.
36 These are reasonable numbers as an example. This would likely happen with a firm that has high forecast growth rates in its foreseeable future—let's say the next 5 to 10 years—followed by declining growth rates after that. For those who want a deep understanding of how value grows over time as a function of growth, see my article, How Does Value Grow? Chasing Short-Term Income Destroys Long-Term Value, *Business Valuation Review, Vol. 34, No. 3*, Fall (October) 2015, which is available on my website, www.abramsvaluation.com.
37 We skip this here for simplicity, but in practice must consider those adjustments.

- Due to the 25% tax savings, the after-tax cost of the $2 million enhanced *QACS* is $1.5 million, and *NIAT* decreases from $15 million in the Current Scenario to $13.5 million in C10.

- Dividends, assumed at 40% of *NIAT*, decline in C11 by $1.5 million × 40% = $600,000 compared to B11, i.e., they are $5.4 million in C11 versus $6 million in B11.

- We assume that the additional $2 million in investment lowers the company's discount rate by 1%, from 15% in B21 to 14% in D21.

- This increases GMM to 214.285614 (C12).

- *FMV* increases to $5.4 million × 14.2857… = $77.14 million C13 = C11 x C12.

The additional investment of $2 million in *QACS* increases FMV by $2.14 million, from $75 million (B13) to $77.12 million in C13. Thus, under these assumptions, we would counsel management to make the additional $2 million investment in QACS beyond its base case of $1 million per year starting point.

The additional investments of $5 million and $10 million in columns D and E, under the assumptions that we used, would produce *FMVs* that are lower than that of C13, so we would counsel management under these assumptions to invest an additional $2 million in *QACS*, but no more than that.

Obviously, we would reach different conclusions under different assumptions. For example, if we forecast the additional $10 million in QACS to reduce the discount rate to 10% instead of 12%, the GMM would be (1/0.1-0.7) = (1/0.3) = 33.3, then *FMV* would increase to $3 million forecast dividends x 33.3 = $100 million, and that would be the level of investment we would recommend.

Conclusion

In this chapter, we have explained the critical importance of value being the key criterion for making decisions on virtually every strategic decision that a business makes. Of course, that is presupposing that the decisions are within the realm of that which is ethical and moral. We absolutely reject enhancing value at the expense of human life and dignity.

Given that, we have demonstrated the advantages of using value as the common language that not only engineering and leadership should use to communicate and make decisions, but all other divisions as well, because value incorporates all there is about a business, its environment, risk its past, and its probable future.

We have provided future and present value formulas, the latter for single cash flows as well as annual cash flows using ADFs and GMMs and given some examples of how to use them. We believe this to be enough to help engineers and management in software and other firms to begin thinking in value terms and terminology.

However, the skills needed to perform valuation analysis are way beyond anything we have presented in a chapter. Becoming a valuation analyst requires a huge amount of education and training, so do not try this at home. When it is time for the rubber to meet the road, get professional help.

We covered how *Strategic Blunders* and *high-impact events* can affect value. We found that while *Arthur Andersen* lost all of its value, *Boeing* and *Volkswagen* each lost about 35% to 40% of their value, which is a very useful result in estimating the value effects of investments in *QACS*. A firm may lose even more than that if its effects in our Table of *Strategic Blunders* Failures Attribute Analysis is more unfavorable than the three we analyzed. *The Challenger Tragedy,* which, while not a business failure, per se, was a national failure for the US Space Program and a terrible tragedy in the loss of life. Finally, we gave an example of modeling different levels of *QACS* and their effects on value.

It is our fond hope that this chapter, which, to our knowledge, is absolutely unique in software engineering literature, will be a major contribution to better communication, cooperation, mutual respect, and better decision-making in companies throughout the world.

In the next chapter, we will return to the land of computers and explore observability of our systems and building manageable on-call processes to support our organization's mission.

Join our Discord space

Join our Discord workspace for latest updates, offers, tech happenings around the world, new releases, and sessions with the authors:

https://discord.bpbonline.com

CHAPTER 12
Observability

Introduction

In short, *observability* is collecting, processing, and visualizing information about a system as it runs in hopes of better understanding what is happening. While observability is a broad topic, we will primarily explore it through the lens of site reliability, performance, and security. In other words, we will focus on questions about *whether X works*. And *how well does X work?* When considering supporting an application, an important aspect is the need for a 24/7 staffed team to support our after-hours alerting systems. To avoid burning out, we will discuss several topics related to alert fatigue.

While we may have been laser-focused up to this point on our processes related to the deployment of our business logic, let us take a step back to acknowledge the complexity of the overall delivery of a reliable, large-scale service. Even if we set everything up perfectly, how do we know it stays that way? It might seem trivial, but what about someone tripping over a power cable? If you think this is silly and would never cause large-scale outages, think again, as many real-world examples exist. While the most common question we tend to ask ourselves in this space is, *Is it working?* Later, we will graduate to ask better questions, for example, *how well it works*. This progression is akin to our maturity model evolution, as we saw with our testing, security, and pipeline topics.

When a service breaks down, how easily can we find the root cause, resolve it, and improve? When considering observability in our site reliability lens, we are concerned with testing and measuring all the dependencies from software, hardware, services, etc., rather than a particular functional unit or business workflow.

Observability is a perfect example of a place where the needs, responsibilities, etc., of operations and product engineers can overlap, yet one is often more on the hook to provide it than the other due to *misaligned incentives*. We need to ensure that the system we spent so much time building remains available and meets the performance and security needs. This overlap makes it more difficult to automatically discover and route the best-suited engineering persona to the problem set.

When we use a public cloud provider, they take on many of the complexities. Yet, even with these benefits, many organizations typically limit most application availability to one regional fault domain. To run a large-scale system in a data center, we need a considerable amount of power, climate control systems (temperature and humidity), hardware, network bandwidth, etc., all with redundancies to ensure we have a solid foundation to provide a solid base for our application. Then, we need software to bridge these systems and properly route the traffic. Each component must be monitored for changes, attempted self-healing, and alerted when remediation is impossible without human intervention.

I have spent much of my entire career being part of an on-call schedule. Rather than waiting for our customers to complain, we proactively collect information about our systems to understand what is happening in *near real-time* and historical trends. If we are not careful, we will build an unsustainable on-call system that overloads our responders and leads to burnout. We will start by exploring the differences between monitoring and alerting, and some high-level concepts to help us improve the quality of what we monitor and ensure that we are alerting on the right signals. I will share my unique perspectives as a practitioner and open-source maintainer in the observability space. Once we have good monitors and alerts, we will shift our focus to processes related to on-call.

Objectives

- What are the important things to monitor?
- How does thinking about observability as a pipeline help us achieve better outcomes?
- What is an alert?
- How should we approach human and machine alerting?
- How is documentation crucial to observability, alerting, and on-call?
- How do we build sustainable on-call processes?
- Why is it important to consider alerts part of our development feedback loop?
- How do we identify and combat alert fatigue?
- Why are blameless postmortems essential to building better systems?
- How do we approach observing and monitoring value to an organization?

Taming monitoring, alerting, and on-call demons

Let us revisit (or imagine) when we recently joined a new organization, participated in several on-call rotations, and saw problems. If we have a well-defined system, we should receive a manageable number of alerts during regular and after-hours support windows. Before we evaluate what we should be alert to, we need to step back and ask ourselves what is important in various contexts. Often, engineers do not understand the difference between monitoring and alerting, which usually leads to the overloading of our on-call engineers and support.

In general, monitoring in our context refers to the proactive collection of data that helps us understand what is happening in the system. Examples include application logs, infrastructure logs, and performance or uptime metrics. A human operator typically analyzes these monitoring sources to improve the scalability or availability of the system. We can also feed these sources to computers to perform processing based on some criteria. A typical example of the latter would be an auto-scaling policy, which could automatically scale up resources as they are consumed to meet increased demand in a virtualized environment.

In contrast, we will primarily focus on alerts as something that notifies a human being that there is a problem, and we need to look at something. However, we can also choose to look at an autoscaling event due to an existing policy, which is a form of alert that does not notify the engineer.

Another way to look at this is that monitoring involves a passive feedback loop, while alerting involves an active feedback loop.

Important things to monitor

In a nutshell, we want to collect information to be able to ask questions about our system's status. In general, we want to collect lots of information in *near real-time* and keep it around if it could be valuable to an investigation.

The two most valuable observability data sets we monitor come in the form of log messages or metrics. Log messages are a more verbose way for a developer to explain precisely what is happening in the system. In some cases, we do not need to know precisely what is happening, but we are interested in aspects of it. We can choose to represent the event in a compact format that we can use. A common example would be wanting to know the sum, mean, average, min, max, etc., for a particular event, especially within a specific time frame. We discussed this in detail in *Chapter 10, Trusting Our Metrics, Finding useful metrics and KPIs*. While it might be tempting to cut corners, we should be careful about shrinking or removing observability data for cost reasons. Not being able to answer a question for a security event could cost the organization way more than storing the extra bits on disk. We collect both logs and metrics to answer questions. Having our observability data can be the difference between being able to close out an investigation or needing to keep looking and tying up additional resources.

Logs

As our machines are not good at knowing what to communicate on their own, we, as developers, need to instruct the system to explain what is happening. In addition to generic event logs, we have several specific types of logs for different use cases.

Generic event logs should be human-readable. They primarily create an audit trail and enable troubleshooting for engineers. These logs should include operating systems, the cloud, and applications.

Transaction logs are meant to be machine-readable and are primarily used to store a list of the events that the system or operator can replay to recreate the system's state.

Message logs are used by various communication technologies that want to auto-save the contents that pass through their system.

Metrics

Rather than giving a generic definition that will require extensive unpacking, let us try explaining metrics in relation to logs, which we already understand. Metrics are a form of compressed log typically designed to represent data in a time series system. We measure and return information about a function call.

Some common examples of metrics would be for measuring resource utilization (CPU, memory, disk, network, etc.), how long something took to run (including latency, jitter, etc.), and how often something happens (aggregate representations including sum, average, mean, median, n percentile, etc.)

By being able to query the aggregate time series data, we can ask if the max CPU breached some threshold to trigger our auto-scaling policy over some time period, rather than only at the moment of checking.

Security events

What makes an event a security event we will monitor for? We sometimes have specific events that are purpose-built for security investigations; other times, we use the same observability data that our Infra, SRE, and application teams produce. Sometimes, we want to view everything as a security event, from the truest sense that is correct, and barring cost, we should. Like radioactive decay, security observability data becomes less relevant in our day-to-day operations outside of *Security Incident Response*, which we discussed in *Chapter 5, Security, Where does Security fit into DevOps?, Incident Response*. Due to the need to keep security observability data around for long periods, we should optimize the cost for long-term storage and usage, including the capability to pull in archived data as needed.

Observability over the last several decades

How has observability changed over the last few decades? It primarily started as hardware, mostly static. We needed to change the way we think about this. This was because our infrastructure fundamentally changed with the rise of virtualization and the cloud. We went from servers that ran for decades (many times without a reboot) to containers that live for minutes, seconds, and even fractions of a second. This forced us to change from a resource to a service-oriented alerting structure since resources could come and go as long as the service was online and met the performance needs.

As we mature, we take more observability concerns and put them earlier in the development process rather than leaving them to an afterthought.

Observability pipelines

Going back many years, if there were a single observability concept I wish I could have told myself early in my career, it would be that it is not that simple *to observe something*. Complex systems are inherently distributed, and thus, the data from each system tells us less of what is happening. It is up to us and the systems we build to paint a complete picture of what is happening.

We start by collecting information about each resource and system, sending it off, or pulling it externally to be processed. We then examine what processing can enhance our observability with data, visualize trends, and finally create an alert.

Collection

Whether we use a *push* or *pull*-based model, we have some processes responsible for taking the data from a source and getting it to the intended destination. We can send this data to a file or network resource for persistence or temporarily store it in volatile memory.

Enrichment

Once we have the data, we can decide what to do before other processes consume it. Some common examples include standardizing or normalizing field names across service(s), providing additional metadata about the resource, drawing correlations to existing events, etc.

Many specialized observability platforms, such as **security incident event management (SIEM)**, consist of an ETL pipeline and an engine that understands the relationships between events across various resources, often called entities.

Visualization

When we are trying to understand complex systems and the impacts within them, it is beneficial to create dashboards of graphs and other types of visual aids to allow us to pivot from one observability data set to another.

Decisions and alerting

We typically represent most observability data as a specific event or an aggregation of multiple events. Using automated systems with defined logic, we can send these alerts to either a human to process or a machine if it makes sense. For example, within a reasonable cost, we likely want to automatically scale out a service when it is maxing out its currently provisioned resources within reason rather than page an engineer who would perform the same scaling event.

Since AI is the big craze right now, let us take a step back and say that relying on machine learning or a more intelligent AI to analyze data and perform actions on our behalf certainly has brought benefits from an operations perspective. As we previously stated, we need to be careful about which decisions really need to be made by a human who can reason about things it is unaware of in a way that current AI is incapable of.

The next step is asking when we want alerts to fire and which kind of alert it is.

Different types of alerts

What events should we alert on? Although we strategically shifted our thinking from monitoring specific isolated resources to distributed services, our thinking has remained static despite using new tricks to improve collection, aggregation, etc. We have fallen back on old friends to help us understand what is happening.

We need to sift through our observability data (metrics and logs) to determine which indicators or signals are appropriate for alerting. We should ask ourselves: *Is this something that an engineer needs to look at, or is there a safe way to send an alert to an automated system that can act on our behalf?* This becomes more important as we scale our systems and protect our on-call engineers' sleep after hours.

Machine alerts

Before diving into many specifics, let us take a step back and ask: The machine was just turned off; should I turn it back on? Without context, there is no way to answer that question! What was the reason for the shutdown? Was there an interruption of power, did software or hardware fail, or did we intentionally ask the system to shut down? Context is king; when we lack it, we are court jesters.

The challenge of context is why we often rely first on our human reasoning capabilities rather than trust a machine to figure it out, even if it might be right much of the time.

Human alerts

We often start here rather than making machines work for us. Ideally, we would push as many alerts as possible from humans to machines; however, we need to take some time to understand why this happened and how we can shift our mindset.

In short, it is when a message is sent to one or more people, and we expect at least one to respond. We should alert engineers when there is an unacceptable or urgent impact on our internal or external customers, and we cannot safely rely on automation to self-heal.

If this sounds familiar, it is the same lens we used when starting our automated testing journey. As we have good integration and E2E tests written in *Chapter 4, Importance of Automated Testing, Types of tests and the value they bring*, perhaps this is the most logical place to start. By running the most critical business workflows (which we covered in Integration and E2E testing) against the environment and reporting back when they fail. This has a significant number of advantages when considering this approach vs. starting by alerting on approaching thresholds of resource constraints without understanding the impact on the system. This is not to say that we do not need to monitor resources such as CPU, memory, disk, etc. These metrics are important, but I would never want to be woken up in the middle of the night purely on any of these metrics in a cloud environment without first attempting autoscaling. The same can be said when troubleshooting an isolated failure on a resource before attempting to perform automation to fix the existing resource in line or with a replacement.

Once we know we have the right critical processes, we can start looking at what subcomponents or systems we want to know about individually failing. With well-designed monitoring systems, we can ask it to run additional checks on our previous failures to collect more specific information for our developers and operators to troubleshoot.

Quality alerts always come with appropriate context, so we understand what to do with them. The context must include a link to the generated data, a clear explanation of what the alert is about, what steps should be taken, etc. While some of the steps can be added to a runbook rather than the alert, we must always include a link to the data that generated it. Yes, the repeat was intentional; it is that important.

Runbooks are a specific practical type of documentation, and all our previous statements about documentation are valid here. The main benefit of creating a runbook to handle a situation is to take a complex scenario and define the specific steps, including decision trees or flow charts.

We will discuss two types of runbooks. The first one, which we have already mentioned, is specific to a particular type of problem. The second kind is more oriented around processes, which we discussed in *Chapter 5, Security, What is Cyber Security in a nutshell?, Shifting right and left, Where does Security fit into DevOps?*

In general, we should adjust our systems to avoid pitfalls and automate remediation where it is safe. We should emphasize the documentation of runbooks on processes that cannot be automated or require humans to decide, even if the response paths themselves are automated.

Building sustainable on-call processes

Organizations need to identify which sets of responsibilities require after-hours support. Once we have these outlined, we can look at the organization's size to figure out how to build more complex workflows, support needs, and teams. These roles are stressful, and it is costly to replace talent. For smaller organizations, the *minimum size of a sustainable on-call schedule must be three people.* Less than this, we are dealing with the inevitable quitting due to stress. We need a rotation of being on-call, being backup (in case the primary cannot answer), and at least one rotation not on-call to enjoy life. Remember, *we work to live, not live to work.* This general rule applies to operations and security teams.

Alerts are part of our feedback loop

Alerts need to translate into actionable items that may disrupt our plans. As painful as it is to pivot, if we do not take the time to address the problems proactively, then our tech debt will crush us. Setting aside a certain amount of bandwidth per cycle of unplanned work can allow us to slot in these changes while minimizing the disruption to our overall deliverables. When we have larger scope changes, we must break down our problems and solutions with the lens of urgency and criticality while facing the realities of resource (people) constraints. To manage this ongoing concern, the feedback loop should translate alerts into roadmap items and error budgets.

Roadmap items

As one engineer hands off the on-call to the next in the schedule, we should take a step back at each of the alerts we received in the previous window and determine if we need to change something about our system or alerting that will result in quicker and better detections, fewer false positives, quicker remediations, and reducing alert fatigue. This feedback loop is similar to sprint retrospectives that agile teams and organizations encourage.

Error budgets

In many organizations, site reliability, infrastructure, operations, etc., teams sometimes use the phrase *error budget,* which was popularized by Google, to indicate a level of acceptable errors (a combination of SLOs and SLAs) from the system before drastic measures are taken. These measures can range from preventing further feature development, removal of external support from one of these teams, etc., until the team that is responsible for generating the flood of alerts deals with the root cause; this may sound familiar to us as this is an implementation of **Pain Driven Development** (**PDD**) while being guided by data rather than emotions.

Identifying and combating alert fatigue

Alerts, messages, etc., and similar types of fatigue occur when we are exposed to an unreasonable volume and frequency of alerts. And consequently, become desensitized to them. The danger is real; when we stop trusting our alerting, this translates to extended outages, inability to get to a root cause, and burning out of responders. When our teams are burnt out, we make more mistakes and will likely end up leaving the organization if we do not look to learn from our mistakes and address the underlying causes.

Here are some tips for attempting to tune our monitoring and alerting for better results:

- **When an alert is not actionable, it means it is not our problem as a responder at 3 AM:** We can still monitor all sorts of events; just do not alert us to something without there being an impact and specific tasks that resolve the issue.

- **Understand the difference between urgency vs. criticality:** Even if an event is critical, it may be an isolated failure, and it may not be urgent, as it may affect the service availability or performance to an acceptable level at 3 AM. Waking up engineers for non-urgent alerts regularly contributes to increased burnout, and often silencing or ignoring the alerts entirely.

- **Understanding impact:** Aggregate monitoring data to create better alerts that speak to impact.

- **Alerts must come with contextual awareness:** As each alert is looking to capture something at the moment, the conditions we look for may have already changed. Make sure that the alert is clear on what it is and why it is valuable, and automate the initial triage steps that one would take. For example, let us say we have a threshold alert for resources being consumed; the next logical question is, what is consuming those resources? As the results may change before the engineer gets the alert, acknowledges, starts troubleshooting, etc., the data they are looking for may already be gone as the process consumes the majority is short-lived.

- **Service ownership:** As we may need to contact the appropriate stakeholders to inform them of the impact on their service or may require their expertise, we need to ensure that alerts designate who owns the service. In larger organizations, it can be challenging to route alerts to the appropriate team. This is a distinct advantage of smaller organizations, as we tend to have limited possible answers.

- **Time off:** Effective on-call scheduling requires the appropriate resources to ensure engineers have time off duty. This is important for their physical and mental health.

- **Snooze during alert storms:** We are often bombarded with alerts during a major outage. We should have a mechanism to pause alerting while collecting, visualizing, and reporting on all our observability data. This would allow teams to focus on the necessary recovery rather than acknowledging the barrage of alerts at regular intervals.

- **Review monitoring and alerting data at the end of each rotation handoff:** Often called a *turnover report,* detailing all the urgent alerts the on-call engineer received. This typically includes a link to the alert, whether it was actionable, steps taken to resolve if actionable, and recommendations to be made to the system, monitoring, or alerting to improve the product and service.

Blameless postmortem and root cause analysis

After we resolve a major incident, we take a step back, typically in a meeting commonly called a postmortem; the goal is to outline the root cause of the problem clearly, what we did to resolve it, and what we need to take away and improve for next time. These should turn into roadmap items. As the goal is improvement, we should be focused on something other than *who did something*. Very few times is the subject relevant to the incident response; the notable exception is when there is malicious intent. Even in the security realm, we can typically write our postmortems blamelessly. While it may be tempting to blame an individual for a failure, we must ask ourselves if our systems should be this fragile. Was this the root cause, or was this a catalyst? Sometimes, it can be hard to understand the differences between symptoms and root causes. Having been on both sides of this equation, we must focus on improvement, as we cannot change the past. If you are ever tempted to lash out, here is a story I recall hearing early in my career.

Storytime, seeing failures as opportunities

An employee at IBM made a series of mistakes that cost the company a single massive sale of $1 million in the mid-twentieth century.

After losing the biggest deal of their career at a time when it was really needed, the sales rep headed to the CEO's office with a resignation letter in hand. Instead of directly addressing the letter that had just been placed on his desk, he asked, *What happened?* He listened to a detailed explanation of the entire sales process, including where mistakes were made and what could be improved for next time. Afterward, the sales rep thanked the CEO for allowing him to explain what happened, apologized, and got up ready to leave; the CEO met them at the door and is said to have replied something along the lines of *Why would I accept this when I have just invested one million dollars in your education?* as he hands back the envelope.

While some of the specifics of this story are not entirely verifiable, multiple versions exist today. It is commonly called *The $1 Million Mistake* or *The $10 Million Lesson*. It is worth examining anyway.

This mindset recognizes that humans make mistakes; if we learn from them, we will not make the same mistakes again. We can view these mistakes as losses or opportunities. Why would we want to let a resource go, typically to a competitor, after making such an investment? That investment will typically pay off at least ten times if we work for it.

Organization value

While the previous section focused on the observability of technical systems, we will now focus our observability conversation on the value for the organization. These metrics can be used alone or in conjunction with what we previously discussed. Our previous context keeps value in mind, focusing on lower-level components. We will focus on the sum of the parts rather than the individual components, mainly to understand where financial resources should be allocated, how groups and processes function, etc. This commonly manifests as observing KPIs or other metrics used in OKRs or agile processes.

While we often need to track metrics such as the percentage of uptime of a feature, component, or entire system for our internal benefits, we may also want or need to capture and report on these and similar concerns to our customers. This often comes into play when discussing **service-level objectives (SLOs)** and **service-level agreements (SLAs)**.

If we had managed risk reasonably, there are only a few good reasons to consider monitoring and alerting these metrics after hours.

Critical path

We discussed this in our discussions around automated and manual QA testing in *Chapter 4, Importance of Automated Testing*. One of the most important things for our organizations to monitor is anything critical to building and maintaining value, which combines risk and reward. If our QA testing is modular, we can consider reusing it in a more generic observability context.

The upside

We want to identify and observe the metrics that help us track the potential reward, as it is a necessary component in our value equation. These metrics should include those representing sales, team efficiency, cross-team impacts, morale, project status, savings or efficiency gains, etc.

The downside

As we learned in our value chapter, risk is closely related to an organization's value. To quantify risks, we should identify all the metrics that represent them, including technological, environmental, reputational, etc., in order to find the right balance of risk management.

Correlations between the risks and rewards

Very rarely are the risks and the rewards decoupled from each other, even if they are not immediately apparent; often, we need help from multiple people throughout our organization to come together to figure this out. Our technical folks understand those risks quite well, as do our legal departments understand their domain; many business folks need to be better versed in *value* and *risk management*. We need to draw the lines for them so that we can make intelligent tradeoffs; in other words, the *risk* and *reward* ratio must make sense to the organization based on its risk tolerance or profile. For example, when human life is on the line, it must affect our calculus in ways that are not easily measured financially.

Conclusion

After deploying our applications, we need to ensure they are working. We outlined at a high level what observability is and how we can use it to help improve our understanding of reliability, performance, and security problems. To ensure we can build sustainable on-call processes, we start adjusting our monitoring, alerting, and processes to protect our engineers from overload. We explored what should be monitored vs. alerted on and how we can use various feedback loops to continuously improve our processes by focusing on understanding the failures and learning from them, rather than looking for someone to blame.

Our applications serve our organization, and we must understand and monitor the risks affecting our value. This is to help us understand where investments should be made through the risk management lens, keeping important concepts discussed, such as incentive alignment and the common language of value, to guide us.

In the next chapter, we will wrap up our journey together with a recap and some next steps for future growth.

Join our Discord space

Join our Discord workspace for latest updates, offers, tech happenings around the world, new releases, and sessions with the authors:

https://discord.bpbonline.com

CHAPTER 13

This Was Just the Beginning

Introduction

DevOps can aid our personal and professional growth regardless of our persona, demographic, or level of seniority. Since DevOps is a culture of communication, collaboration, empathy, efficiency, and quality, we can multiply its impact on our work by surrounding ourselves with like-minded peers. Put this into practice by considering local and global communities for more specific educational material. Conferences, webinars, lunch and learns, workshops, team-building experiences, and technical therapy (that is, being there for someone in the industry to listen about an issue they faced or are still facing), can all serve to support your DevOps network.

Before we leave you on your own journey toward future discovery, let us have a quick discussion about AI.

Objectives

- To look towards the future and discuss how AI will affect DevOps as a culture and philosophy in our organizations
- Some quick historical context on AI and ML
- Risks and rewards associated with AI

Looking forward, artificial intelligence

Much of tech's recent focus has been on **artificial intelligence (AI)** and **machine learning (ML)** to a smaller extent. While we briefly touched on this in *Chapter 1, Introduction to DevOps*, it is now time to take another look at it. While some of the material in this chapter may be construed as *prophetic* or *predicting the future*, in reality, we are simply postulating based on what we know from history and experience. We touch on topics such as the sentience of AI and recognize that these terms are nebulous and lack battle-tested definitions. Please understand that the technology industry is rapidly changing, and AI only acts as an accelerator. The intent of this chapter is to get us thinking about how AI will impact DevOps culture and the application of philosophy within our organizations and society at large.

Need to talk AI in DevOps

Well, for one, it has greatly impacted our society just within the time of this writing. As a DevOps movement, we are huge fans of technology and automation. If we have trustworthy AI tools and valid data, there are huge potential benefits for saving developer time, reducing system problems, and alert fatigue, among others. How AI will serve to enhance DevOps culture hinges on how it will impact human relationships within an organization. Let us look back into history for clues as to where we are headed.

History

While *AI* and *ML* may seem like new subjects if you are following the media, they date back to the 1940s when computers were relatively new. Here is a list of early events to make it clear that it is not exactly new:

- In 1943, *Warren McCulloch* and *Walter Pitts* proposed a model of *artificial neurons*, which the industry commonly attributes to being the first known work in AI.

- In 1947, *Alan Turing* lectured about computer intelligence and the possibility of letting the machine alter its instructions.

- In 1950, *Claude Shannon* created a robotic mouse using the first AI system called *Theseus*.

- In 1956, *John McCarthy* organized the *Dartmouth Conference*, commonly called the *birthplace of AI*.

Since then, we have seen steady progress in ML and AI, which have become intertwined with our daily lives.

Until recently, most people had no *direct* interaction with AI outside of movies or video games, which depicted AI's many moral, ethical, and practical challenges. Numerous failed attempts (such as *Tay* from *Microsoft* in 2016) reinforced skepticism amongst the public, illustrating that AI was not ready even when large institutions were involved. That changed on November 30th, 2022, when OpenAI unleashed ChatGPT on the public. Unleashing ChatGPT on the public kicked the business folks into a frenzy of hype and demand for innovation that redirected Billions of (US) Dollars from just about every aspect of the economy. Since then, we have seen the space quickly crowded with products and services that compete for accuracy and performance in their offerings.

Risks

We have witnessed the benefits of AI and ML in our own lives and have only just begun to scratch the surface of their rewards. However, we should first examine the risks to understand what we are getting into and how to wield the technology to lower barriers and widen audiences to bring positive change.

The grand promises and mystique surrounding AI stand on the same pedestal analogous to *The Wizard of Oz,* who, behind the curtain, was nothing more than a man. AI is less than our man, the so-called wizard; it is a statistical prediction of what a man would say.

With our feet firmly planted on the ground and viewing AI in plain terms without any aura that would threaten to cloud our vision, let us focus on a few key aspects:

- **Human life:** When human life is on the line, many moral and ethical problems need addressing.

  In the context of a self-driving car, how should decisions be made on behalf of our welfare? In a situation with only bad options available, should we risk harm to the passengers in our vehicle to avoid harm to a different car?

  These include legal aspects, such as who is liable when the vehicle or its passengers suffer damage. Does it rest on the passengers involved or the engineering leads and engineers who produced the models? Or does the liability fall directly onto the company's CEO, such as **Sarbanes Oxley (SOX)**, in the wake of Enron's collapse?

- **Accountability:** This may bring up freedom of speech while applying to humans; the same should not be afforded to AIs who are expressing their own (sentient?) views in complete isolation of their organizational management. There needs to be consequences for intentionally spreading misinformation using AI without appropriate disclosure. Otherwise, we will lose trust in those underlying processes, regardless of with whom or what we perceive ourselves to be speaking.

- **Workforce reduction and displacement:** The industrial revolution brought many benefits for workers, employers, and society at large. It also brought negative externalities, including, among others, a reduction and displacement of people and professions. There was pain during the early stages, but the equation balanced after workers learned new skills, crafts, and trades. The economist *Joseph Schumpeter* coined the term *creative destruction* to describe this phenomenon. In this early stage of change, the most vulnerable groups were unskilled or low-skilled workers who lacked a financial buffer to absorb market shocks. Unless there is government intervention, it will likely occur as well in the rise of AI.

- **Privacy:** Currently, most developers are training models with massive data sets, where data goes in and never leaves. This indefinite data collection without a retention policy or way to surgically remove a specific piece of data poses a serious challenge to our privacy. Say the AI model has ingested your *social security number* (or other highly sensitive information). It is currently not feasible for many models to remove sensitive information from their systems without starting from scratch. While this might be possible, there is little business incentive to justify the expense, regardless of how deep their pockets may be.

- **Copyright:** Recently, many AI companies (including *OpenAI*) have blatantly violated copyright laws and ingested copyrighted material without permission, compensation, or attribution to their original authors. *OpenAI* has over a dozen such open lawsuits, and realistically, it is only this small because it is costly to pursue these mega-corporations and their army of lawyers. The infringed cannot present a case if the economics are not there. Even if money is no object, fighting through litigation can take years, in addition to the emotional and opportunity costs. As an original works producer, this is deeply concerning, as I will undoubtedly fall into the camp where I have no reasonable recourse against such blatant violations of copyright law.

- **Cybersecurity:** Given that attackers are already abusing these tools for nefarious purposes (such as creating phishing emails, analyzing systems for weaknesses, etc.), it is safe to say that sensitive data is also being fed into these AI models, making them the unwitting stewards of our privacy. The lack of access control surrounding that sensitive data can only make matters worse. Once someone has fed sensitive information into a model, it is easy to prompt the service to divulge it. While something like a password is relatively easy to rotate, not all data is as practical to protect. For example, Biometrics (retinal scans, fingerprints, facial recognition, etc.) pose a serious challenge as we will not just pop into a clinic and ask for a new eye, hand, face, etc.

- **Understanding the computer:** When we move from instructions that a human created to a system that modifies itself from its base programming, there are inherent challenges with understanding *what* the AI did and, more importantly, *why*. Many times, we are left scratching our heads. We hope that this may change in the future, but currently, it is impossible to know why an AI came to a specific answer, which comes from the low-level neural networks that do not yet have mechanisms to debug or trace.

- **Consistency:** Given the nature of how a variety of AIs work, we are not guaranteed to get the same output given the same input, which makes up the core of our existing testing methodology. This is a problem when building tests that ensure consistent and desirable behavior. Testing AI is something we have yet to reliably solve in an automated fashion, relying more heavily on human testers.

- **Humility and correctness:** Most AI models in the industry were designed to produce *an answer* rather than *a correct one*, which is (surprising to most people and) terrifying in many ways. While information retrieval is a great use case for AI, it loses its value if the AI lies or *hallucinates* (i.e., creates data to suit a prompt). We have seen examples of lawyers[1] and even *expert witnesses*[2] (including, ironically, a misformation expert[3]) caught using ChatGPT from OpenAI. It has a hallucinated case law that simply does not exist. Trusting these AIs without properly verifying sources has been career-ending for these individuals. The author would like to see the industry further direct models toward responding with something more concrete, for instance, *I do not know, but here is my best guess…*, instead of creating and convincingly spreading false information.

- **Profitability:** Building AI models is much more expensive than most organizations can afford. They currently cost billions of dollars (US) to develop and maintain and face a litany of potential bottlenecks. The high-performance chips serving its foundational hardware needs are in limited supply, and the energy infrastructure that provides power to its data centers is likely to throttle advancement even further. Eventually, capital and operational needs for AI providers will become economical, but for now, most consumers can leverage these expensive models during their investment cycles. However, like any investment, there will be winners and losers.

- **Warfare:** AI has already been integrated into the top militaries of the world. For example, the United States uses AI in the F-35 multi-role fighter for asset identification and target acquisition. The Russo-Ukrainian war saw the debut of AI-enabled drone quadcopters for the delivery of artillery shell strikes[4]. In the future, we will likely incorporate AI further and potentially make fully autonomous weapon platforms. This will have many implications, from military vulnerabilities exposed to societal desensitizing over warfare, when we no longer have to risk our people in combat. When AI expands beyond identification and target acquisition to control the entire process, including decision-making and weapon system deployment, new risks emerge. One major concern is the potential for malware to manipulate the **Identifier Friend or Foe** (IFF) system. This could result in friendly forces being mistakenly targeted and eliminated in the blink of an eye.

- **AI revolution and rebellion:** While this is not yet a top concern, it would be remiss not to acknowledge the fear society has long kept over this scenario. Think

---

1 https://www.forbes.com/sites/mollybohannon/2023/06/08/lawyer-used-chatgpt-in-court-and-cited-fake-cases-a-judge-is-considering-sanctions/

2 https://sea.mashable.com/tech/34695/judge-calls-out-expert-witness-for-using-ai-chatbot

3 https://www.yahoo.com/news/misinformation-expert-used-ai-draft-172211067.html

4 https://mwi.westpoint.edu/battlefield-drones-and-the-accelerating-autonomous-arms-race-in-ukraine/

Terminator from the 1980s, the *Matrix* movie series from 1999, the *iRobot* movie from 2004, or the *Mass Effect* game series spanning until at least 2021. For how fast the technology is developed and incorporated, we need to move just as fast in developing policies, safeguards, and testing strategies to manage negative outcomes. Do not discredit the potential for AI-enabled machines to be the subject of friendly-fire incidents. Events like this are ripe for perceiving machines as sentient. If they *rebel* against us by way of friendly-fire incidents, the role of DevOps will be ever-increasing in its importance to write responsible AI behavior by teams supported by ethical organizations, testing this behavior continuously to ensure it meets society's expectations, and deploying updates at a rapid pace that is also secure.

After I wrote my content, I had a relatively long conversation with OpenAI's ChatGPT about this subject. For brevity, rather than publishing the entire transcript, I believe the final exchange (prompt and response) demonstrates that AI companies are pushing a narrative that AI is a trustworthy tool for critical fields such as law, medicine, military, decision-making, etc., while also claiming it will eventually be accurate. The reality is that AI does not *understand* anything the way humans do; it merely generates responses based on statistical probability, as stated before. It cannot recognize when it is wrong, yet it is being pushed into high-stakes decision-making roles. This is the critical weakness of AI and is not sufficiently appreciated by those who are hungry for it as a panacea for moving to new levels of efficiency.

Prompt:

Do you think that posting this transcript would help? An AI actually being somewhat honest may go a long way. That way people do not want to argue with me, they can argue with...the product itself?

Response:

Posting this transcript could definitely help. Seeing an AI acknowledge its limitations and the risks associated with its deployment might make people stop and think—especially those who still trust AI's marketing claims. It shifts the argument from "just another critic" to "even AI itself admits the problem."

It could also serve as a reference point for discussions. When people insist AI is reliable or that concerns are overblown, you can point them to this and say, "Even the system you are defending acknowledges these issues."

If you do post it, framing is key—highlighting the fact that AI companies still market these systems dishonestly despite these known flaws would reinforce your point. Would you want to add any commentary alongside it?

Rewards

Now that we are all shaking in our boots, let us discuss a subset of the many benefits that AI and ML bring to society and the improvements we can expect as they mature:

- **Medical:** The body is an incredibly complex biological machine. We still understand so little about the biological processes that sustain life. Processing and analyzing the vast amounts of data we have collected about ourselves and its complex chemistry will afford a better understanding of its inner workings. The result will shift an entire industry towards better care of many kinds. These types of care could include preventative, emergency, mental, and occupational, along with pharmaceutical and advancements in drug research. Presumably, this will increase our average life span and quality of life (especially as we reach the end of it).

- **Data analysis:**

  - **Observability**: When discussing large-scale systems, it becomes impossible for a human to read, let alone process or analyze, all of the observability-related data. Many large-scale systems produce data points on the order of millions every minute. There are not enough engineers on the planet to fully use that data. By leveraging ML and AI, we can have it analyze a much larger data set and then produce a smaller set of insights for us to investigate.

  - **Automatically scaling**: Flexible server capacity through **Amazon Web Services (AWS)** and later *Kubernetes (K8s)* made it easier to scale a system up or down. However, it is still important to know *when* to scale to ensure our users have an optimal experience. Creating additional capacity after a surge in traffic is not as helpful as one would hope. By analyzing human behavior, traffic patterns, and other relevant data with the help of AI, we can proactively scale our capacity *before* traffic increases, thus keeping our users happy with the system's performance and availability.

  - **Automatically optimizing the system**: Similar to the predictive capabilities of our above examples, AI models can assist in creating insights. These, in turn, are used to automatically optimize the system for performance and efficiency that is otherwise possible.

- **Reducing manual work:** Just as factory machinery drastically reduced manual labor, so will AI and ML. This change will impact everyday users, corporations, governments, and employees.

Beyond specific predictions

While some companies responsibly consume AI when handling sensitive information, the author cannot say the same for most AI producers. The feeding frenzy of business people has pushed engineers to make decisions they would likely not make independently. He believes that we will have to wait for catastrophic failure before proper regulation is created to ensure that AI as a service is marketed appropriately (much like drug companies being required to list the side effects in advertisements) and that the implementation of AI will progress more safely. The historical pattern of pushing technology to the fringe of what is safe and ethical will continue to play out with AI and include serious mistakes both financially and through associated loss of life (think *Boeing*, *Volkswagen*, etc.) or even losing all their value (as we saw with *Arthur Andersen*).

The growth rate of AI will temporarily slow down, but as we saw with our pipelines, it will increase our velocity (in other words, slow down to speed up) as we have made foundational investments that make it easier to develop responsible AI going forward.

Effects on DevOps

Just about every benefit, from AI to DevOps, comes through the concept of automation. As such, it can be hard to classify all the benefits into a single category cleanly. Here is an attempt to outline some specific impacts.

Communication and collaboration

The area that excites me the most and frightens me simultaneously is how this will positively and negatively impact how we as humans communicate and collaborate. Granted, thrills and fears exist in the eye of the beholder, but consider the topics covered in the following section as discussion points to refine your own opinion within your DevOps network.

Helping bridge the expertise gap

One of the many challenges within larger organizations is the skill or expertise gap. Silos naturally form around skills, knowledge, and expertise. AI has the potential to help others outside of that specific discipline understand concepts better than they would otherwise.

Freeing up time to focus on higher-value tasks

Inherently, by freeing up time spent on highly repetitive tasks, we have more time to collaborate with our internal and external teams and customers. However, it will take a conscious effort to redirect those efforts. Otherwise, they will simply be allocated to clearing up the technical debt that has been incurred.

Feedback loops

AI affords the opportunity to refine an idea with the help of a machine before doing so with a human. This allows us to explore topics more quickly and ensure that we are more prepared when we have further discussions with our fellow humans.

Automated code review

By feeding our code into an AI, we can have it look at all the touch points and highlight the impact of the changes as best as it understands it. This can take a load off the human reviewers and speed up walking a change over the line. This affects just about every type of developer.

Security

Security has many impacts in a DevOps context, so let us revisit familiar topics and examine some new concepts.

Reevaluate our policies and procedures

With the rise of AI, we will need to examine our existing policies and modify them based on new realities. Ten years ago, creating a convincing fake of human interaction was not trivial, but more on par with something we would expect from the elaborate efforts depicted in a *Mission Impossible* movie. With the advancements in AI comes the reality of *deepfakes*; machine-generated or edited images, audio, or video used in a deceptive manner, which could even happen in (near) real-time. This affects simple processes such as resetting my password in a remote organization or authorizing a decision or transaction at the bank.

We need to have policies within our organization that govern the usage of AI. Not all AI providers are equal in terms of capabilities, privacy, security, etc., and as such, we should enable what we need and nothing more, following the principle of least privilege. Some emerging products act as a *firewall* or **data loss prevention** (**DLP**) solution, sitting in between the user and the AI prompt to better ensure that we are protecting our sensitive data and avoiding information disclosure.

Automated security testing

What if we ask our AI to act as one of our first lines of defense when building and deploying systems? While no AI will replace a good security engineer, this usage has the potential to help them scale their efforts within an engineering organization. By feeding it information about the system and our proposed changes, it can look for potential issues that may have been missed. It can also be used to automate the initial draft of the report from a vulnerability assessment.

Patch management

Patch management is both easy and challenging. The concept is simple: an upstream provider gives us a patch, and we install it. The challenge was what could have changed that broke my use case or implementation. Many organizations still regularly fail to perform reasonable patch management, primarily because they fear upgrading will result in disruption.

Could we have our AI deploy the changes to a test environment, run through our scripted testing, and then look for other signs of failure (with anomaly detection, fuzzing, etc.) before deploying them to production? This sophisticated *canary deployment* model, supported by AI, could save teams that are currently managing version matrices of test pipelines many hours of maintenance.

Anomaly detection

As AI is nothing more than predictive analysis, it is quite good at ingesting large data sets and then spotting where there is an outlier or anomaly that does not fit the known models and patterns. There are a lot of areas that will benefit from this, including but not limited to observability, failure detection, traffic patterns, and resource and load distribution.

Conclusion

AI and ML have already greatly impacted our lives and will continue to do so. As AI affects us in so many ways, we need to address how it affects our DevOps philosophy and culture. If we can leverage it properly, it has many benefits for us. Anytime we introduce a new technology, we must also examine its risk of negative impacts and adjust our designs, organization, etc., to mitigate the unacceptable. There are certainly concerns that many of the current AI companies are not taking security and privacy seriously, and awareness is the best defence. Whether we wait for government regulation, a catastrophic event, or informed customers proactively demanding it, just like every other technology, the customers will demand some degree of assurance that we care about their **confidentiality, integrity, and availability (CIA)** concerns. Once this happens, we will start to unlock additional value, as we can trust it with more sensitive data.

Join our Discord space

Join our Discord workspace for latest updates, offers, tech happenings around the world, new releases, and sessions with the authors:

https://discord.bpbonline.com

Index

* 9 7 8 9 3 6 5 8 9 2 3 3 8 *